Praise for *There When He Needs You*

"As a psychologist and father of two grown sons I was very impressed with this book. Dr. Bernstein shares his own personal and clinical experiences to capture the significant role that fathers play in the lives of their sons. He offers realistic suggestions for both fathers and mothers for enhancing the father-son relationship and he does so with warmth, empathy, and humor. This very readable book is an invaluable resource."

—Robert Brooks, co-author of *Raising Resilient Children*
and *The Power of Resilience*

"Hurray! A book all fathers deserve! Thanks to Dr. Neil Bernstein's wise advice and warm stories, today's fathers can feel reassured. All parents want to feel that special connection with their children; all fathers want to be 'good enough—and better'—and now they can. Thank goodness Dr. Bernstein is there when we need him!"

—Sandra Burt and Linda Perlis, authors of
*Raising A Successful Child: Discover
and Nurture Your Child's Talents*

"Finally, a father-friendly book on the topic of dads raising sons! Neil Bernstein is wise and passionate as he reminds fathers how much good we do when we seize the chance to connect with our sons."

—Neil Chethik, author of *FatherLoss: How
Sons Deal with the Deaths of Their Dads*

How to Keep Your Teenager Out of Trouble
and What to Do If You Can't

Treating the Unmanageable Adolescent:
A Guide to Oppositional Defiant and Conduct Disorders

There
When He
Needs You

How to Be an Available, Involved, and Emotionally Connected Father to Your Son

NEIL I. BERNSTEIN, Ph.D.

with Brooke Lea Foster

FREE PRESS
New York   London   Toronto   Sydney

FREE PRESS
A Division of Simon & Schuster, Inc.
1230 Avenue of the Americas
New York, NY 10020

First Free Press hardcover edition May 2008

FREE PRESS and colophon are trademarks of Simon & Schuster, Inc.

For information about special discounts for bulk purchases,
please contact Simon & Schuster Special Sales at 1-800-456-6798
or business@simonandschuster.com

Manufactured in the United States of America

1   3   5   7   9   10   8   6   4   2

Library of Congress Cataloging-in-Publication Data

Bernstein, Neil I.
There when he needs you : how to be an available, involved, and emotionally connected
father to your son / Neil I. Bernstein; with Brooke Lea Foster.
p.   cm.
Includes bibliographical references and index.
1. Fathers.   2. Fathers and sons.   I. Title.
HQ756.B463 2008
649'.10851—dc22   2007048226

ISBN-13: 978-1-4165-6073-9
ISBN-10: 1-4165-6073-4

To the memory of my parents,
who taught me about love and devotion

To my children,
Daniel and Julie,
who make "being there" a joy

Contents

Introduction   1

Chapter One: A Dad Is Not a Male Mother: From Half-There
    Fathers and Peripheral Parents to Good Enough and Better   5

Chapter Two: Generational Mistakes: Facing Your Regrets
    About Your Own Father So You Can Become a Better Dad   27

Chapter Three: Sons in Progress: Fathering Through
    the Developmental Stages   53

Chapter Four: What Dads Won't Say: Fathers' Secret Fears
    and How to Face Them   93

Chapter Five: Sons Speak Out: When Dads Hurt
    and Disappoint Them   119

Chapter Six: Boys and Their Tech Toys   141

Chapter Seven: The Father-Son Competition   165

Chapter Eight: Love, Dad: Unlocking the Language of Feelings   181

Chapter Nine: The Father Project: A Mother's Role   203

Chapter Ten: Top Ten Fathering Tips   225

Acknowledgments   229
Index   231

There When He Needs You

Introduction

My father was from the old school. My mother ran our home and he followed her directions. She did the cooking, cleaning, child rearing, and any other domestic chore that came down the pike. He dutifully went to work each day—a nine-to-fiver—and turned the paycheck over to my mom. When I was upset, Mom was first in line to comfort me. Dad was in the background, always there to be called upon, but rarely initiating activities and conversations. A good man, he put others' needs before his own, but did not provide me with a role model for a strong, emotionally expressive father. Sure, he attended my sports events, chauffeured my friends and me around, and was always willing to help out when I asked. But on some level, I resented his shadow status. I wanted more but didn't have a clue how to ask for it.

At times, my dad embarrassed me. He was uneducated, wore dated clothing, and had a corny sense of humor. I didn't have much as a child and was often envious of the things some of my friends had—better baseball gloves, bigger allowances, stylish clothing, and dinner out once a week. I never complained but on one occasion my father picked up on my sadness. During my fifth-grade year, two of my close friends were flying to Florida with their parents for Christmas vacation—I had never been on an airplane. I was invited to join them but had to decline because the trip was too expensive. Knowing I wanted to go, my father put his arm around me and said, "I'm sorry, I wish I . . ." He never finished the sentence, because he was too choked up and I was crying. But because I knew how much he felt for me, somehow it cushioned my disappointment.

After I had a son and daughter of my own, I saw a different side of

1

Dad. My mother had passed away before my children's birth and so he was on his own again. At seventy-seven years old he was crawling around on the floor with his grandchildren, laughing, playing, and having a grand old time. On one occasion, I asked him if he had done that with me when I was little. "Sure," he said. "You loved to wrestle with me."

"Did we talk much, Dad?" I queried.

"We mostly played, but you always knew I'd be there when you needed me."

Dad was right. My father was a man of few words, but he always offered them at the opportune moments. When I struck out in a Little League World Series game, he reminded me that Mickey Mantle had done the same thing the previous year, and no one had laughed at him. Years later, he moved to Florida. Dad remembered the time when he couldn't afford to send me there, joking, "Now you can come to Florida whenever you want and stay for free." I laughed then—and I can laugh now, fifteen years after my father's death. But my heart still aches for my father. I wish I'd had the courage to tell him, "Dad, if I turn out to be as good a man as you are, I'll consider myself fortunate."

Let me confess at the outset—I'm not a perfect father. My father wasn't a perfect father. And I'm certainly not expecting anyone reading this book to be. But I am here to say that it doesn't take 24/7 devotion to be a better dad. It just takes a little extra work. Like many fathers today, I missed some of my son's games, worked late several nights a week, and failed to seize a few opportunities to teach some life lessons. Oh, sure, being a child psychologist has helped a little, but there were still times when I felt that I wasn't as good a father as I might have been. There were the feelings I didn't express, the times I failed to heed their mother's advice, and the times I was too indulgent and failed to set adequate limits on their behavior. But I can look back on those tiring, gratifying years and assure myself that I did the best I could. I think my children would agree. No one showed me how to be an active, involved father, and there were no father-son books—although there were some fine dads out there—to tell me how to balance career and family, which feelings to share and which to withhold, and the secrets to making my peace with my own father.

So I winged it. And I got by. I rushed home from work, tried to make time for special events, volunteered in school, and had more than a few awkward talks with my son.

The good news is that I learned from my experiences and my mistakes as a parent and I learned from my clients over the years—and you can, too. Today, as a dad, you face a whole new ball game. The expectations that society and our own families have of fathers have changed: you're supposed to be actively involved, express your feelings, and balance career and family—as if you're a kind of Superman and Superdad. Many men are struggling to be the best fathers they can be in the face of these sometimes overwhelming expectations. Some are getting it done, but far more know that they're not quite pulling it off. Some had good role models, some vowed to do it differently from their fathers, but others are entrenched in a high-stakes juggling act where each day is an adventure in multitasking.

You can be a great father without having to become a superdad. You can learn what compromises to make, learn to express your feelings in a different way, and enlist your wife or significant other as your greatest ally. I know you can because I've helped other fathers and mothers accomplish this and get closer to their sons. Thirty years of a therapy practice with more than two thousand children and families have taught me the dos and don'ts of good fathering, how powerful life experiences can shape a father-son relationship, and what sons and fathers really need to form lifelong bonds. There's a language of feelings to be learned, and although it's uncomfortable for many men, they can become fluent by taking a few risks and staying the course.

On the following pages, you'll hear stories of fathers lost and found, of men overwhelmed and underwhelmed, of parents who will do anything for their sons. In each story lies a slice of life, a lesson, sometimes a whiff of sadness at missed opportunities to connect, sometimes a sprinkle of humor. I wrote this book for the millions of evolving dads, and the mothers (and sons) who spend hours trying to decipher: "What is Dad thinking?" These mothers and sons often ask me, Why is it that the greatest man in a boy's life is also the hardest to be close to?

To help dads understand themselves and get closer to their sons, I decided to write this book.

CHAPTER ONE

A Dad
Is Not a Male Mother

*From Half-There Fathers and Peripheral
Parents to Good Enough and Better*

I met Kevin on a cool autumn afternoon. His wife, Larissa, and his fourteen-year-old son, Jason, had arrived in my office at four o'clock. We were meeting to talk about what was going on with Jason. A ninth-grader, he had grown moody, stopped talking to his mom and his dad, and his grades had dropped.

Jason looked uncomfortable in my office, trying to sit straight on the squishy black leather couch. Wearing a Borat T-shirt and bowling shoes—he liked the way they looked, he said—he rarely looked up when I talked to him. I made small talk with him about school, friends. Larissa, a prim woman in a pale pink sweater set, often answered for him.

Kevin arrived fifteen minutes late. He charged in, out of breath and still wearing a suit from work. "I'm sorry," he said. "There was a meeting at the office and it ran late and I had to excuse myself to get here and anyway, I'm here. I'm sorry."

Larissa and Jason were unfazed by his explanation. A tax attorney at a large firm, Kevin was often late. It wasn't uncommon for him to miss dinner. If he did make it home, he was exhausted. Larissa also worked as an attorney but had a flexible schedule. She and Jason spent most family time alone. "We're used to him not being around," she said.

That comment put Kevin on the defensive. He lapsed into an explanation of how hard he worked to make sure his family had a good life—"the nice house, safe neighborhood, megavacations, saving for Jason's college." He said he knew that Larissa wanted those things as much as he did. He was willing to make the sacrifice.

I suggested that it must be hard for him to relax and spend time with his family. Kevin sighed. "I try to go to as many of his basketball games as I can," he said, "but there's only so much time in a day." *Trying to go to basketball games*, Larissa informed me, meant he'd gone to one all season. Of course, Kevin wanted to go and because of that he'd felt like he'd gone to many more. But the truth was he was torn between work and family.

I felt similarly when my kids were young. I'd leave for the office in the morning and my son would hang on to my legs. I'd rush home to read him a bedtime story and sometimes find him already asleep. I'd go to sleep with a knot in my stomach. I felt a tug—as if my love for my son was pitted against the power of my obligations.

"Kevin's a good man," Larissa chimed in. "I try to support him, but he's not around enough. I wind up doing almost everything for Jason. I cover for his dad in a way, and try to be his mother and his father. And it's not easy being a—"

"—single parent," Kevin said. His cheeks turned crimson. "That's what she says sometimes—that she feels like a single parent."

Jason tucked his hands under his thighs. He gazed down at his feet and said he was used to hearing his parents bicker over how little time his dad spent with him. I asked him how that makes him feel. "Can I listen to my iPod while you talk about this?" he asked me. His parents shot each other a look.

Kevin told his son that he wished he could spend more time with him, that he feels as if he's always apologizing. He said he'd be there if he could, and that "I'm doing the best I can."

MOVING AWAY FROM
OLD STEREOTYPES ABOUT FATHERS

Forty to fifty years ago, fathers were silent when it came to family matters. It was a mother's job to wake the children, dress them for school, pack their lunches, and draw their baths. Mothers stroked their sons' foreheads when they struck out in Little League, and instructed their boys to be like their fathers. A son's job was to understand what it meant to be a father by observing his father from afar, by following him around the golf course or watching him flip steaks behind the grill. These "cavemen dads" would come home from work, plop themselves in front of the TV or behind a newspaper, and nurse a scotch or martini. These dads started to become obsolete as more women entered the workforce and as the divorce rate rose, making it necessary for fathers to become more engaged in everyday routines with their children.

Cavemen dads generally didn't learn good parenting skills, because their wives took care of the emotive, expressive, and intuitive aspect of caring for another family member, including their own sons. Whenever boys had a problem, cavemen dads would tell them to "suck it up," "take it like a man," or "talk to your mom about it." Mothers allowed their boys to cry and express a range of emotions. Cavemen dads grunted or gesticulated their feelings. *All in the Family*'s Archie Bunker defined this prototype for a generation of men; *Married with Children*'s Al Bundy defined it for another. These men were generally considered beloved, harmless, and laughable. They worked hard, had their bigoted opinions, but were there for their families in the only way they knew how to be. Their wives and children often made excuses for them.

Even today, many grown sons will protect their fathers' cavemenlike behaviors. "He was a good man," one forty-five-year-old man said of his dad, after he had spent thirty minutes listing all the ways his father hadn't been there for him.

Being a good man doesn't mean you're a good dad, I reminded him.

Expectations of fathers have evolved over the last few hundred years. Dads in the 1600s were expected to educate their sons in trades, and emphasize respect and authority. In the next hundred years, fathers shed that persona and became their sons' best friends and moral guides. In the 1800s, fathers returned to an authoritarian role, but at the turn of the twentieth century, "masculine domesticity" took hold, and—believe it or not—fathers and mothers ran households together. But in the mid-1900s, increasing consumerism led fathers away from the domestic role and returned him to a "provider" role. Even with the rise of the two-income family in recent decades, fathers remain the primary breadwinner. Women today earn only seventy-five cents for every dollar earned by a man.

Fathers who focus on "providing" tend to raise lonely sons. They offer birthday parties and baseball mitts, summer trips and fishing poles, but don't always give time to their sons. I'm reminded of the father-and-son pair in the classic holiday film, *A Christmas Story*. Twelve-year-old Ralphie dreams of owning a BB gun. His mother, his teacher, and even Santa Claus, tell Ralphie, "You'll shoot your eye out." Ralphie's father surprises him with the gun on Christmas morning, but when Ralphie goes outside to try it out, his father doesn't follow. He doesn't give his son a lesson or watch him shoot. Ralphie gets hurt shooting the gun and his mother comes running out to comfort him. His father's job is done.

Most sons of cavemen dads vowed never to be like their fathers. These boys fantasized about having fathers as sympathetic and responsive as Ward Cleaver, Andy Griffith, or Charles Ingalls. They aspired to be the ideal father: someone who was the man of the house, breadwinner, mentor, father figure, handyman, and role model. Their imaginations were fueled by the 1978 hit film *Superman*. They may have seen their fathers in Al Bundy but they saw themselves in Clark Kent. He was a role model who transformed their ideas about manhood. Superman had a successful career as a reporter, a passionate love life. He could save the world—and he could do it all in one day.

This generation of men came to a silent consensus: They weren't going to be great dads. Just as women expected to have it all—career, love life, and family—and be supermoms, these men were going to be superdads—mythical perfect fathers.

Alan felt he was losing touch with his twelve-year-old. Every time he got home from work, Alan would find his son in his room, door closed, playing Xbox or surfing the Web, music playing in the background. When he'd knock to say hello, he'd barely get David to say hi, much less turn to look at his father. So last February, Alan told his wife, Mary, that he wanted to take David on a ski trip. Just the two of them. It would be the perfect bonding experience for father and son.

David seemed indifferent when Alan raised the idea to him. Could he bring a friend? David asked. Of course not, Alan responded. The question hurt Alan but he pretended not to care. He told his son that this was their time together. David reluctantly agreed. In the week leading up to the trip, Alan threw himself into planning and scheduling. He created a spreadsheet listing all the items and gear they had to pack, prepaid for lift tickets online, and surfed the ski resort website to study maps of the slopes. He called the lodge to make dinner reservations, making sure the restaurant served steaks, as he wanted to buy his son a thick juicy one after a long day of skiing. He fantasized about the types of conversations they'd have in the car—deep meaningful conversations about life, the kind Alan never had with his own dad.

On the day they were to leave, Alan got home later than he had expected from work and was perturbed they were already off schedule. As he rushed to pack the car, he kept pestering David to get moving faster. After stopping by a gas station for snacks, they were ready to hit the highway by five-thirty with a five-hour drive ahead of them.

As soon as they got moving, David turned on the car stereo and tuned out everything else. Alan tried to start a conversation by talking about which slopes they'd ski—black expert or blue intermediate?— and where he wanted to stop to eat. David didn't seem to care much about either decision. He took sips of his Mountain Dew and stared out the window. Then he fell asleep.

Snow started to fall.

When David woke up, there was a soft white blanket of snow on the road. Alan wanted to have a meaningful, intimate talk, but didn't know where to begin. Instead, he brought up all the old topics he knew David would relate to. They talked about how poorly the Knicks were doing, about David's favorite Xbox video game, and what David's friends were doing that weekend. Alan felt a twinge of disappointment: their talk was no different from the terse, forced conversations they'd been having recently at home.

The snow was coming down harder and Alan was having trouble seeing the road. They pulled into a McDonald's for a quick bite and bathroom break. By the time they got back on the road, they were only two hours from the resort. From here, they would drive on a twisting two-lane road that cut through valleys and mountains.

"Dad, there's a lot of snow on the ground."

Alan pretended to shrug it off. The snowflakes looked like cotton balls, he told David, but he didn't say that they were coming down so hard and fast, straight into the windshield, that Alan was having a hard time seeing the road. "Dad," David finally piped up, "are we going to be okay?"

"Sure we are. This car can get us anywhere. That's why your mom and I bought it." But Alan was getting nervous. He was driving only fifteen miles an hour but he could feel their four-wheel drive barely gaining traction on the road.

"I'm scared," David confessed.

Alan didn't respond. The truth was that he was just as scared as David but he didn't want to let him know. Finally, after a few minutes of silence, he confessed, "You know, Dave, I'm a little scared, too."

His son perked up. "Have you ever been this scared before?"

"When I was fifteen," Alan said, "a few friends and I went swimming in the Hudson River. I wasn't such a hot swimmer but I figured I had to go along with the guys. The current started pulling me farther and farther out. I couldn't get back and I thought it was the end. Then I felt a strong arm pull me under his shoulder. It was my friend Bobby. My heart was pounding. I really thought that was the end for me."

"How come you never told me this before?" asked David.

The question stumped him. "I guess I never wanted to admit to you that I've been scared."

"There were a lot of times I've been scared but I never said anything."

"Like when?" the father asked.

"Like when I had to give that speech in school or the morning of my baseball playoff game."

"Why didn't you tell me about how you felt?"

"Because I thought you'd think I was weak."

There was a loud crunching noise outside the car, then a thump. The SUV came to a stop. Alan got out and took a look. The snow was too deep to pass through. "We're stuck. We're going to have to wait here until a snowplow arrives." It was eleven o'clock at night.

Alan could sense his son was nervous. He encouraged him to put his seat back and get some sleep. Alan thought of a Leo Tolstoy story he'd once read, *Master and Man,* about a wealthy man and his servant whose horse and carriage get stuck in a blizzard. They don't know when help will arrive so they huddle together to stay warm. The following morning, the master wakes up to find the servant frozen to death, his body covering the master to keep him warm. Alan knew it was ridiculous to think in such drastic terms. He loved his son so much he knew he'd do anything to make sure he was safe overnight. He'd do the same for his son, if he had to.

"The plows will wake us up when they get here," Alan said reassuringly. Snow continued to blanket their windows as wind whipped and whistled through the pitch-black forest around them. David seemed afraid so Alan pulled his son closer to him. The boy let his head fall into his dad's shoulders. It was the first time in years that he and David had been this physically close. David leaned closer to him for support and comfort.

As Alan held his son, he closed his eyes and thought about the last time he felt this way as a dad. It had been when David was only two years old. Every day when Alan would get home from work, David would beam his bright smile, race to the door with his chubby little legs, and give his dad a welcome-home hug. It was the best feeling in the world, and it made Alan want to be the best dad in the world. The memory warmed him inside, but it also made Alan wonder how he'd gone from feeling an indescribable love for his son to feeling vexed and estranged from him. For now the answer didn't matter. Alan gripped his son even tighter, not letting go. He wanted this moment to last. And it did—even after the plows arrived.

THE HALF-THERE DAD

Today's dads could never be called cavemen. They're forward thinking. They define masculinity differently. They're living in a world transformed by women's rights and so are often equal partners in running the household. Fathers today shuttle their kids to piano lessons and the soccer field. They sit at their son's desk at open-school night, teach their boys to ride bikes, finger paint, and fish. If a boy hurts himself, a father will wipe his tears just as quickly as his mother would.

But something unexpected happens on the way to men becoming great dads. These fathers find themselves falling short of their expectations—and their wives' and sons' expectations. Why? It's impossible to play all their roles well. They feel the pressure to be successful at work, to be attentive to their wives, and to be model citizens in their community. Most important, they feel the pressure to be great fathers. The only problem is, their own fathers did not give them the tools to be great dads. So they've improved but often find themselves stuck.

In spite of all the positive changes in being a father today, 56 percent of dads surveyed by the National Center for Fathering said they spend less time with their children than their fathers spent with them. According to a 2001 Child Trends study, fathers are half as likely to be involved in their child's school activities as mothers. One 2004 study reported that fathers with sons spend more time in the office than fathers with daughters—researchers speculate that fathers unconsciously believe it's important to demonstrate to a son a man's role in society. Sadly, only 37 percent of men surveyed in a recent study said that they're satisfied with their ability to talk to their own fathers. In another national study of fathering trends, only 44 percent of fathers reported knowing what's going on in their children's lives.

Many dads deceive themselves into believing that they'll change and become more involved in their sons' lives next year. And then the next year goes by without any change.

Nonetheless, today's dads have come a long way. They're a major step beyond the caveman dad of old, and most important, they want to be *more* involved in their sons' world. But, like today's mothers, they're struggling to juggle work and family. Mothers often describe their husbands as rushing around trying to do all the right things but not quite pulling off anything well. Their families often feel as if they never get "all of him." Yet one recent study found that 74 percent of fathers prefer a "father-friendly" job to a "fast-track" job, a good illustration of how much men want to be better dads.

But the study said nothing about how many fathers actually have "father-friendly" jobs—and few do. Less than 50 percent of the fathers who come into my practice have jobs that make them available to their families. With everything from real estate to gas prices shooting up over the last several years, parents are under increasing pressure to provide. Men who wish they had "father-friendly" jobs are caught "keeping up with the Joneses." Some fathers approach spending quality time with their sons the way they approach a meeting at work—if it's not scheduled, it won't happen.

Many fathers delude themselves into believing that being success-

ful or having a powerful job will raise their stature in their sons' eyes
or inspire their sons to be successful. But this is often simply a rationalization for their own obsessive drive to prove themselves, and for their
being more comfortable at work than at home. Too many men confuse
giving material things with giving the most precious thing they have
to offer—time. They buy their sons laptops, expensive sports equipment, cars, hoping that their sons will overlook their absence or lack of
attention. But boys don't overlook this. They yearn for their fathers.
Think of it as "father longing." Father longing colors a son's existence.
His grades suffer. He's more susceptible to peer influence. Maybe he
does just fine—maybe he becomes highly successful, eventually—
but he may spend his life analyzing why he wasn't good enough for his
dad, what was more important to his dad than he was. And that
legacy is likely to affect his relationship with his own son.

Because fathers today are so wrapped up in work and getting ahead,
they're often only "half there" for their sons. A struggling dad is the
guy you see at the playground talking to the parents more than he is
interacting with his boy. He's the parent at the soccer game who has
got his head buried in his BlackBerry or is jabbering on the phone. He
may not be plopped in front of the TV nursing a scotch, but he has no
problem forcing his son to watch the Patriots game rather than watching *Ice Age* for the ten-thousandth time. He physically "shows up" for
his son but he's not exactly sure what to do while he's there. These dads
aren't "good-enough" fathers.

Half-there dads don't realize that their sons would feel just as
resentful and hurt when they see their dads typing on their BlackBerries at a basketball game as they would if their dads hadn't shown up
at all. "Sometimes my son looks me in the eye and asks me if I'm listening to him," says one forty-three-year-old father. "I'll say, 'Sure,'
knowing full well that he caught me drifting again."

The half-there father is a man in the middle. On one hand, he's
determined to be a good father, available to his son and actively

involved in his boy's life. On the other hand, he doesn't know how to be. He's expecting better parenting skills to come naturally to him and doesn't know how to ask for help. Some dads are so overwhelmed by how far they are from their parenting ideals that they stop trying at all. Others try so hard but still fail to connect with their sons, which causes them to give up on fathering altogether.

One of my patients recently told me a story that illustrates the half-there father perfectly: Steve is CEO of a small company. His seven-year-old, Matty, wanted to learn how to ride a bike, so they went to the park one afternoon. Matty said he was nervous and Steve reassured him he would never let him fall. Matty climbed onto the bike and his dad held the handlebars to keep him balanced. When his father tried to lift his hands, Matty screamed. He didn't want his dad to let go.

After half an hour, Steve started growing impatient with his son; he was acting like a baby. Matty said he wanted to go home but Steve insisted that he try it a few more times. On the next try, he let go of Matty's bike. The boy glided ten yards. Matty started screaming for his dad, but it was too late. He crashed into the curb, scraping his leg. He lay on the ground crying.

"Matty," he yelled. "Get up and ride that bike. Are you a man or a mouse?"

The seven-year-old looked at his father angrily. "I'm a mouse," the boy said. "Deal with it."

This is a great example of a half-there dad. He took his son out to teach him and spend quality time with him. It was a moment they would remember forever. But this potentially wonderful memory turned sour, mostly because Steve treated his son as he would an underperforming employee. Steve's lack of patience is a side effect of his stressful job, but also demonstrates how tenuous is his hold on being unlike his father. Steve promised himself that he would parent differently from his father and would swear to me that he was nothing like his own father, but, when stressed, he instinctually became a caveman.

He called on old definitions of masculinity to push Matty to do something he didn't want and didn't have to do. And the result was disastrous; he lost his son's trust.

What would have been the correct way to handle a situation like this? Let me retell the story in a way that might help you understand and glimpse a "360-degree dad," or a dad who turns his parenting around.

Stuart is a CEO of a small company and one afternoon he decides to teach his seven-year-old, Mark, how to ride a bike. They walk a couple of blocks to the park. Mark says he's nervous. "I'll never let you fall," Stuart reassures him. Mark climbs on the bike and his dad holds the handlebars to keep him balanced. When his father tries to lift his hands, Mark screams, because he doesn't want his dad to let go.

After half an hour, Stuart starts growing impatient with his son, who he thinks is acting like a baby. Mark says he wants to go home but Stuart wants him to give it another try. He doesn't push it, but he encourages Mark to take a break. The two walk over to the swings. And as Mark glides back and forth, Stuart asks him what is scaring him. "I feel like I'm going to tip," Mark says.

Stuart tells him that he was just as nervous when he was learning to ride. He had fallen several times before he could stay up. Stuart describes to Mark how good it feels when you finally get it right. "What's the matter with falling anyway?" Stuart asks. "You just get back up and try again."

After a half hour, Stuart encourages Mark to give it one more whirl and he does. Stuart grabs hold of the handlebars. "Okay, Mark, now pedal," he says. "I'm going to let go as soon as I think you're steady." Mark nods nervously and begins to pedal. Stuart lifts his hands for a few seconds but doesn't leave his son's side. When Mark's bike wobbles, Stuart catches it before he falls.

"How about one more time?" Stuart asks.

When Mark says he's had enough, Stuart gives him a hug. "That was brave of you," he says. "You'll get it next time."

See the difference? In the first story, Steve is a stressed CEO who grows impatient with his son. In the second, Stuart reframes what could have been a tense moment into what educators call a "teaching" moment in a day and a lesson that his son will want to remember forever.

Now let me set the record straight. I'm not saying boys shouldn't be raised to be strong. I'm just saying that if fathers and sons want to connect on a more meaningful level—and many do—then they need a new framework for doing so. When Matty told his dad he was a mouse, he was sending a powerful signal. He hadn't yet learned that he was supposed to be tough. He was a little boy enjoying an afternoon with his dad. But he learned that his dad wanted him to be something else. And that moment may stay with the child forever. It's certainly haunted Steve. He remembered that he'd tried to teach Matty how to bat a year before, but that, too, ended in frustration for both of them. Then he remembered how demanding his own father had been—and how much he had hated him for it.

Men like Steve and Alan don't understand why they're not connecting to their sons. They all want to know: "What am I doing wrong?"

Last year, Bernie, forty-three, came to talk to me about his eleven-year-old son, Patrick. From the outside, Bernie had the perfect life, a sprawling house, a new promotion at work. He played golf on Sundays and coached his son's Little League team. But he felt anxious and wasn't sleeping at night. He always felt as if he wasn't doing enough for his son. "When my son was born," he told me, "I vowed to myself that I'd be a different kind of father than my dad was to me. But despite my promise, I'm still struggling with the same things that he did—getting ahead in my career, being a good provider, and finding enough time to spend with my son. Much as I hate to admit it, I often feel rushed and I have trouble letting go of work and other self-imposed obligations so that I can be with my son a hundred percent." His relationship with his son has suffered and Patrick rarely asks Bernie for help anymore. When Bernie asked him why, Patrick said, "It's easier to ask Mom." Bernie knows it's because his wife is always around. Bernie isn't.

Men are working harder than ever and it's keeping them from their families. A 2003 survey of over three hundred fathers conducted by the website CareerBuilder.com found that 65 percent of fathers worked more than forty hours a week; 25 percent worked more than fifty hours. And that's counting time spent only in the office. Add in the time we spend checking e-mail at home or responding to BlackBerries in the middle of dinner. Men are often on the road; 54 percent of fathers travel out of town for work. Surveyors confirmed what I see in my practice every day: the most common question children ask is, "When will Dad be home?" It's often Mom who has to do all the explaining.

WHY WIVES ARE FRUSTRATED

The following is an excerpt from a therapy session with Joe and Kathy Littles. They have two boys—a nine-year-old named Clay and a six-year-old named Giles.

Kathy's take:

Joe promised me he'd wake the kids this morning at eight A.M. and get them ready. But when I check on them at twenty after eight, they're still puttering around in their pajamas. Clay is playing Game Boy. Giles is looking for his socks. We've got to be out the door in twenty minutes. So where's my husband?

Joe's in the kitchen reading the paper.

I hustle the kids to get ready. When the kids and I walk into the kitchen, Joe smiles at us, as if the kids miraculously got dressed on their own. I feel like wringing his neck. I want to yell, "Am I the only competent parent here?" But the kids have only ten minutes to eat before we have to load them in the car. So I don't say anything at all. But again, I feel like I just can't count on Joe to get things right.

A Dad Is Not a Male Mother

Joe's take:

I got the kids up on time and told them to get ready and come down-stairs in fifteen minutes to eat. They're not babies anymore. They ought to be able to do things on their own. Then before I know it, Kathy comes in the kitchen and gives me a dirty look. She's rushing everyone to get ready like we're going to miss a plane or something. We haven't been in the car five minutes before she's on the phone yelling at me because we forgot Clay's cleats. She doesn't appreciate anything I do. Let her do the damn stuff herself.

Joe isn't exactly a caveman dad, but his perception of his role as a father and partner in parenting needs some readjustment.

Women have a right to feel frustrated with their husbands. Their ideals for men have evolved just as rapidly as their husbands' ideas about fathering. Two decades ago, more women entered the workforce, creating two-income families. These women wanted it all, to be great moms *and* career successes, to be "supermoms." Many men expect this of their wives, too. But to ensure that both careers move forward requires equal partnership at home and in parenting.

Husbands and wives want to run their households as couples. Dads cook some nights. Mothers take out the trash. Dads take the kids to soccer games and doctors' appointments.

That is the general expectation on both sides, but what I'm seeing play out is quite different. Dads do want to participate in child rearing, so they will cook dinner and slip out of an office meeting in order to make a parent-teacher conference. They will mow the lawn Saturday morning and shop for the kids in the afternoon. They've certainly stepped up their role inside the home. But few women would say that they married men who are their parenting equals. Instead, many women often feel betrayed, as if their husbands somehow deceived them into thinking they'd do more when they promised that they'd be highly evolved, available fathers—a new breed of dad.

Men weren't being purposely duplicitous. They thought that better fathering would come easily to them. For some it has. But the majority of men I see in my practice are struggling. They didn't realize how unrealistic it was to think they could do it all and still be a different kind of dad.

Still, you can't blame women for their mounting frustration; they're married but they often feel like single moms. Lots of women say that they appreciate what their husbands do to help, but it's just not enough. Many of them are in the same predicament their own mothers were in—overstretched. "I get up and go to work," says one twenty-nine-year-old mother. "Then I get home, play with the baby, feed the baby, put the baby to bed, cook my husband dinner, clean the house. By the time I'm done, it's ten P.M. . . . time to go to bed. Then I do it all over again the next day. I feel like I'm doing everything by myself. If things don't change soon, I'm going to flip."

An underlying assumption in many marriages is that mothers do, and fathers do when they're asked. A mother is going to know if her son's laundry needs to be done and throw a load in. Today's father will happily do his son's laundry, but he won't think of it on his own. Television shows such as *Nanny 911* depict incompetent dads in nearly every episode. The nanny gives advice to mothers, who in turn filter the information to their husbands. That line of communication would be expected if they were stay-at-home moms, but many mothers on the show—and in America—continue to be working moms. So even though the expectations of fathering roles have changed, fathers still parent from the periphery, and mothers still are considered the alpha parent. And their resentment over it is building.

Take Joe and Kathy, the couple featured in the story above. Kathy asks Joe to get the kids dressed and take Clay to his soccer game, but Joe drags his feet. He doesn't feel the same sense of urgency to get Clay to his game on time or to remember that Clay has to take his cleats. This makes Kathy furious that she has to stop what she's doing and work double-time to make up for his lax parenting. Things get tense between the couple because Joe, who considers himself a modern, available father, doesn't comprehend what he did wrong. He got the kids up, told them to eat breakfast, and drove his son to his game. Joe believes he's helped out—his job is done. What Joe doesn't realize is that his ideas on "doing the job" are based on an outdated assumption that "helping out" is fathering.

Kathy expects Joe to be an equal parenting partner. She expects him to think three steps ahead of her to meet their kids' needs, just as she does. When Joe forgets the cleats, it illustrates that Joe's parenting is still dependent on Kathy's direction. Joe didn't get the kids up independently, feed them breakfast, and then shout out to Kathy that he was taking the boys to soccer, while she read the paper. Kathy had to give him a checklist of assignments. When Kathy expresses her disappointment, her husband says she's unappreciative and next time he won't help at all—as if his role in caretaking is optional rather than a requirement.

That's not good fathering—Joe is another example of a half-there dad.

I don't blame men for being confused. They're stuck in what I call "the father trap": they're drawn to fatherhood by their desire to outfather their own dads, but when they do become parents, they realize they have no idea how to go about being different. They're parenting in the dark, often not having had a positive role model, uncertain of what's considered "good enough," "not good enough," or "more than enough." Many men still don't define their self-worth based on how good a father they are. Unsure how to attain the closeness that they crave with their sons, they are still putting more pressure on themselves to perform as well at home as they do at work. They want to do better.

You should know that your feelings of frustration are legitimate and that you're not alone in feeling them. The parents' stories in this chapter are meant to help you identify the problems you're having, so that you can move forward in solving them.

My hope is that you will be honest with yourself about your strengths and weaknesses and, in turn, take your fathering to the next level. I often tell men, You can become the father you've always wanted to be, the role model that your son needs. But you need to open yourself to change. By the end of this book, you'll see that in becoming a better father, you'll become a better man.

DEFINING GOOD FATHERING

Harvey was camping for the weekend with his son's Boy Scout troop. He didn't have time to be a troop leader, because he was a software sales-man and on the road most of the week. When his son, Hal, told him that fathers were invited on the next camping trip, Harvey jumped at the chance. He rarely had his twelve-year-old to himself.

On the first night, the boys stayed up talking around the campfire. Harvey enjoyed watching his son interact with the other boys. When one of the children bullied another about his weight, Hal intervened, making a joke about the bully's zits. "Nobody's perfect," his son said. Harvey had told Hal that the week before when his son had spilled milk on the couch. When he and his son locked eyes, Harvey gave him the "thumbs-up." His son smiled.

When the boys fell asleep, Harvey stayed up talking with the other fathers. A few complained about their wives. One was going through a divorce. Then they started comparing what video game systems they'd bought their sons and where they'd taken their families on vacation. The conversation turned to what cars they drove, what percentage rate they got on an equity loan, how you shouldn't take out an equity loan. Harvey listened. He drove a nice car and he had a big house but he didn't feel the need to tell the world about it. He changed the subject.

"Do you think you're a good father?" Harvey asked a guy wearing a John Deere cap. Every time Harvey took off in an airplane, he'd think about the possibility of it crashing, which made him worry about his family. What would they do without him? He'd flown often lately and he'd been thinking a lot about his relationship with his son. Am I a good father? he'd recently asked himself midflight.

The men shifted uncomfortably around the fire. One said, "I'm here, aren't I? If that doesn't make me a good dad, I don't know what does." A couple of guys laughed. Someone asked if anyone had seen the Redskins game.

Harvey told me this story when he was talking about his fears one afternoon in my office. He had come in several months after this trip because he was worried about his son, who had become distant from him and his wife. Hal was giving one-word answers and holing up in his room. They didn't know how to deal with this change.

Harvey tried to be there for his son. He attended most of his son's events but missed some because he worked hard and traveled often. So he'd send his son e-mails, offering anecdotes about whom he'd met that day, the place he was in, or just saying he missed him. "I don't let work run my life," he told me. "Some men I work with stay in the office just to avoid going home. It sickens me."

I would later talk to his son, whose behavior had nothing to do with his father or mother. Hal was on the verge of puberty, and was pulling away naturally, as adolescents do. I mentioned this possibility to Harvey and we set an appointment for Hal.

Harvey seemed satisfied. He began to stand to leave. Then he sat back down.

"Doc," he said. "Am I good enough?"

Harvey needed encouragement. I told him truthfully that I'd be happy if I had him for a dad. He wasn't perfect but he didn't have to be. He was fully present when he was with his son. Hal didn't have to vie for Harvey's attention and never felt like an afterthought. Harvey left my office breathing a sigh of relief.

Says Harvey: "Sometimes you just need to know that you're doing okay."

*   *   *

You don't need to be perfect to be a good father. You just need to work harder and with more awareness than you are now. Forget about being superdad, the perfect dad. There's no such thing as the dad who thinks of everything, gives everything, sacrifices everything, succeeds at everything. If that person existed, he'd be miserable. He'd be living for everyone but himself.

Fathers who burden themselves with unrealistic expectations often feel guilt and heartache. They're uncertain in their role and constantly second-guess their parenting skills. Sometimes they mask their self-doubt by acting overconfident. Lots of men I see want me to tell them that they're good fathers, but I have them ask themselves whether they are. They—and you—can usually answer that question. If you feel guilty, you're probably not giving your son something he needs. If you feel close to your son, you're probably giving him enough of yourself. If you have never considered your son's feelings then you're probably not giving him much at all.

Men are task-oriented, so I'm giving you some tasks that will help you learn to be a better father. You don't have to be the best. But you do need to be good enough. Here are your assignments:

- A "good-enough dad" finds balance between being there for his son and nourishing his own spirit.
- A "good-enough dad" should commit to being home at dinner at least two or three nights a week.
- A "good-enough dad" keeps his promises and shows up when he says he's going to.
- A "good-enough dad" listens attentively and makes his son feel important and understood.
- A "good-enough dad" expresses his feelings openly and encourages his son to do the same.

Fathering is a study in contradictions—gentle and rough, serious and silly, strict and lenient. A father is often moved by his son's hurts and disappointments, and is always looking to protect him from the cruel world. No matter how many mistakes a father makes, he will always play an indispensable role in his son's development. Even a flawed father can be good enough.

As you read on, you'll meet dads who have struggled to balance career and family; men who are having trouble making peace with their own fathers; men learning to openly express their feelings to their boys. And you'll hear from mothers and sons who catalyze a father's transformation.

You can find the courage to change, and new ways to become a dad for all seasons and still be comfortable in your own skin and "all there" for your son. No need for excuses or guilt. Just get to it. Your son is waiting.

It's time to get the father monkey off your back.

CHAPTER TWO

Generational Mistakes

Facing Your Regrets About Your Own Father
So You Can Become a Better Dad

I was flying to visit my daughter at the University of Michigan when I met Steve, who told me his thirty-one-year-old son had gone to the same school, but that he had never visited him there. He had a thick gray beard, so I figured he was in his sixties. I told him he had missed out—even the football games were exciting, more than a hundred thousand people cheering for a single team. Steve looked out the window. I went back to my book.

Then Steve looked over at me. "I'm visiting my son this weekend— for the first time in a few years," he said. What kept them apart so long? I asked. He looked at me suspiciously.

"What do you do?" he asked. When I told him I was a psychologist, he laughed. "Man, I could have used one of you," he said, and we spent the rest of the flight talking about his son. Steve opened up to me on that short airplane ride; he was extremely anxious about seeing his son.

"I'm going to level with you," he told me. He and his son had never felt 100 percent comfortable around each other, but it had started when his son was a teenager. Over the years, they could talk about sports and 401(k) plans and that was about it. "I'd invite him to games and concerts," Steve said, "but he always had something else going on. He wasn't home much after he left for college."

Steve always thought that their relationship would change, promising himself that he'd work harder to improve it. But then his son would come home for a visit and they'd fall back into the same old pattern. It didn't help that they had little in common: his son was an artist and had little interest in football anymore; Steve tried to be interested in his son's paintings but they were so abstract he didn't really understand them.

We got talking about the regrets we'd had as fathers. I told him that I wished I'd known my own father better. He said he wished he could have known his son.

"It's never too late to start," I said.

Steve looked out the window again. Then he looked back at me, his brow furrowed.

"I have a feeling he's going to get engaged one of these days," he said, "and I'm not even going to know his girlfriend."

CHANGING THE PAST

The bottom line is that we all have regrets when it comes to our own parenting and decisions. Men call it Monday morning quarterbacking. Women think of it as learning the hard way. Nearly every father I've worked with dreams of "do-overs," moments with their sons that they wish they could do differently. They go through their day-to-day lives feeling weighed down by decisions they made years ago, beating themselves up over career choices they've made that kept them from their families, failures to seize opportunities to connect meaningfully with their sons. A father's love for his son is so great that even thirty years later, he can still remember the look on his son's face when he said he couldn't make it to his soccer championship. Years later, that father will wonder out loud, "What could have been that important that it kept me from being there?" Yet many men realize they are doing to their sons what their fathers did to them. Still, they don't know how to break the pattern.

Regrets often surface long after a father has conditioned his son to give up on him. Fathers rarely admit where they went wrong. They're not so good at showing vulnerability and few have the courage to apologize. Instead, many men ball up their regrets, file them away in their hearts, and spend a lifetime aching. Besides the pain caused by not expressing feelings of regret, tensions between father and son build, sometimes to the point that the two grow estranged. Many men die without ever telling their sons that they're sorry. And because of that, sons don't always know the tremendous sacrifices their fathers made for them in the name of love.

It's important for you to admit your regrets and get to the heart of them. Your son can glean a powerful lesson from your willingness to admit that you've made mistakes. He may see himself in your admission, for instance, and learn from the stories you tell him—he may learn practical lessons as well as emotional ones that will stay with him forever.

Fathers make some of the same mistakes from generation to generation. They spend too much time at work and not enough time at home. They push their sons by criticizing them. They never say "I love you." And many don't have a clue that they're damaging their sons. They think they're doing what's best for them only to find out years later that those very actions hurt them terribly.

You can face up to your regrets about your own father and about your own fathering of your son. To help you recognize your own disappointments—so that you can avoid perpetuating them—I've pulled together a number of different stories of fathers and sons. Think of these stories as parables, maybe even cautionary tales. As you're reading, track your reactions and figure out where you and yours fall. Remember: it's never too late for you to change course and transform your relationship with your father and your son.

TELLING DAD WHAT YOU NEED AS AN ADULT—
BEFORE IT'S TOO LATE

Lowell was a thirty-eight-year-old investment banker. His father, Shorty, as his friends had always called him, was a sixty-six-year-old retired construction foreman. Father and son couldn't be more different. For years, they'd argued about anything there was to argue about. Lowell would bash conservative Republican politics, just to annoy his father. His father would hammer back with criticisms of the Democratic Party. If Lowell talked about getting a new car, Shorty would go on about how crappy they made cars today, point to his 1978 Chevy Nova, and say, "That gal is still running as good as the day I got her." Lowell would roll his eyes; the car was a jalopy and his father knew it. Shorty had lots of opinions about Lowell's children. Lowell was too lenient on them. "You're making spoiled brats out of 'em," Shorty said. "And why do they do so many after-school activities?"

Shorty was good at making his son feel bad. But as I sat talking to Lowell about his eleven-year-old son, Brady, I realized that Lowell was doing the same thing to his son. He often argued with the boy and heaped on criticism, just as his dad had done with him. And Brady was feeling just as rejected as Lowell had when he was younger. I was certain that Lowell's unresolved antagonism with his father was getting in the way of his relationship with Brady.

"It sounds like your relationship with your father has always been strained," I said to Lowell. "Have you ever tried talking to him?"

Lowell shook his head. "He's impossible to talk to. He's always right," he said.

"But do you think your dad really understands how he makes you feel?"

"I doubt it," Lowell said. "He's been doing it since I was a little kid."

"And so he'll keep doing it until the day he dies?"

"I guess so," Lowell said.

You shouldn't allow your father to treat you in a way that you would object to if anyone else tried it, I told Lowell. His wife, Lisa, who was sitting in on the session, said that Lowell puts up with things from his dad that he wouldn't from anyone else. "His dad is always perfectly nice around me," she says. "Then Lowell gets home and Dad's nasty side comes out."

Lowell admitted that it had always been difficult for him to stand up to his father. In fact, he'd never been able to. I asked if Brady had ever stood up to Lowell. Not yet, Lowell said.

Sometimes you—and plenty of other men—need to hear things that you don't want to hear. Lowell was every bit his father's equal now. He was no longer a child and he needed to make it clear to his father that he couldn't push him around as he always had. "Maybe he has no idea how he's affected you over the years," I said. "But he needs to hear it and you need to say it." Lowell smiled slyly.

"I know," I added, "you're going to tell me that talking to him is a complete waste of time."

"Come on, Lowell," Lisa chimed in. "Don't tell me you're still afraid of him."

"I'm not," Lowell said. "It's just that . . ."

"Just what?"

"I just hate feeling like I'm in battle with him. I have trouble finding the right words and even if I do, he changes the subject or turns it into an argument."

I told Lowell what I tell all my patients longing to be closer to their fathers: Your father isn't going to live forever. If he died tomorrow, wouldn't you regret not telling him how you felt? Wouldn't you want to have a stronger relationship with him in the years that the two of you have left?

I asked Lowell to try a role-playing exercise: Lisa would play his dad. Lowell would finally tell his dad how he was feeling. Think of it as practice, I told him.

Lowell clenched his hands. Nervous, he began tentatively. "Dad, I've never really been able to talk to you," he said. "When I was growing up, you were always so busy. When we did talk, you turned it into a lecture. My opinions and feelings didn't seem to matter."

Lowell stopped. He was blushing. "I can't do this," he said. "It's silly." I pointed out that he'd never said these feelings aloud before. It was important to do so.

"I used to wonder why you had me," Lowell continued. "To this day, we can't talk without arguing. I'm pretty successful and I still don't think you respect what I think or believe. I've always wanted a real father, someone who'd be there for me when I needed him."

I was struck by what Lowell had said and I encouraged him to say those very things to his dad.

Several weeks later, Lowell stopped at his father's house after work. He'd tried talking to his father a few times already but had lost his nerve each time. This afternoon, his dad was in his garden, pruning his tomato plants. Lowell leaned down next to him and began to weed. "Now don't go ripping up my good plants," Shorty scolded.

"Why are you always so harsh with me?" Lowell snapped. It had slipped out and Lowell's heart began to pound inside his chest. Lowell didn't look up at his father but he knew he had got his attention. Shorty's shears had fallen silent.

"I'm not being harsh," his father said, gently. "I'm just making sure you know the difference between a healthy plant and a weed."

"I wish you wouldn't," Lowell said.

To his surprise, his father didn't start an argument. In fact, he didn't say anything at all. The two stayed in the garden, pruning and weeding in silence, for the next half hour. Then Lowell got up. "I got to get home for dinner," he said. His father nodded.

It may not have seemed like much but for the two of them it had been a breakthrough. Lowell began stopping by and joining his father in the garden more frequently. He felt more comfortable asking other questions. What was grandpa like? Did you like working in construction? His father didn't pour his heart out but answered what he could. Shorty said his own father picked apart everything he did, just as, he admitted, he'd picked at Lowell. Over the next six months, Lowell got to know his dad better. They still bickered but the arguments felt more like debates—a battle of two equals.

Lowell's relationship with his father changed forever when they were sitting in the emergency room together one morning several months after our session. His son, Brady, was getting stitches in his knee after he had fallen off his bike. Lowell was clearly upset, beating himself up for not having watched Brady more closely.

Shorty put his hand on Lowell's knee. "We all have regrets about our sons," his father told him. That was the apology that Lowell had needed all these years later. It allowed Lowell to let go of his anger at Shorty, and, having finally acknowledged his own shortcomings, Shorty became gentler with his son, which Lowell appreciated.

Soon after, Lowell walked into my office humming. Brady had quickly bounced back from his fall, and was spending more and more time with Shorty. The three of them had plans to go on a fishing trip together that weekend.

The full-circle change was inspiring, but it could happen only after both father and son had let go of the past. Because Lowell felt less angry about his relationship with his dad, he was also less angry at Brady. He worked hard to correct his own tendency to be hypercritical, trying his best to catch himself if he criticized Brady, and even apologizing a few times after he had been harsh inadvertently.

Brady was a bit shocked at first. "Dad's been acting weird," he told me. But as his trust toward his dad increased, he welcomed him back into his life. Sure, they still argued, but their battles had shifted from one-upsmanship to a respectful interchange.

Think for a few moments of your own father. What made you laugh or warmed your heart? One of my patients couldn't stop laughing when he told me how his father would walk around the house with his boxer shorts pulled up high above his waist. "It was out of Revenge of the Nerds," he said. Another man remembered how his father would return home from business trips with a surprise for him in his pocket. "That was always exciting," he said. His father would pull out the trinket and tell a story about where it came from. It made him curious about the world and today, he too travels for his job, and always brings home a gift for his children. "It helps me feel close to them," he says.

You've probably also had moments with your dad that still make your blood boil. Unfortunately, these are the times we tend to remember most. Getting past the anger of the memory, however, is important. You want to see a pattern behind it and you want to make sure that that pattern is not one that you yourself have fallen into.

When fathers are struggling in their relationships with their sons, I often challenge them to probe what their own father was like. We typically don't consider our father's parenting style. Dad is just dad. But think about it. Was he controlling? Was he a pushover? Did you put him on a pedestal? Did you fear him? Often, the issue that's dogging a man and his son is the same issue that dogs that man and his own father. Fathering patterns are passed down through the generations. An emotionally open father will typically create an emotionally open son. Scientific studies, as well as my own experience as a therapist, show that abuse perpetuates abuse. The point is simple: you may try to parent differently than your father, but if he's your only role model, how else are you likely to behave?

Jed came in to see me last year with a big chip on his shoulder. He was always angry. He could rant about everything from the driver who had cut him off as he was turning into the grocery store's parking lot to the boss who was hassling him about meeting his sales quotas. Jed came in because his son was getting into fights at school, and his wife wanted Jed to help him calm down. But Jed and his son were often arguing themselves.

Not surprisingly, Jed's father had often put him down in front of others as a child. Whenever Jed succeeded at something, his father made light of it. Jed's father had a lot of mechanical knowledge, but Jed was more gifted with numbers. His father called him "good for nothing." It took Jed months to realize how much his everyday anger was rooted in the way his father had treated him. "How dare he do that to me?" he lamented one afternoon.

What Jed hadn't thought about was how much his own father had influenced the way he was fathering—and how that had affected the temper of his own son. Every time Jed blew up at someone, his son was watching. Now, whenever his son got angry, he did the same thing as Jed.

Jed was forced to take a good look in the mirror. At first he didn't like what he saw, but gradually he made the connection between his behavior and his son's and began trying to control his temper. He learned to take deep breaths or punch his fist into his hand to give his feelings an outlet and give himself time to collect his thoughts and maintain his cool. He sat his son down and shared these same techniques, admitting that his own behavior had been a problem. They agreed that they would work together to change that and decided that, when one of them was about to lose his temper, the other would yell a code word—"Boil"—to put the behavior in check. Jed also talked a lot about his own father and apologized to his son for the way he tended to snap at him. "Too much anger can get you in a lot of trouble," he said. "It's getting me into trouble and it's getting you into trouble." They committed to helping each other break their family legacy of anger.

HELP YOURSELF

Are you doing to your son what your dad did to you?

You don't want to think that you could be hurting your son, but there's a chance that you are if you're caught in a generational fathering pattern as Jed was. Want to break the cycle? Start by figuring out what those patterns are. Ask yourself the following questions:

- Has your wife ever commented that you're acting just like your father? If so, when does she say it? If not, ask her if she sees any similarities—and listen attentively.
- Think about the things that your father did to make you angry. How does it make you feel today when you think about them? Do you ever act that way to your son?
- When do you get angriest with your son? Do you see yourself in him? In what ways: good, bad, or just neutral?
- Tell your son that you want to become more aware of the things you do that upset him so that you can make your time together more enjoyable. Can he name a few?
- What are some of your traits that you're not proud of (e.g., anger, cynicism, rigidity)? Think about where they come from and if they relate to your father.

THE FATHER YOU NEVER WANTED TO BE

Ryan wasn't exactly happy to see me, having had to leave work early to get to my office by four. At forty-seven, he had dark rings under his eyes; yesterday, he'd stayed at the law firm until midnight. He sat down, still in his suit and tie, and made it clear that he wasn't a fan of therapists—his brother was one and psychoanalyzed just about everything—but his wife had begged him to come. Their teenage son, Will, was cutting school, talking back, and leaving the house when he was supposed to be grounded. Ryan said he was willing to try anything to change this dynamic—Will was driving him ballistic.

"Tell me about your own dad," I asked him.

Ryan smacked his leg impatiently and stared hard at me. I knew what he was thinking: I left work early for *this*? "What does my son have to do with my father?" he asked.

"More than you might think," I said. "Go with me on this."

Ryan shook his head. "My relationship with my father was crazy," he said.

"You would have had to grow up with an ax murderer to make it into my patient hall of fame," I said. We laughed, which made him relax a little. Then he began.

Ryan and his siblings had spent their childhoods tiptoeing around their father. His mother feared that the children would make her husband angry so she kept them in their bedrooms doing their homework. Ryan could still hear the sound of ice hitting the bottom of a highball glass as his father mixed himself a gin and tonic whenever he got home from work. With a few more before dinner, he'd be drunk by eight. "I wasn't so good at minding my business," admitted Ryan. "The man had no patience when he was drinking and guess who was his target?"

I pointed at Ryan. He nodded.

"Did he ever participate in your school activities?"

"He'd come to basketball games now and then," he said. "I still remember the one time he stood up in the stands after I scored a winning basket. He yelled, 'That's my son!' Man, that felt good."

"So he was proud of you?"

"Maybe," he said, "but he rarely showed it."

"Do you let your son know when you're proud of him?"

Ryan grew quiet. He said he did once in a while. "It's not easy," he said.

"Now we know why," I said.

As a boy, Ryan had vowed never to be like his father. He promised himself that he wouldn't drink, would compliment his son often, would never be unrealistic in his expectations. He'd accept Will for who he was and encourage him when he was trying his best. But as Ryan's star began rising at his law firm, he grew impatient with his son. He

37

didn't have time to push Will to be the best—Will should *want* to be the best. Ryan had become a perfectionist at work and at home—he wanted everything done right. "No shortcuts," Ryan often told Will. At the end of a football game, Ryan didn't tell Will, "Good save, son." He said, "Why don't you tackle more aggressively?"

Ryan was doing to Will what his father had done to him and it was keeping the two of them from growing close. Yet Ryan hadn't lost sight of his father's behaviors that he didn't want to repeat—he wasn't an alcoholic, he did show up for his son, he didn't humiliate his son. Ryan was not responsible for his father's actions but he was responsible for his own, and he would find a way to be a good father, despite his own tainted legacy. Ryan would have to monitor his own interactions with his son carefully to make certain he was not replicating the emotional hardships he had endured. Still, Ryan had plenty of time to make changes within his own family. Will and Ryan came in to talk together with me and we were able to clear the air of resentment between them. Will was able to say that he wanted his dad's support, but didn't want to feel pushed all the time. Ryan was able to step back from some of his own expectations of his son and allow Will to pursue interests of his own without feeling hurt that they weren't the same as his. He was also able to establish a new way of talking with Will that communicated his affection and concern for his son without being hypercritical.

Generational mistakes tend to persist if you don't make a conscious effort to dismantle them. The sons of workaholic fathers tend to fill their emotional voids with big, stressful jobs. Children of divorced parents can spend their lives wondering what they would have been like if their parents had stayed together. The sons of stoic fathers often mourn the lack of fatherly love. Adult children of alcoholics share a panoply of emotional and psychological issues.

One patient told me that his father would scream at the whole family when he got home, insisting that no one else but him was doing a fair share of chores. My patient found himself doing the same thing to his family, and hated it. He'd get easily frustrated with his wife and son when they complained that he wasn't home enough, hearing in their voices the faint echo of his own father: "You're not doing enough." He had begun to feel as resentful of them as he had been of his own dad and realized that he couldn't just dismiss their requests or their feelings.

Then there was the father who spanked his son for being disobedient and then felt so sickened at what he'd done that he couldn't sleep all night. He had once promised himself he'd never hit his children the way his own father had hit him. His father had actually chased him around the house with a belt strap, terrifying him. As a child, he had never understood what he'd done wrong. Yet as an adult, if someone in his family tried to give him feedback on something he'd done wrong, he'd grow defensive. He could barely listen to his son's point of view in an argument. Because he saw himself as the perpetual victim, always the boy who was attacked unfairly, he overreacted, even when the criticisms he heard as an adult were far from abusive. Once he realized this, he worked to change his perspective of himself and his place in the world, which also improved his relationship with his son.

One patient talked angrily to me about his father's penchant for putting him down in front of others. He vividly recalled how his father would find fault with almost anything he did. "If I got three A's and one B, he would complain about the B. If I cleaned my room, he would look around like a drill sergeant until he found the one thing I forgot to do. I guess that was his way of keeping me in his place and making himself feel better." But this patient had become just as critical of his own son—which shocked him when he realized the unconscious generational mistake he'd been making.

Criticism and emotional neglect deflate self-confidence, weaken trust, and fuel depression. Sadly, too many men repeat negative patterns that their fathers established for them. Be honest with yourself about how you parent. Are you making the same mistakes your father made with you?

And how do you break the cycle? First, you need to understand what kind of dad your father was. It's one thing to assess a man; it's another to evaluate a father. You need to name the pattern that you disliked in your dad, recognize why it affected you negatively, and track when you do the same thing to your son. It may be difficult but your wife—or even your son himself—will probably be able to help point out those moments. Here's an exercise to help you.

HELP YOURSELF

The Soul Search

I have done this soul-searching exercise with many fathers and it really helps. You can answer these questions alone or ask your wife to explore them with you:

- In what ways did your father let you down?
- When have you felt your father's strength?
- What's the best moment you ever spent with your dad? Why was it special?
- In what ways have you let your son down?
- Can you think of a few things you didn't like about the way your father raised you? Are you doing any of these with your son?
- How are you like your father?
- Can you recall any powerful lessons your father taught you?
- What were your father's expectations of you and how did they affect you?
- How did your father treat your mother? Is it similar to the way you treat your wife?
- Do you feel you had your father's support and approval?
- Did your father ever talk about his father? What do you recall?
- Are you happy with your relationship with your own son?

- Take a close look at yourself. Is there anything about you that you should change?

DON'T KNOW DAD? LEARN ABOUT HIM

Many men don't know their fathers very well, even though they love them and spend time with them. If you really think about it, can you explain much about who your father is as a person? Men like to do activities when they're together—watch the ball game, play a round of golf, swim laps at the YMCA—but they don't typically sit around the dining table asking each other deep personal questions. We envy our wives when they do that with their fathers, though.

You can still get to know your dad. Every family has its historian, the person with the facts and insights who can tell the family story—Grandma or Aunt Sadie, Uncle John or the next-door neighbor of forty years. Whoever it is, court him. Milk him for every bit of family folklore that he can recall. Put together the pieces. If you understand your roots, you may understand long-standing resentments. You'll get a sense of what drove your father to act the way he did, which can lead to understanding and even, if necessary, forgiveness. This sort of research is a relatively pain-free way to get to him. You don't have to talk to him if he's difficult. You get to talk about him. Often, it provides just enough incentive to initiate a peaceful dialogue with the man you want to know most.

Take Peter, who, at thirty-three, didn't understand his father. The two were cordial but never close. Peter talked to his mother often, but if he asked about his father, his mother gave him little insight. "He's a good, quiet man," she'd always say. That made Peter think that his mother didn't understand him, either.

One night, Peter asked his Aunt Elsie, his father's sister and the family gossip, to meet him for dinner. She'd told Peter funny stories about his father over the years but he had never really inquired about why his father had seemed so distant, as if his mind was somewhere else. "He's always kept to himself," Peter told Aunt Elsie. "I'm starting to think there is a reason why." Elsie nodded knowingly. She told Peter that his father was a tortured soul.

"He was always quiet," she said. Growing up, he never got into trouble. He worked hard at the corner store and never asked for much. He'd come to Elsie for advice about girls but mostly he didn't let things get to him. He had a small group of friends with whom he played basketball but otherwise he was a loner. Peter asked Elsie what she thought his father's biggest regret was. Elsie hesitated. She wasn't sure if she should tell Peter. When Peter sensed she was holding back, he repeated the question.

"He walked away from the love of his life," she said. It was the summer of 1973 and Peter's dad was backpacking across Europe. He was writing in his journal at a Parisian brasserie when a woman with black eyes and red lipstick asked if he wanted more coffee. For the rest of the afternoon, Peter couldn't keep his eyes off her. He asked if she would join him for dinner that evening. At dinner, he learned that she was an art student. She invited him to see her sculptures. They spent the next several months together.

"When your father returned," Elsie said, "he brought her with him. I believe her name was Juliette. She was beautiful." Juliette didn't like the States. She missed the pace of Parisian life. Ultimately, she moved back. She begged him to come with her. But he didn't want to leave behind his family. They exchanged letters but after several months, they drifted apart. "That's when your father met your mother," Elsie said. "Your mother was very different from Juliette." Juliette was a free spirit who encouraged Peter's father to work on his music and not take the world so seriously. "Your mother took charge from the start," Elsie said. "She wanted a nice home, fine jewelry. She pushed him into his first sales job."

Peter was fascinated by this information and felt that he finally understood why his father was the way he was. His father was more than the staid salesman he'd grown up with: he had had a romantic side. He'd been an adventurer. He'd felt pain. It was a relief to know that his dad was—gulp—human.

Not only did hearing this story help Peter understand his dad, it gave him something to ask his dad about. When Peter brought it up, his father spent the afternoon reminiscing about picking olives in Tuscany, of swims he took in crystalline Alpine streams. He was shy when it came to talking about Juliette, but Peter understood. He told me that for the first time in his life, he felt that he had no regrets about his relationship with his dad. Said Peter: "We had more in common than I ever thought. He wasn't just a quiet man. And he felt that he had lived a full life."

UNRESOLVED REGRETS

Let's be frank. It's hard work building a father-and-son relationship later in life. Despite your best efforts, there are times when the obstacles will be too formidable. When this happens, you must make peace with your father as he is. In essence, you must give up on repairing the relationship. I don't advocate this often but sometimes the attempt to improve relations with your father can be such a strain that things between you grow worse. Sometimes you have to accept what you can't change. And that takes a lot of strength.

Jimmy talks about his failed attempts to connect with his dad freely now—but he went through a lot of agony about them. Like Lowell and Shorty, Jimmy and his dad were polar opposites. His dad was a successful businessman and flag-waving conservative. Jimmy listened to the Grateful Dead as a teen, took a couple of cross-country trips as a college student, and was drawn to liberal causes as an adult, volunteering for both of Bill Clinton's presidential campaigns. After law school, Jimmy got a job as a public defender and today runs a staff of twelve overworked and underpaid true believers.

His father never approved of any of it and Jimmy grew tired of his father's contempt for his life and decisions. They had argued for years and as a result had drifted apart. Still, Jimmy called his dad on the phone and tried to talk. He wouldn't talk about his job, but would tell his father about his daughter's first day of school or how she was taking ballet lessons. His father wouldn't respond much; he'd ask to talk to his granddaughter and then hang up. As far as the father was concerned, he was going to punish Jimmy for the rest of his life for being so different from him. After months of therapy, Jimmy realized that he was banging his head against a brick wall. He had tried to meet his father halfway for years. His father wasn't willing to budge. Jimmy's daughter continues to have a good relationship with her grandfather, nonetheless.

Gil also had to give up trying to change his dad. A thirty-seven-year-old attorney who has two young sons of his own, Gil rarely sees his father. His parents divorced when he was nine years old and Gil went to live with his mother, who eventually remarried; his father moved out of state. His father wasn't a deadbeat—he had provided child support and sent plane tickets for Gil and his older sister to come visit him on holidays. But they had never really felt like a family. Gil remembers being uncomfortable in his father's house; for example, he had to sit up straight on the couch while watching TV. There was no traumatic falling out, no especially hurtful behavior, but there was very little bond between them; Gil looked at his stepfather as his dad. As Gil entered college, he and his father talked once or twice a year. But when Gil became a father, he wanted to connect with his dad in a more meaningful way. He would call more often, invite him out to his home for holidays, chat with him about golf (since it was all his father did these days). But his father didn't seem interested. He often turned down the invitations, saying he had too much going on to fly across the country for a visit. After a while, Gil gave up.

Several years later, Gil came to see me. He wanted to know if it was wrong for him to write his father out of his life. "I feel guilty," he told me. "Should I keep trying?"

The answer is no. There are times when all you can do is accept the reality, even if it is painful. Sometimes our fathers do not turn out how we had hoped. Both Gil and Jimmy were haunted by their feelings of disappointment in their dads. So they gave up—and broke free from their anger. They had lives of their own now. They had sons who needed good parenting. And they were relieved to hear that they had done the right thing.

Anger can consume much of your emotional energy, wreak havoc in relationships, and color your existence. I do believe in working out long-standing, unresolved issues, but sometimes either the father or the son makes resolution impossible. One will refuse to be in the other's presence. Another allows his grievances to affect his relationship with his siblings or grandchildren. Sometimes the only way to make peace is to agree to disagree and to avoid each other. But men, if you are in a stalemate, you need to recognize how you've contributed to it and not simply blame the other person.

If things can be worked out, someone has to compromise, to give in. Before you give up on your dad, I suggest that you try to be the one to give in. Being right is rarely as important as being close.

There's an ancient Jewish tradition observed on Yom Kippur, the Day of the Atonement, during services at Temple. Family members are asked to turn to one another and say the Hebrew word *Selichah*—the loose translation is, "Please forgive the hurt I may have caused you this year." The other person responds with *Mechilah*, meaning, "I forgive you." It's an emotional, symbolic ritual designed to help us take responsibility for our own behavior and open the door to reconciliation.

Perhaps there's an opportunity for you to do this with your father or your son. It offers both of you the possibility of a new beginning.

HELP YOURSELF

A Graveside Chat

Some men lose their fathers before they're able to resolve the problems between them. It's a difficult burden to bear but you can come to terms with it so it doesn't feel like a life sentence. Early in my career, a supervisor suggested that I visit my mother's grave and talk to her about the things that were never said between us. First I balked at the idea. Then I tried it.

It was awkward, initially. I kept turning around to see if anyone was looking. But I found myself pouring out my heart—I apologized to her. I thanked her. I updated her on my life. When my father joined her there ten years later, I did the same thing with him. I've told my dad about my son's graduation from college and my daughter's acceptance into one. One day I told him that I wished he had been stronger and hadn't always given in to my mother. I told him I had forgiven him for what he wasn't—he was neither a successful businessman nor an emotionally expressive dad—and then I thanked him for what he was—a kind, generous man. "You were doing the best you could," I said. "I see that now with my son. I'm doing the best I can, too." I talk to my parents once a year and I make peace with some of the issues I had with my parents that have followed me through the years.

These talks would have been wonderful to have had in person, but this is all I have. The cemetery is a safe, peaceful haven where you have the sacred opportunity to feel your parents' spirits. I encourage you to do the same.

WHAT KIND OF REGRETS WILL YOU HAVE?

We've talked a lot in this chapter of our regrets about our fathers. But do you have regrets about the way you're parenting now?

Generational Mistakes

When I meet with younger fathers, I encourage them to think about what kind of father they want to be, and then to assess the kind of father they actually are. I ask them to imagine that they're approaching the pearly-white gates of heaven and they're handed a scorecard with the following questions:

- How were you there for your son when he needed you?
- How did you live a life that set a positive example for your son?
- Looking back, would you say you did the best you could?
- Would you and your son agree that you had a good relationship?

I tell men to be honest with themselves as they rate their fathering. They don't get extra points for the size of their house, the cars they drive, or the fullness of their bank accounts. Over the years, the men to whom I've given these questions have reacted in three ways. Some are made uncomfortable just by looking at the questions; they have trouble facing their peripheral, half-there parenting. Others are hard on themselves and admit that they're already regretful about not being around enough for their sons. And only a few have said that they wouldn't change a thing.

The father-son bond is unspoken, an accepted fact but largely undiscussed. Fathers often *assume* that their sons know how they feel about them. They assume that their sons understand why they're too tired to talk about their sons' victories on the soccer field or failures in math. But sons don't understand why. They only know as much as you did when you were that age and assume you are blowing them off. Your long day at the office isn't an excuse.

Sometimes it takes a near tragedy to make us realize what's most important.

Carl was the creative brains behind a large advertising firm. At forty-five, he loved his job but it required long hours. "I'll slow down one of these days," he would tell his wife, who was always begging him to spend more time with their two boys—one in fourth grade, one in sixth.

47

Instead, he spent most of his time running from place to place. He would make it to his children's events but then rush back to work immediately afterward. He would watch his son in the school play but skip the congratulatory party and sundae afterward.

In bed one night talking to his wife, Carl felt a sharp pain in his chest. He was a young guy—heartburn, he reassured himself, and popped a few Rolaids. But the pain persisted. A few hours later, he woke up, holding his chest, feeling faint. His wife got him in the car and drove him to the emergency room. As soon as he arrived, Carl was hooked up to a heart monitor, convinced he was going to collapse from a heart attack at any moment. A nurse took his vital signs.

"What if I—" he started to say. His wife silenced him. But Carl couldn't help but think of all the times in the last couple of years that he had skipped the "congratulatory sundae" with his kids. He couldn't remember the last time he'd spent alone time with his boys. What if I never got another minute with them, he thought?

A few minutes later, the doctor came in with the EKG. He smiled. "You're not having a heart attack," the doctor said. "It's a panic attack. Have you been under a lot of stress?" Carl gave him a quick run-down of his job, his hours, his life. He looked at his wife: "Things have to change," he said. It was a pivotal moment. Carl was coming home—from the hospital but also in spirit. Said Carl: "I want to know my boys."

GRANDFATHERS RECLAIMING SONS

As the end of life draws near, some men are comfortable admitting their regrets—at least to themselves. Some actively work at developing better relationships with their adult children, to make up for a lifetime of estrangement, spending more time with family. Fathers who struggled in their relationships with their sons often make up for their failures by becoming attentive grandfathers. They have the wisdom of experience. They know what worked in their relationships with their sons and what didn't. They have the opportunity to get things right.

A man may feel his father's love only through his children. One patient told me that his father, a stoic disciplinarian, revealed a softer side whenever he spent time with his grandson. "He took him out for ice cream and bought him stuffed animals," he says. "I was floored. He never once did that for me." Clearly his dad was making up for lost time.

Eighty-four-year-old Dennis had been married twice and is engaged to marry again. He enjoyed a successful medical career and lived a full life, but has regrets about his son Mark, now fifty-four. Mark was coming up just as Dennis's medical practice began to take hold and grow. "I didn't pay him much attention," Dennis says. "At least, not as much as I should have." Their relationship was further strained because Dennis didn't relate to Mark, who was a jock, always competing in basketball tournaments or begging to attend baseball camp. Dennis preferred the creative pursuits of his older son, Paul. "He was who I always wanted to be," Dennis says.

Mark went to college and became a professor. Paul fell into drugs and lived at home until his death from hepatitis C in 1997. Still, Dennis protected Paul. "He was a kid who liked to sow his wild oats," he says. "I never got to do that. I related to that."

Looking back, Dennis thinks his son Mark picked up on his preference—and it caused tension in their relationship. Further tensions arose when Dennis divorced Mark's mother, an alcoholic. After years of begging her to get help, Dennis gave up. He never told his son Mark about his mother's addiction, preferring to keep his son from the pain. But Mark grew to hate his father for leaving his mother. "I regret not telling him," Dennis says. "I think our relationship would have improved dramatically. I've told my daughter about these feelings but not Mark. I've just never been comfortable around him."

In recent years, Dennis decided he wanted to be closer to Mark. "A man of my age doesn't have much time left," he says. He began visiting Mark, his wife, and his two granddaughters as often as he could.

Mark would take his dad golfing with a group of his friends, but was careful never to spend time alone with his dad, which Dennis understood. When his son mentioned that he was worried about layoffs at work, Dennis encouraged him to talk about it. "I made sure to listen to everything he was saying," Dennis says. "I became the confidant, which was more than I'd ever been before."

Dennis said the greatest moment he ever spent with his son was when Mark had planned a day of golf for his dad and friends but his friends dropped out at the last minute, leaving father and son to play alone in the early morning of a crisp Virginia winter day. Dennis actually didn't play, but simply watched his son. Mark pointed out the secrets behind shooting par on every hole. They stared at the distant mountains and talked about nature's beauty. Mark was so excited sharing his world with his father that he seemed innocent, like a young child—and in that moment it felt to Dennis that he was able to be the attentive father he'd always wanted to be. "It sounds like nothing," Dennis says. "But it meant the world to me. I followed him around and listened. We agreed on everything. It was wonderful. We'd never felt so in sync."

Bud, a seventy-year-old retired CIA analyst, says it's much easier being a grandfather than a father, especially because you don't have to do it every day. His kids have always been important to him but he dotes on his three-year-old grandson more than anyone else in his life. He spends one day a week with him and really looks forward to everything they do together. They go to the park, the zoo, and watch TV. I asked him if he spent as much time with his son as he did his grandson. "And take a day off from work?" he smiled. "Never!"

Many grandfathers I've spoken to echoed similar feelings. It's easier to do this stuff when you have more time, and when you're old enough to see where you went wrong the first time around. "I really enjoy it," said one sixty-eight-year-old grandfather, "but it's good to know you're returning them to their parents." Another grandpa told me, "I probably spend more time with my grandchildren than I did with my son. When you get older, your time gets more precious, and you think seriously about how you're going to spend it." Most telling, one grandfather confided: "I feel like I'm repaying my grandchildren for the time I didn't spend with their father."

Sadly, many grandfathers' regrets are the same. They say, I wish I had been more involved. "I spent too much time worrying about how much money I was making. I probably let my wife run things with my kids too much. It's always easier to look back and say what you should have done. There's still time left, though. I'm thinking I can make up for some of the things I didn't do."

A seventy-three-year-old retired researcher told me that he looked forward to spending time with his grandson, because he could be alone with him—without his ex-wife present. When his grandson was a baby, he enjoyed doing basic child-care stuff such as giving bottles, changing diapers, etc. "My wife wouldn't even let me in the room when my son was a baby. I'd never changed a diaper in my life. Now I feel more involved. I actually feel more competent as a grandfather than I did as a father."

In the book *Letters to Sam*, author Daniel Gottlieb writes thoughtful letters to his real-life grandson, sharing wisdom on everything from discovering girls to remaining young at heart. One of the most powerful moments in the book involves stories he tells of his own father, whom he calls Pop-Pop. He and Pop-Pop show each other very little affection. When Pop-Pop passes away in his apartment in Atlantic City, Gottlieb learns that we don't realize what we'll regret until what we love is gone.

He and I had our last visit the day before he died. It was a very windy day. When I got to the apartment, he was sitting in the front of the window, warmed by the sunshine. I pulled my chair next to him. After I rested my arm on his shoulder, we gazed down at the beach together, not saying much.

A strong wind was blowing sand directly into the ocean, erasing all footprints. It seemed if the wind kept up, all the sand would blow into the sea. The beach was being swept clean. As I watched the beach renew itself, I moved my hand to my father's chest, drawing him closer. Without looking up, he took my hand, kissed my left thumb—the only area on my hand where I have sensation—and gently rubbed his cheek on it.

The next day, his nurse found him dead in the same place, sitting in his favorite chair in the living room, facing the ocean. . . . But for several days after his death, whenever someone asked whether I needed anything, I began to cry. "Yes," I thought. "I need to feel his cheek on my thumb one more time."

As long as I am alive, whenever I am with you, I will be glad to tell you about your pop-pop. He was a small man—small in stature and small in the mark he made on the world. He did not lead any groups or organizations. All he did was marry a woman he adored and raise two children who were capable of love and compassion. He lived and loved. He left the world pretty much as he found it.

Some day, Sam, you will take the measure of your own father. You will see the role he plays in his family's life, in your life, and in your mother's life. You will know the dimensions of his impact on the world. But I know that none of those judgments or measurements matters very much. What matters is the way you look at the ocean together.*

So you see, a good father is not judged by his accomplishments or the material possessions that he's accumulated over the years. He is remembered for what he was—a man devoted to his wife, who taught his kids through his example, or who was there when his kids needed him. The measure of a man comes from who he is on the inside, not who he projects on the outside. Too many "cavemen," "superdads," and "half-there" dads give their sons opportunities instead of emotions, a generational legacy that we need to stop. Appreciate your father for who he was and recognize who he wasn't—and use this information to rewrite the relationship you have with your own son today and every day thereafter.

*From *Letters to Sam* ©2006 by Daniel Gottlieb. Used with permission from Sterling Publishing Co., Inc.

CHAPTER THREE

Sons in Progress

Fathering Through the Developmental Stages

> My father gave me the greatest gift anyone could give
> another person—he believed in me.
> —Jim Valvano, basketball coach,
>   North Carolina State University,
>   NCAA Championship basketball team

Hank was thirty-two when his wife got pregnant. Even though they married in their twenties, they had purposely waited until later to have children, because, he believed, he would be more mature and financially stable. In other words, he'd be ready. "Boy, was I mistaken," he told me.

Having watched his buddies with their babies, and thinking they seemed to be having fun, Hank had envisioned taking his son on trips to the ballpark and sleeping with him in tents under the stars. He hadn't considered that, before they could do that, his son would first appear as a crying, needy infant. Hank found his newborn hard work. By the time he came to see me, he was overwhelmed. "I come home from the office exhausted and my wife expects me to take over after dinner," he said. "I don't want to take over. I need a break."

Sometimes his wife placed the baby in his arms, pecked him on the cheek, and left to go to the gym. Then Hank didn't know what to do.

His son would cry and cry and Hank would grow terrified when the tears went on too long. He'd call his wife's cell phone every few minutes—"Honey, where is his binky?" "Which bottle do I feed him?" "Honey, he won't stop crying."

When their son turned one, Hank's wife decided her husband needed "bonding" time with him. Plus, she wanted Saturday mornings to sleep in. It was his job to get up, feed the baby, change him, and play with him. Hank loved his son but admitted that he was a reluctant father. He felt like he'd had to give up so much. "My son would wake up and want to play immediately," Hank told me. "I want to wait a few hours before doing anything. Relax. Read the paper. Then I can crank it up. But fatherhood doesn't work that way."

The research is definitive. Boys who lack involved fathers and adequate male role models don't do as well in school. They're at greater risk of getting into trouble. They're more likely to have difficulty with relationships later in life. Boys, and even men, struggle without their fathers. Fathers parent differently than mothers. They're generally not the world's greatest nurturers, but fathers can do for their sons what mothers can't. They teach them to defend themselves and to pee, to knot their ties and to shave. They can reminisce about getting erections in class and how to deal with that. A father is not a male mother, nor should he be. Nonetheless, there are situations in which fathers can try to be more nurturing to their sons. For instance, when a toddler falls and injures himself, that's not the time or age to be telling him not to cry. You want to learn how to comfort and encourage your son at every stage. You'll learn your own style of nurturing from experience—listen carefully to your son's voice, observe other dads, and adapt to the situation.

All men want to get fathering right. But fathering is difficult. We don't get a manual when our children are born telling us what to do, how to feel, and when to shift our priorities. But we ought to have one, and that's what I'm going to give you in this chapter.

THE INFANT/TODDLER YEARS

I'll never forget the first time I changed my son's diaper. I had spread out the essential paraphernalia—diapers, baby wipes, powder, all of it foreign to me—laid down my son, and tried to operate at warp speed. I held him with one hand while reaching for the supplies with the other, worrying that his tiny squishy body might fall off the changing table. What if I hurt him? So I moved him onto a blanket on the floor and started all over again.

His cries, my fears, his kicking legs—we were in sensory overload, and I still had to get the fresh diaper on him, which I quickly learned was an art form. I would lift his bottom and slide the diaper underneath, but as I lowered him he'd somehow kick it out from under him. I would reposition it and he'd do it again. It was frustrating: "How hard can it be to change a damn diaper?"

I was a bumbling father in my early years, as many men are when first grappling with baby care. Babies explode into our lives. They turn our worlds upside down. Men who are used to sidling up to their wives for impromptu moments of intimacy are suddenly hovering around changing tables. They're warming baby bottles instead of Irish coffees by the fireplace. And when the baby cries in the middle of the night . . . Mom isn't the only one expected to get up.

Yet many men still take a backseat in caring for their sons in the infant years. They rely on their wives to take on the bulk of the child care, claiming that women's "motherly instincts" trump their own shaky skills. They write themselves out of the parenting equation. On the other hand, sometimes a wife's new "motherly instincts" can keep a father from spending time with his newborn.

For instance, Craig, a thirty-four-year-old dad, says, "My wife and my baby boy are having a love affair." From the moment his son was born, he felt like a third wheel. Gillian was always around the baby, breast-feeding, fawning over him, talking about him. The baby defined her. Craig had been used to getting most of his wife's attention, but now with the baby, "she was too exhausted for me," Craig said. "Sometimes I wonder if they realize that I'm around. Sure, I help with chores, errands, and logistics, but there's always this nagging feeling that I'm dispensable."

Fathers aren't supposed to admit this about becoming new dads, but they have trouble sharing their wives with their sons and daughters. As much as a man celebrates the birth of his first child, he also mourns the loss of his wife as he knows her. "You're different ever since you had the baby," one thirty-five-year-old man told his wife. "I can't pinpoint it. But we're different." Women reconfigure their world around their newborns. And if a mother is the moon to her son's earth, then fathers are frequently the more distant stars.

Existing on the periphery at home is a big change for most men. They don't want to say it because they think they sound ridiculous, but they are initially jealous of the relationship between their wives and sons. It's not just because their wives' energies are now divided, but because they don't always know how to connect with the infant. "Why doesn't it come that easily to me?" one young father asked.

You need to know from the start that you're a major player in your son's life. You do not have to be on the periphery. Your wife needs you and so does your son. You can't pull away, get scared, and leave your wife to fend for herself. Mothers bond with babies because they work at that bonding. They spend time doing it through all the little chores of taking care of the infant. Most mothers—like fathers—are learning how to parent on the job. They're not just naturally better at it. You can and need to do these little things, too. Forget about being superman. Men like to make checklists, run errands, pay the bills, do the gardening, change diapers, warm bottles—all of which is extremely helpful—but they need to spend time with their babies, too. You can't just expect a bond to emerge. Your baby needs to know that his dad feels comfortable with him. If your baby screams after being placed in your arms, you need more time with him—not less.

Here are five ways to keep your wife close and your son even closer:

Seize Every Opportunity

Watch and listen to him. Grow familiar with his actions. Hang out—it's that simple. Play an active role in your son's life from the start. Offer to take him to the pediatrician, feed him. Forget being afraid to ask questions. It's okay to not know what to do.

When holding your son, talk to him and comfort him. Play with him. Babies will become acutely aware of your presence this way. A baby will fix his eyes on his father and keep them there while his dad is interacting with him. In a month or two, the child will be smiling and gurgling when his dad arrives home. Fathers who take the time to bond with a baby in this way are greatly rewarded. "I felt like I'd won the lottery when my son's first words were 'Da-da,'" one man told me.

Adjust your schedule. Get up in the middle of the night when the baby cries. Learn to get by with less sleep. It builds character. If your baby is waking up at six in the morning and falls asleep by seven at night, you need to make time to catch him awake. If you don't, you'll find yourself a "weekend parent."

He's Not "Just a Baby"

Don't make the mistake of saying, "He's just a baby. I plan to do more with him when he gets older." This is a weak rationalization for not being involved. You are laying the foundation for your relationship with your son, setting the tone for a lifetime of interaction. Babies are in tune with the people around them even during their earliest years.

Will your son wait eagerly for your return home from work, or will he scarcely notice your arrival?

Colin, twenty-nine, didn't realize how important his son's early years were. "I didn't spend much time with him when he was a baby," he admits. "I left almost everything to my wife, figuring she was the expert and would get the job done. Even though I felt left out, I told myself that I had more important things to do than changing diapers, like building my career and paying the bills. By the time my son was three, my wife was angry with me for my lack of involvement and my son naturally gravitated toward her. I felt like I had to pry him away from her just to get his attention. If I did, he'd say, 'Where's Mommy?' It took a year before I could make up for some of the precious time I lost. But now we're expecting another child. This time, I'm going to get in on the action from the start. I learned the hard way."

Talk Baby Talk

I've heard many men say that talking baby talk is dumb. That's like saying football talk or sex talk is dumb. It's not. Baby talk is the language of babies. You may as well learn it sooner rather than later. Babies respond to the sound and tone of our voices as much as they do to the words themselves. Repeating "Hi, Baby," "Peek-a-boo," or "Bye-bye" hundreds of times will do more good than you think. When your son makes a cooing sound, coo right back. I'm not suggesting that you shouldn't talk normally to your babies, too. In fact, you should—it's another way for you to connect with your son. Name the objects in the room; talk about them. Talk about your day, your feelings, where you plan to take him that weekend. Of course, he won't understand, but that doesn't matter. As you talk with your baby, you're setting a pattern of easy communication for the future. You're telling your son nonverbally that you enjoy being with him, and the two of you will feel increasingly comfortable in each other's presence.

As babies grow into toddlers, they begin to use their voices—and at times you will feel as if you need an interpreter. When my son was a year old, he would shout gibberish out the car window whenever we drove down a certain street. My wife and I were puzzled until we heard him do it when an ambulance drove by and we realized it was the way he expressed excitement. Lots of fathers are excited themselves when they decipher their sons' ramblings. One recalled how his son would shout "bird" whenever Big Bird appeared on *Sesame Street,* and suddenly connected that bird to the real ones flying around them in the park. Another laughed heartily when he told me how his son would say "Bye-bye" to the truck that hauled off their trash every week. It's fascinating to watch your guy begin to make sense of the world around him— which includes you.

As your son begins finding his voice, encourage and converse with him. I tell dads to talk to their toddlers the way they would an eight-year-old. Tell him about your life; ask and answer questions for him so he gets used to the give-and-take of being with other people. Learn what makes him laugh—it'll end up making you both laugh.

Be a Kid Again

The world is wonderful and fascinating to little tots. Every day they're on a new adventure. Why not join your little one on his journey? Some of the best dads are the ones willing to meet their sons in the land of play. Get down on your hands and knees, crawl around, make animal noises, laugh your heart out. You don't need an arsenal of toys to be a good father. What you do with the toys is more important than the toys themselves. You can turn basic stuffed animals and puppets into a world of action. Toddlers love when you give these animals voices and make them talk to one another.

Mothers sometimes complain that their husbands are too rough. One mom told me that her heart would drop every time her husband threw her giggling toddler up in the air, but her husband would catch him every time. There's nothing wrong with this "roughhousing." It's how many men play. But do be careful. Pediatricians have told me stories of kids being injured inadvertently by overzealous fathers.

Take Your Son with You

Whether it's the grocery store or the backyard, find a way to include your son. It's part of the bonding process. Put your son to work with you in the garden or take him to the grocery. Yes, it's more work to keep him busy, but I can't overemphasize the importance of spending time with each other. Follow your children into their worlds. Go to the playgroup to which your wife usually goes with your son and observe your son at play. You'll meet other fathers and share stories. Plus, Mom gets a break.

CHILDHOOD CUES FOR DAD'S ATTENTION

When my son was four, he was scared of the dark. I would tuck him in, read him a bedtime story, and, when he was unable to keep his eyes open any longer, tiptoe out of his room. Often he'd wake up right after I closed his door. One night he called me back because he said he heard a noise, certain there was something or someone in his closet. At first I told him he was being silly. There was nothing in there, but my son was upset and convinced something was in there. Then I realized that I had to abandon logic and think like a four-year-old.

I decided to put on a show and went in the closet like gangbusters. I opened the door with courageous effect, and screamed, "All right you, you get out of there!" My son stared at me. When there was no response, I said, "You put one hand on my son and I'm going to break your nose and make you cry. You better never ever come back here or you'll be sorry. I'll turn you into dog poop!" My son began laughing hysterically. Then he snuggled with his pillow and closed his eyes, assured that the intruder would never return. There I was, Dad the dragon slayer. It was the closest I ever came to playing a superhero—and I loved every minute of it.

Babies grow into toddlers and toddlers into young children faster than new parents can imagine. Within a few years, a father will have a full-fledged little boy following him around who craves his dad's attention and hangs on his every word. More than anything, boys desire love and acceptance from their fathers and will often ask for it directly. When fathers join their sons' worlds, they often hear, "Daddy pick me up," or "Daddy, will you tickle me?" or "Daddy, hold me tight," or "Will you take me to the zoo today, Daddy?" But boys learn to stop asking for these things when fathers fail to respond. They begin keeping their feelings to themselves and stop asking Dad for what they need.

Worse, they may also learn the unfortunate lesson that any attention is better than no attention at all. That's why little boys sometimes misbehave—just to grab their father's attention—which is the beginning of the cycle that many men had with their own fathers: a physically close, yet distant, relationship, in which they spend time with Dad but don't always tell him what is on their minds.

Play Attention

Fathers can have an open, close relationship with their sons from the start, but too many fail to realize that these interactions need to begin early. When a boy says, "Hold me tight, Daddy," most fathers will scoop up their son and squeeze him in response to a touching, clear cue. But it's also important to respond to the smaller, seemingly unimportant cues, such as, "Play car with me, Daddy," or "I want to see the tigers today, Daddy." This is your son's way of asking for your attention. A boy isn't going to jump up and down and yell, "Notice me!" Instead, he tries to establish a relationship with his father by asking to be tickled or to be held—it's something innate that makes him want to be close to his dad.

Of course Daddy is tired when he gets home from work and playing car might seem insignificant at a time when mortgage payments and management challenges are running through his head. But playing car is very important. Even though you can sit on the couch, turn on the television, and have your son playing next to you—happy just to be near you—watching TV together doesn't foster your relationship with your son. You're merely existing with your son, not burrowing into his world and responding to his need for attention.

Many fathers waste moments with their sons. I know I have over the years. But you can get better at recognizing your young son's cues. Then you can keep track of how often you're turning down your son, and be sure you are saying yes more often than no.

In early childhood, children's imaginations run wild, and good fathers find a way to fuel their sons' fantasies rather than squash them. They say "Yes" as often as they can. Whether it's Santa Claus, the tooth fairy, or the "boogie man," you become a player in the game—it's your job to honor the cherished and feared myths of childhood. One father I know told his son that the tooth fairy was a "bunch of bullshit" and he wasn't going to be a part of "the stupid tradition." If his son wanted money, the boy could do a chore around the house. This was a dad who had forgotten how to be a kid and who would eventually infect his boy with his own rotten attitude.

I'm reminded of Tennyson, who wrote, "How many a father have I seen, / A sober man, among his boys, / Whose youth was full of foolish noise." He reminds us that too many men forget what it's like to be children—full of hope and optimism and open to possibilities. I had, too, all those years ago, until my son helped me realize that I needed to enter his imaginary world in order to slay the dragon he heard in his closet. That moment changed my perspective—and brought us closer.

Set Limits

In addition to helping your son develop his imagination and dreams, one of the most important lessons you teach your son in his early years is about accepting limits and learning self-control. What do I mean by limits? Well, it's important that your son know such things as what behaviors are appropriate and what are not, when he can be mischievous and when he cannot, when his requests are reasonable and when he's asking for too much. We've all seen kids in the local grocery store throwing temper tantrums. Watch the father. He'll either ignore the kid, making everyone listen to the shrieks, or he'll lose his temper right back. Either way, he is not setting proper limits for his son. You need to be consistent so that your son learns self-control.

A patient named Mickey recalled how he and his son would often have wrestling matches. They'd roll around on the floor, pin one another down, yell and scream. "When it came time to quit," he told me, "my son's engine was still revved up. It would take a few minutes to settle him down." Mickey was uncertain about how to calm his son. In other words, he needed a lesson in setting limits. I told Mickey to sit his son down before they began playing next time and to tell him that when Dad said it was enough, it was enough. Mickey went home and practiced with his boy that night. He talked to his son about knowing when to quit. They got into a wrestling match. When Mickey said it was time to stop, his son hit him over the head with a pillow. Mickey understood the first time his son didn't listen, but on the second, he grew firm. He reiterated his talk about calming down. He did the same thing the next time and the time after that. It took a few weeks but soon his son got used to stopping when his father told him to.

Play can teach your son how to rein in his actions, express his feelings, and respect the rights of others. Talk to any kindergarten teacher and you hear the same thing: Kids like limits. They crave them. They like feeling that there's a wrong and a right way and that they're choosing the right one. With young children, you can transform any moment into a teaching moment.

Take Billy, whose nine-year-old son, Lee, would get so frustrated when he was playing video games that he would throw the control on the ground and pitch a fit. Billy and his wife wanted Lee to stop that and realized that they could teach him a lesson in expression—just from playing video games. Billy had a one-on-one talk with Lee and asked him what about the video games was making him so angry. Lee said he didn't know, so Billy asked the same question a couple of different ways: "What upsets you?" "Do you dislike the characters?" "Do you get mad at yourself?" Finally, Lee admitted what was wrong. "I feel stupid because I can't beat the game," Lee told his dad.

Billy had had a feeling that's what was bothering Lee and told his son that he knew how he felt. "I always wanted to win prizes when I went to the arcade as a kid," he said. "I often came up empty-handed."

"But there are a lot of things I can't do, Dad," Lee said. "It makes me mad—really mad. Sometimes other kids tease me. That makes me want to scream."

Billy was touched by his son's disclosure. Billy hadn't had to say anything deep; he had just needed to be honest about himself, listen to his son, and tell him what was in his heart. "You know Lee, you may not be the best at everything but as long as you're really trying, I'm proud of you," he said. "If you ever want to practice at something and try to get better, let me know. I'll help you."

The Value of Patience

Sons remember the moments when they felt their fathers' love and pride in them. Chris, a thirty-one-year-old history teacher, will never forget an experience at age nine. "I had never pitched before and the coach called on me to pitch," he says. "I complied only because I had to, but I was so scared I was going to fail. It's one of those things you never forget. I don't remember what field we were on, but I remember the back-stop on the field. It was getting dark and the ump was a young guy who was really into it. I pitched that inning for the first time and struck out the first three batters I faced. I remember the crowd was very loud. It was a heated Little League game, and I was embarrassed at the attention and also excited by it. I vividly remember my dad sitting on a picnic table behind home plate and raising his hands in the air after every pitch and then jumping up and down for that last strike. I felt like I had made him so proud, like he was the happiest he had ever been with me. I know he has been happy since, but that twenty-year-old memory still sticks . . ."

This was a defining moment for Chris—but it could have gone differently. Patience goes a long way when it comes to fathering, but I've seen fathers ruin times like this for their kids and the rest of the team. They scream at their sons to throw the ball harder or yell, when a boy misses a pitch and gets upset, "Stop being a crybaby." Humiliated children don't learn very well. Their self-confidence suffers and they don't want to be around fathers who embarrass them. I'm not suggesting that you never yell at your son, but make sure you develop patience in dealing with your son. It's vital to being a good father.

If patience is not your strong suit, consider the following advice in advance of the next time your son gets upset: Think about how it feels when someone loses his temper and yells at you. Anger magnifies a negative experience. Your son is already probably hurt and sad that he's disappointed himself or you in some way, so your anger may make him less likely to make an effort in the future. Is that how you want him to feel? You can probably remember a time when your father yelled at you and how awful you felt. You have so much guidance, caring, and courage to give your son. Why undercut your authority and his trust in you by showing your anger? The next time you get angry with him, try this: Count backward to keep your cool. Or imagine something pleasant for about a minute before you react. Since the most likely outcome of your screaming will be to make the situation worse, make a neutral comment or ask him questions about his behavior and motivation.

If you can't stay calm, you may want to consider taking meditation, yoga, anger-control classes, or getting into therapy in order to get to the root of your anger. You don't want to perpetuate this kind of uncontrolled emotion in your son.

Kyle, a reformed screamer, explained that the hardest thing for him to do was lower his expectations of his son. He would always lose his temper when his son didn't live up to his potential. "I don't know why I expect him to be so perfect," he confessed. "I'm certainly not." Yet he'd lose his patience again and again. After working on it for a few months, Kyle began to notice when his temper was flaring and would gain control of it before hurting his son's feelings. Sometimes he regressed but he gradually reined in his impatient behavior. As his wife said, when he was beating himself up for losing his temper, "You're trying your best to improve. That gets you points with me and our son. So give yourself some credit, too."

Father-and-Son Talk

My son was five when I got a call from my neighbor about him. He and his best girl friend had been found together playing naked in her closet. By all accounts, the perpetrators were partners in the crime but it was obvious we needed to have a talk. I went into his room and gently asked him what they had been doing in the closet. "Playing there," he responded.

"But you both had your clothes off," I said.

"I know," he said. "It was hot in there."

"You shouldn't do things like that."

"Why?" my son wanted to know. "It was fun."

I found myself tripping over my words. I didn't know where to start to explain that "why."

We all stumble along a bit in the early years. Even though I was a well-trained child psychologist who had talked numerous times with parents and boys about sexuality and should have been more comfortable, somehow the same rules didn't seem to apply to my own son and me.

It's okay to struggle. You may not make your point the first time around, and bumble or mumble. Your son may render you speechless at times. What's important is that you realize that it's okay if you don't know how to handle something. Those are the moments that you should seek advice from your wife or your own father, a therapist or a school counselor. Even if you want to avoid a topic of conversation altogether—maybe you're uncomfortable explaining sex or maybe you don't know how to explain why you're getting divorced—you need to get through the conversation, and not drop the subject. Your son is not going to "drop" a behavior or miraculously understand it. When my five-year-old son asked me why he shouldn't play naked in the closet, I wanted to bolt. I didn't want to have this conversation. But I let it play out. I knew that he needed to understand why it was wrong.

"Boys and girls shouldn't play naked together," I told my son that day. "It's not respectful."

"What does that mean, Dad?"

"It means we don't do things to hurt another person," I said.

"But she's my friend," he said, looking confused. "We didn't hurt each other."

"I know but you could have," I told him. "What if she didn't really want to take off her clothes? What if you didn't? One of you might have been hurt."

He nodded. "I want you to respect girls, okay?" I said. There were a few minutes of silence. He nodded again.

That's what we fathers need to do—try to explain right and wrong in words and in our own actions. We need to stay connected with our sons in the daily situations and challenges of growing up. If fathers reach out to their sons, there are so many lessons for their sons to soak up. Les did a wonderful job dealing with his eleven-year-old son, Tim, when he learned that he was bullying a younger boy at the bus stop. Rather than yell at Tim, Les asked him how he thought the other boy felt about being picked on by someone bigger than him with others watching. At first his son was reluctant to answer. Les persisted. "Would you rather I just punish you?" Les asked Tim.

"No," Tim said.

"Well, try to answer my question," he said. You could hear anger growing in Les's voice.

"You don't have to yell, Dad," Tim said. The boy began to cry.

Les stopped himself and realized what was driving his reaction. And he told his son that when Les himself was a kid, three boys held him down in the street. They took off his pants and ran away with them. "I was so upset and embarrassed," Les told his son. "So answer my question. How do you think I felt?"

Tim got what his dad was getting at, and said that the boy was probably mad because there wasn't much he could do about it. "I'm sure he was embarrassed, too," Les said. "I'm sure some of his friends were laughing at him."

Les asked his son to think about how it would feel if someone bullied him. Tim admitted that he wouldn't like it. Les hugged his son. He felt as if he and his boy had had a good meeting of the minds and that Tim now knew more about the kind of person his father wanted him to be. But he made Tim do one more thing. "I want you to go over to his house tomorrow and apologize," Les said. Tim refused at first. Then he reluctantly agreed. That afternoon Les taught his son an important lesson—the power of empathy and respect for others and their feelings. It's essential in building good character.

Listen

Listen carefully. Sometimes boys ask questions that reveal larger worries or fears. "Can someone break their nose if they get punched in the face but don't bleed?" Lenny's eight-year-old son asked him one day.

Lenny didn't answer, but asked his son if anyone had punched him in the nose lately. His son grinned. "Yeah," he said. "Michael hit me yesterday!" Boys sometimes try to tell their fathers things without really telling them. But you can play detective and read between the lines.

PREPARING CHILDREN FOR THE TEEN WORLD

As children grow older, their penchant for disagreeing with adults and asserting their independence becomes almost full-time. Fathers often say that even preteens want to know "why," and protest that a father's action "is not fair." As the old adage goes, "At eight, they have all the questions. At eighteen, they have all the answers."

Boys begin to test one another as they become more competent and learn to master their environment. Whether it's in the lunchroom, on the athletic field, or at a friend's house, the battle of one-upmanship begins. Boys in their tweens—or preadolescence—will stretch their vocal cords and flex their physical muscles, and fathers need to help them tone it down a bit and learn to use their hands at the same time. As one ten-year-old boy once told me, "When we're at recess, we're always arguing about who's the best and who's going to be on which team. It's very important that we stand up for ourselves, or the other guys will think we're a wimp." That's fairly normal, but your son needs to know that he can object if the bragging and posturing crosses the line, becomes bullying or threatening. Standing up for himself doesn't always mean standing with the crowd and going along with what they do because they've always done it.

In your son's preadolescence, you have to set limits. You have to help your son learn to control his impulses and understand how to behave in the larger world around him, outside the family home. Like the father in the previous section who taught his son how to calm down after wrestling together, this sort of instruction in self-restraint and emotional intelligence generally is necessary to carry through the tween years.

A couple of years ago I met Manny, one of the brightest students in his fourth-grade class, a leader whom many of his classmates looked up to. But at eleven, he was also the class clown, often disrupting lessons with his wisecracks. His teacher had tired of his lack of respect for her authority, and sent home a note complaining that he had always been a chatterbox, and that his bright personality usually got him off the hook, "But I can barely get through a lesson anymore."

Manny's father, Bruce, was incensed at his son. Why would Manny act like this when he knew he would get in trouble? Did he need attention that badly? Was there something about the teacher distressing him? All these questions were on the table in my office a few days later when Bruce and Manny came to see me. I asked Bruce if he engaged in similar behaviors at Manny's age. He smiled slightly and nodded. "I was the class clown, too," he said, "but I never got into trouble like Manny here."

Manny said he knew about his father's history. "So you take after your dad a little, don't you?" I asked. Manny proudly nodded. I was wracking my head for some sort of solution, since I wouldn't want to suggest something that would alter this sense of connection Manny had with his father. Bruce chimed in.

"When I was in sixth grade, my teacher would call me to the front of the class every few days and ask me to tell jokes for a minute or two," Bruce said. "It helped calm me down and it was lots of fun. Do you think something like that could help you, Manny?"

Manny said he believed it might and agreed that it would be okay for his dad to call his teacher and ask for a similar arrangement. Father and son forged a deal. A few weeks later, Bruce called to report that he'd spoken to the teacher, who had agreed to the experiment. Manny was the center of attention for a few minutes twice a week. "It's actually working," Bruce told me. "His teacher reported that his behavior is more tolerable."

To have a conversation like the one between Manny and his dad, you and your son don't need to go to a therapist's office. In fact, the best talks often don't fit the stereotype of the serious sitdown, look-him-in-the-eye, man-to-man chat. Fathers and sons typically spend more time doing activities together than actually having conversations about their feelings, but during these activities, a needed talk can happen and necessary understandings can be reached. Spend time with your son doing things that offer the opportunity for conversation—go to movies and sporting events, play ball or cards, build tree houses or science projects, shop (yes, men do it too), take walks or runs, go swimming or browse in electronics stores. Your son can certainly join you in some of your activities, even if he says they're boring. There's no reason to have your relationship revolve completely around his. After all, he needs to learn about the give-and-take of relationships, about compromise, and different ways of spending time together. So whether you're at home, on the run, or on vacation, seize those opportunities.

There's also nothing wrong with sometimes watching TV together, playing video games, Ping-Pong, or even working on separate projects in the same room. Avoid setting up elaborate media and entertainment centers in your kids' rooms, however, as this discourages them from interacting with family and forces you to flush them out. Set up a common space in your home where the computer, wide-screen TV, and most comfortable chairs are located. Then everyone will always be in the same room. Parents who make family time a ritual when their children are young struggle less when their children enter adolescence. You won't have to battle about spending family time together when your children are already accustomed to it.

Adolescent Awakenings and Challenges

If childhood is the time when father and son find one another, then adolescence is the time when they lose one another. Many parents dread their children's adolescence. Could all those horrible stories about teenagers be true? Is adolescence a hormonal joyride, with liberal sexual attitudes, rampant drinking, and marijuana use? Are today's teens an entitled, opportunistic generation concerned only with themselves?

The answer is yes and no, depending on whom you ask. The Partnership for a Drug-Free America reports that alcohol and drug use has declined over the past few years. More high school students than ever are attending college and going on to seek advanced training in graduate schools. But in a riveting book titled *Generation Me*, social psychologist Jean Twenge reveals that today's youth culture in general is more casual about sex, that they distrust authority and traditional social mores, and that although their egos and self-esteem are greater than any previous generation's, they are also more anxious and depressed.

To me and other psychologists and educators, there's no question that too many youth today feel highly entitled. Parents who give their children everything they want assume they will be better off for it, but often they're not. Their generosity may be met with increased demands for *more* brand-name clothing, shoes, gadgets, and money—goods that kids don't need. As you set limits on your son's behavior, you have to set limits also on his expectations. If you give your son everything up front, you only set him up for future disappointment. He's not going to understand the importance of setting goals and working hard to attain them—he'll assume everything will be handed to him, including an acceptance letter from a top-tier college.

Bill Marriott Jr., the patriarch behind Marriott hotels, insisted that every one of his children and all of his grandchildren work in one of the family's hotels every summer. They would each adopt an alias so no one knew they were Marriotts, and so no one would treat them any differently from the other employees. All of his kids credit their father with making the Marriott family who they are today—a hardworking set of siblings determined to be number one in the lodgings industry.

So think about what you're teaching your son whenever you give him gifts. What do you want him to feel about himself and about you? Does he appreciate what he's given? Does he thank friends or family who give him things and want to reciprocate? What kind of impact will a monetary gift have in the long run?

What You Need to Know About Teenage Boys

I've known, loved, and cared for teens with all types of issues including depression, rebellion, substance abuse, school failure, family conflicts, and minor crises of confidence. I've also crossed paths with plenty of teens who toe the mark and do their parents proud. Their similarities are often greater than their differences. But you may need to make an extra effort to understand your teenage son and introduce some new ways of dealing with him on a daily basis.

A father told me that he used to hate watching the teenagers at the mall walk around in herds dressed like gangsters and tramps. Then his son became one of them—and he felt as if he didn't know him anymore. This sentiment is a common refrain of parents of teens over the years. Adolescence is a time of great change. The cute little boys we knew and loved grow up and become unrecognizable. Between twelve and fifteen years your son's body develops rapidly but his mind doesn't keep pace. Parts of the adolescent brain—the corpus callosum and the prefrontal cortex—aren't fully developed until young adulthood. This is especially significant when you consider that those parts of the brain are responsible for emotional control, curbing impulsive behavior, and exercising good judgment. Because your son has an immature brain, you have to set clear limits for him on his behavior. You have to insist he observe the rules you set and you have to enforce consequences for disobedience. Because he can't anticipate the consequences of following his impulses, the limits you set help him protect himself.

Younger teenage boys are particularly concerned about their bodies and the accompanying changes ushered in by puberty. They're a self-conscious bunch, often comparing themselves to their peers, seeking acceptance, and constantly looking over their shoulders to see what the other guy is doing. Whether it's their complexion, the clothes they wear, or the size of their muscles, they put themselves under a microscope. If they don't like what they see, they often blame Mom and Dad for their perceived shortcomings.

A father told me that his fourteen-year-old son demanded that he get him a set of weights to work out with. His son screamed at him, insisting that it was his father's fault that his friends teased him for being so skinny. "What am I supposed to do?" the father asked me. According to medical doctors, early teens shouldn't be lifting heavy weights, so I suggested he could buy his son two ten-pound dumbbells to work out with, and if the boy was still using them in three months, he could consider getting him a small weight set for Christmas. Naturally, his son balked at the proposal, but was smart enough to know that something was better than nothing. He worked out for a few weeks with the ten-pound dumbbells but lost interest in a matter of weeks. Teenagers are fickle.

They're also sarcastic. It's not unusual for teen boys to mock their parents. At a certain age, they become masters of the wisecrack. To them, fathers are out-of-touch control freaks who get kicks out of ruining their sons' lives. Dads can't tell them what's dangerous—particularly if their friends are doing those very things. If a father asks to speak to a classmate's parents to find out if they really do allow their son to set his own curfew or drink at home, his son will say that he's violating his space. You'll have to ignore that and investigate for yourself.

It's a mistake to meet a teen's sarcasm with sarcasm. As tough as he'll try to appear, a teenage boy's feelings bruise easily. In a rather extreme example, I watched a fifteen-year-old boy attack his parents for everything they stood for. With sarcasm and hostility, he insisted that his parents were both posers. Much of his anger stemmed from the "unfair" rules he felt his father was imposing. His father responded angrily. He felt his son was an ungrateful brat who didn't deserve any of the things that he had. The boy's response was "See! That's what I mean—they're always putting me down and they never take me seriously." He had completely forgotten about his verbal attacks from a few minutes before. After a few more visits, we came to a consensus: Each family member had to acknowledge his role in the problem. Dad needed to listen more attentively to his son's requests, without dismissing them. His son needed to be able to plead his case without accusations, and accept no for an answer. After a few months, a newfound mutual respect began to improve their relationship—although every so often they'd fall into the same pattern, rehash their shortcomings, and promise to change all over again. But their overall relationship improved as they became more and more conscious of what they were doing to one another.

Much of this jockeying is a son's attempt to begin to separate from his father and define himself as an independent person. As difficult as it is at times, it's part of a healthy transition toward middle adolescence—roughly fourteen to sixteen years old. Fathers can usually ride out their sons' protests by letting them blow off steam. Tell them that you do understand their frustrations. But you have to set limits also about what can and cannot be said in an argument. Your son can disagree vehemently with a rule or an opinion, but that does not justify cursing, threatening, throwing things, or otherwise behaving abusively or violently. The same holds true for parents. You must set an example for arguing appropriately and constructively. You must specify what you will tolerate and what the consequences are when your son crosses the line: First, give him a warning. After that, impose the consequence. Young people are less likely to push the envelope when they know what to expect.

A teen's mood can shift rapidly. Just ask Stuart. One evening his sixteen-year-old son, Rex, sat with him cheerfully at dinner discussing his involvement in an upcoming school play. A few hours later, Stuart ran into his son in the kitchen and asked him, "What's happening?" Rex bit his head off about how his father was so nosy. "Leave me alone," Rex told his dad. Stuart was hurt and confused by the confrontation, but didn't react. He later found out that Rex had just gotten off the phone with his girlfriend, who had told him that she was going out with her friends Friday night—and not with Rex. Rather than talk about his jealousy and hurt, Rex lashed out at his father. Stuart might have responded by picking up on his son's mood. He might say, "You seem upset . . . I guess something must have happened to annoy you." An open-ended sentence like this gives his son a choice about answering. A question may have made Rex feel interrogated. Maybe Rex would have taken the bait and shared his angst, but then again, maybe not. He may have still been defensive. It's always worth a try. Sooner or later, the law of averages will work to a father's advantage.

Teenage boys are struggling to find their identities. They're already playing roles in high school: the jock, the prep, the socialite, the artist or musician, and the college-bound student. Most teenagers have an "image," a prescribed role that they've adopted for their peers' benefit, and constantly evaluate and reevaluate themselves. Whether your son's talking to you about it or not, he is thinking about what type of person he is, where he fits in the world, and how others view him. A teenage boy is trying simultaneously to please his father and rebel against him. During your son's slow coming of age, you provide a model for his behavior. You and your words and actions will guide him even when you think he's not listening or watching.

Herbie vividly recalled going through this phase with his fifteen-year-old son, Jared. Quiet and introspective much of the time, Jared would ask Herbie every now and then about how he decided to be an architect. Herbie would answer Jared's questions and try to get Jared to share what he was thinking about. One day Jared confided to his dad that he had been feeling different from the other kids at school, that he didn't fit in. Herbie didn't know what his son was getting at and asked Jared to clarify what he meant. Jared said it was hard to explain, but in their next conversations Herbie got more insight into Jared's unique mind. A creative type, Jared didn't always relate easily to other kids and was more interested in the interior world of thoughts and imaginings of what his future would hold than in his fellow teens' social dramas. Jared was seeking his father's approval, wanting Herbie to tell him it was okay to be different. Jared might have had a lot more trouble accepting his own differences if his father had not made it clear that he would love him no matter who he was.

Communication: The Root of Good Relationships

Good communication entails trust and a genuine sharing of feelings. Good communication does not mean lecturing your son. Fathers and sons who can talk comfortably with one another have a much easier time getting through the challenges of young adulthood. They can air differences of opinion civilly, negotiate solutions to problems amicably, share experiences truthfully, and be secure in one another's presence. Teenage boys who regularly talk to their fathers are more likely to stay out of trouble and establish healthy, close relationships with other people of both sexes.

Yet more often than not, fathers and teenage sons can't talk to one another. One fifteen-year-old boy told me that his parents were clueless about what was going on in his life, who his friends were, or what was on his mind. Another young teen I counseled insisted that his father didn't know him at all. "He couldn't even tell you what kind of music I listen to," the boy told me. I looked over at his dad, who sadly shook his head in agreement. His dad couldn't name one band. On the other hand, parents can't get their sons to come out of their caves—otherwise known as bedrooms—to talk to them, even when the adults make the effort to find out what's absorbing them so completely in there.

When fathers and sons have formed a close bond during childhood, they can better navigate the more intimate and complex issues of adolescence. But even for closely bonded fathers and sons, the teen years can be particularly difficult. Many boys who openly play and talk with their fathers as children begin to pull away and shut down as adolescents. They're self-conscious, private, and prone to withdraw emotionally as their concerns become increasingly personal to them. You may notice that your son always seems as if he's in a hurry. He may talk to you briefly but cut you off before you have a chance to speak your mind. There will also be times when he is in one of his "moods" and won't talk to anyone at all. You may feel hurt when you hear him on the phone with his friends or see them online talking and laughing. Take heart—these are the ways of teenage boys who seem to love everyone but their mothers and fathers.

Teens hate to talk about school, but their fathers love to, perhaps because some measure their success by their sons' academic achievement, so this sets them at odds with each other. To a ninth-grade student, the future can seem light years away and good grades unimportant. Henry was determined to find out why Ellis had mediocre grades, but Ellis assured him that things would be fine if he just left him alone. Here's one of their typical conversations:

DAD: I hate to be a nag, but don't you have a big paper due in three days?

ELLIS: Yeah, but there's still plenty of time.

DAD: You always leave things till the last minute. I think that's why you're always getting B's and C's instead of A's.

ELLIS: Get off my case, Dad. I'll get it done.

DAD: But I checked your teacher's website and it said you were supposed to hand in an outline yesterday.

ELLIS: Well, I told him it would be late.

DAD: That's what I mean: you never get things done according to the teacher's schedule.

ELLIS: You're always criticizing me. All you ever talk about is school.

DAD: Well, maybe if you did better, I wouldn't bug you so much.

You don't need to be a psychologist to know that this conversation was a lost cause. But let's take a look at how Henry might have approached it differently:

DAD: I guess your classes must be pretty boring. You don't seem very interested in them.

ELLIS: Yeah, I just can't get into school.

DAD: That's too bad. I can remember feeling the same way when I started high school. I wasn't very happy about stuff and ninth grade was my worst year.

ELLIS: What did you do?

DAD: Well, I guess I just squeaked by. And we moved at the end of my freshman year, so I had a new start in tenth grade. Then things got better.

ELLIS: I don't think I'd want to change schools. My friends are here and even though school's not so great, I can try to do better.

DAD: Let's try to figure out something. Maybe I can help. We could get you a tutor, try to change your classes for next year, or meet with the school counselor. I'm open to any ideas that you have.

ELLIS: I have to think about it, Dad. I'm not sure what I want to do. It's not that I don't care about my grades, but I can't seem to psych myself.

DAD: I understand it's a tough situation. Let's talk about it some more in a few days. Meanwhile, let me know if you need any help with that paper that's due this week.

This was a far more productive conversation. Dad listens, doesn't judge or criticize, and offers to help. He keeps the door open for further dialogue and his son is responsive. Both leave the conversation feeling understood and comfortable with each other. They haven't resolved the problem, but father and son are on the same page, ready to work toward getting something done.

Enter their world. Fortunately, there's a lot you can do to narrow the communication gap. Just as you can do various things to enter the world of a young child, you can try to immerse yourself in various aspects of your teen son's world. One way for you to get to know your son is to spend time in his bedroom. What posters are on the wall? Are the names of the rock groups or sports stars unfamiliar to you? These are easy subjects to begin a conversation. Ask your son to tell you about these celebrities. If you fear ridicule for being out of touch, there's an alternate strategy: Google the celebrities' names, or go to Wikipedia. Then you'll be better prepared to start a conversation and not be completely clueless.

It's your responsibility to learn about teen culture. Watch *E! News,* read *Rolling Stone* or *People* magazine, surf the Net. Your son will take you more seriously and be more likely to open up when he feels that you understand him. Learning about your son's world shows that you care.

As teens get older, and difficult as it may be, you need to find new and different ways to show that you love them. Think of the research as a deposit in an emotional bank. You may have to wait a while to make a withdrawal, but the dividends are enormous. So tune in—whether your son collects butterflies or hip-hop hits, eats and sleeps soccer, or is obsessed with "the Goth thing." These are your way into conversation and connection.

Never look down on your son's interests or treat them with contempt or you'll turn him off and weaken his trust in you. In fact, any form of subtle rejection is dangerous. Many boys have told me that their parents gave them birthday gifts that they didn't want to try to redirect them from something they were really crazy about. One boy asked for a new video game and instead received a pair of athletic shoes for a sport he didn't want to play. Now I'm no staunch advocate of video games, but the pressure his parents were exerting for him to give up one pursuit for another that they wanted him to do didn't endear them to him. It showed how little they understood him. Another boy told me that his father would make snide remarks about his son's friends' haircuts. The father thought that he was being funny, but teenagers' feelings bruise easily, and when his father put down his friends, his son felt as if his father was putting him down.

Sometimes fathers really need to go out of their way to connect with their sons. Howard confided in me that he didn't know what to talk to his fourteen-year-old son, J.R., about since they had so little in common. Howard disliked rap music but J.R. loved it and was obsessed with Ludacris and Nelly, Dr. Dre and Jay-Z. He listened to rap, practiced rapping, and attended concerts. Unlike Howard, J.R. wasn't into sports, carpentry, or even playing video games.

I suggested Howard invite J.R. to a rap concert in town, but he immediately shot me down because he didn't want to have to sit through it. "What if it meant connecting with J.R.?" I asked. "Nothing else you've tried has worked." Howard saw my point, flipped through the newspaper, and found an upcoming rap concert. He asked another father-and-son pair to join them—to make it more bearable. His son was enthusiastic, which surprised Howard, who thought he might ridicule his sudden interest.

During the concert, J.R. loosened up around his dad. They laughed about some of the performances and discussed the themes in the music. J.R. told his dad that he thought it was cool that he took him out on a school night and Howard admitted that the music wasn't that bad. Most important, father and son took a step toward a closer relationship. Two weeks later, when J.R. heard that his parents were looking for a new house, he said he would go with them that weekend. J.R. hadn't asked to do something with them in months.

Making conversation. If you're going to develop a solid relationship with your son, you'll need to talk with him on a regular basis. Ten to fifteen minutes a day is a reasonable goal to shoot for. Stop in his bedroom before bed or ask him to come by your study when he has a free second. Get your son's attention away from the computer or television.

Don't try to talk as he's getting ready to walk out the door; he's likely to blow you off, or throw you a crumb with a two-word answer, "Yeah, okay." If you get that a lot, tell him that you'd like to spend a few minutes with him when he can give you his undivided attention. You can also try to talk when you're driving somewhere in the car, when he's having a late-night snack, or when he's run out of things to do and is wandering around the house.

If you ask your son about school or friends and receive grunts in return, change your strategy. Teens are notorious for saying that there's nothing happening and complaining that parents ask the same questions over and over again. Bring up some local news—a fight at the previous night's football game or the drug bust in the mall. Talk about the car you're planning to buy. Then ask for your son's opinion. The four most important words you can use to grease the wheels of conversation are "What do you think?" Teenagers love to share their opinions and show that they know something, too—an opportunity they cherish. And when you're talking to your son, make sure you're having a two-sided conversation. That means dad talks, son listens; son talks, dad listens. No one-sided lecturing.

Share some of your own teenage experiences. Sons are often interested in hearing what their fathers learned when they made similar mistakes. It helps them feel safe in sharing their own concerns. But don't go on about how good a student you were, how tough you had it as a kid, or how you would never have spoken to your parents the way he speaks to you. Teenagers interpret these as self-righteous indictments of their character rather than as invitations to share their own feelings and experiences. In other words, whatever you did well is what they're doing wrong.

It took time for Brett and his thirteen-year-old son, Corey, to learn to talk to each other. One night Corey needed a ride to a sleepover at a friend's house that was forty minutes away. Brett agreed to drive him, on one condition—that Corey keep his iPod off. Desperate for the ride, Corey agreed. At first they drove in silence.

"How many kids are sleeping over your friend's tonight?" Brett asked.

"Maybe three of four," Corey replied.

"That ought to be fun," Brett said. "What do you think you'll do? Watch movies?"

Corey rolled his eyes, sighed. "I'm not sure, Dad. We'll figure it out."

Brett felt rejected. Many fathers give up trying to talk to their sons at moments like these. Some dads might resort to chatter about last night's basketball game. Others won't say anything at all. Brett didn't give up, he trudged on, determined to find something he and his son could talk about.

"You know, when I was a kid," Brett told his son, "we used to do some pretty sneaky things during sleepovers."

Corey sat up. "Like what?" he said.

"We'd make crank phone calls to people whose names we found in the phone book. Take the name Dunn. We'd call and say, 'Are you Dunn?' When they said yes, we'd say, 'Then wipe your butt'—and we'd immediately hang up. We thought it was the funniest thing in the world."

Corey was cracking up. "You didn't get caught?"

"We had a few close calls but there was no caller ID in those days."

"We do things, too," Corey said.

"Like what?"

"A few weeks ago, we sent a kid an e-mail pretending to be a girl he liked, and saying that she wanted to hook up with him. It was hilarious. Sometimes we call and order a pizza and have it delivered to someone's house," the boy said.

"That's a little sneaky," Brett replied.

The two laughed and talked for the rest of the ride. Brett told his son that he knew the pranks were in good fun but he should be careful. He said he might really hurt someone's feelings. "I'm not proud of what I did," his father said. "Can you promise me that you'll be careful and at least think about what you're doing?"

Corey nodded. Then they promised each other to keep talking. "I want to know what's going on in your life," Brett told him.

If Brett had given up early on in the conversation, he would never have connected to his son in such a meaningful way.

When your son shuts you out, find another way in.

Setting Reasonable Limits

You will have to continue to set limits for your son well into his teenage years. Young people must learn to accept rules and constraints on their behavior in preparation for entering the adult world. As the "male voice" of authority who can recall how it feels to be a teenage boy, you are the best person to serve them in this role. Nonetheless, setting limits is both parents' job, and the more that Mom and Dad are on the same page, the more likely a teen is to comply with their expectations. As we've seen in the previous chapters, men often bring their father baggage to the table. If your dad was a hard-liner, you may follow suit—or you may choose to do the opposite. But you need to balance setting limits with giving teens some freedom appropriate to their age. Tyrants don't fare any better than pushovers. A large body of research suggests that excessively controlling parents often create rebellious teenagers and that extremely permissive parents create problem teens. So avoid extremes—take an informed, measured approach.

Base the limits you set—the curfews, driving, party-going, group activities—on your child's age, his level of demonstrated responsibility, and his past performance. It would be unreasonable to allow a thirteen-year-old boy to stay out until eleven at night unsupervised on a weekend, but it would be equally unreasonable to expect a seventeen-year-old to be home by ten, especially if he's a "good kid" and all of his peers are staying out much later. At either age, a parent should at the very least know where this child is going, whom he's going out with, and if his plans change. You need to know what's going on out there, so find out where the boys are hanging out and what other parents consider reasonable freedoms. If you still have doubts about what constitutes "typical," check with your son's school counselor for information.

Laying down the rules is not enough. You have to explain your thinking to teens and allow them the opportunity to plead their case. That doesn't mean that you cave in—but you provide boys the opportunity to vent, to feel listened to and understood. You will probably still hear things like "Leave me alone" or "It's no big deal." That kind of brush-off can signal that you need more dialogue. The old "Because I said so" approach isn't effective. "Because I said so" frustrates teenage boys. They want to understand where your rules are coming from; they want to argue the logic behind them. If rules seem arbitrary or senseless, your son will be more upset by your enforcing them without an explanation.

Here's where you need to set clear expectations and limits:

School. Regular attendance is beyond argument but also let your son know that you expect him to make a sustained effort to do his best, even if that doesn't always mean A's. You don't need to know everything that's going on in school but you should know something. Make it clear to your son that sharing information about his life isn't optional. It's mandatory. You need to know his friends, teammates, and extracurricular activities.

Curfews. Teenagers need them. Period. Negotiating a curfew can be a sticky point between fathers and sons. Every year your teen ages, you can reward him with a loosening of the reins, but only if he demonstrates compliance and responsibility. Giving him more freedom builds trust between you. When you discuss a reasonable curfew with your son, negotiate up, not down. In other words, start early. If you suggest an 11 P.M. curfew, he's likely to say, "Why not midnight?" Then he will feel as if he's helped decide his own curfew when that's the time you had in mind all along.

Drugs and alcohol. Too many teens are experimenting with drugs and alcohol way too soon and everyone agrees that these pose terrible health risks. Don't turn the other way if you know your son is drinking. You need to handle this. Some parents forbid any use. Others recognize that teens are likely to experiment, and offer them extensive guidance about doing this as safely as possible. Again, you don't want to lecture your son, because you can be more effective when you tell stories from your own life. A tale of a friend who had alcohol poisoning can illustrate the dangers of binge drinking. A story about the kid down the street who is in rehab or a disciplinary school for smoking too much marijuana is a lesson about the dangers of addiction. Cautionary tales can be effective. But I urge you to be clear with your son that drugs and alcohol are illegal for you to use. Don't. If you seem to permit experimentation, it can be hard for you to turn him back.

Making rules is only half the battle, perhaps the easier half. The real challenge is effectively enforcing these limits: the punishment should fit the crime. A first-time offense should not be punished with three months of grounding, but a recurrent offense should be taken seriously. Punishment must teach consequences, but it should not be an exercise in the infliction of pain. Always discuss what he did wrong, why he did it, and how he might deal with the same situation differently if it occurred again. Most important, if you find yourself constantly punishing your son, and it's not working—his behavior doesn't change or improve—you need to try another approach.

Sometimes a father grows so fearful that his son is heading down the wrong path that he virtually imprisons him—in the name of love and concern. Andre's sixteen-year-old son, Seth, was a good kid but rarely met his father's expectations, earning mostly B's and C's. He played sax for the school band and ran track. Most of his teachers described him as easygoing; he wasn't the most active participant in class but he always paid attention. Seth had a small circle of friends who pretty much stayed out of trouble, but you wouldn't know it from the way his father treated him.

Andre carefully monitored Seth's activities, believing that he had to protect his son "from the bad influences out there." Seth was expected home by nine-thirty on Friday and Saturday nights. Andre often smelled his breath to be certain there was no sign of alcohol, which Seth found humiliating. He resented that his dad didn't believe him when he said he wasn't drinking. Andre frequently e-mailed Seth's teachers to get feedback on how Seth was doing. Unless the response was glowing, Andre would demand an explanation from Seth, feeling he had to push Seth to do well in school so that he wouldn't throw his life away.

Andre failed to see that many of his conversations with Seth basically revolved around interrogations about homework. Whenever Seth brought home a C, he wasn't allowed to use the computer for a week. Still, Seth was not becoming an academic standout. Instead of trying harder to please his dad or outwardly rebelling against his control, he withdrew. Seth felt his father didn't know him and never talked to him without a purpose that stemmed from Andre's own expectations. The pattern had existed for several years before I met with them—Dad was determined to set stringent limits but his son wasn't buying into them. Andre's wife let her husband be the alpha parent and didn't step in when Andre was being hard on Seth. She let him do what he thought was right.

One Sunday morning, Andre grew irritated that Seth still wasn't up by nine. Andre knew that Seth needed to get started on his oral history project. Andre went into his room and told him to get out of bed. When Seth didn't stir, Andre shook him. Seth's eyes were rolled up in his head. He was hot to the touch and seemed delirious. Andre ran downstairs and called an ambulance. Seth had taken an intentional overdose of Tylenol and at the ER they pumped his stomach.

A few days later, Andre, his wife, and Seth came in to see me. Seth looked pale and drawn and didn't need to say much that day. It took time to unravel the details of their story—Andre's father had been as controlling as Andre. I told Andre that his rules were ineffective and had to change. "That's why we're sitting here," I said. Each family member vented in turn, and then we came up with a plan. Andre would loosen the reins. Seth would take on more responsibility at home. Mom would make sure each kept his promise. Andre agreed to extend Seth's curfew in exchange for his son's commitment to create a study plan. At my insistence, father and son agreed to spend time together every weekend. There was one condition: school could never be discussed.

Over the next six months, Andre and Seth's interactions remained stiff and awkward but gradually relaxed as they began to get beyond the harsh jailer-prisoner roles into which they'd been trapped. Their one-sided views of each other also changed as Andre opened up to modulate his disciplinarian tendencies. Seth felt more comfortable revealing his own likes and dislikes, his boredom with school, and his feeling that school wasn't helping him prepare for the future and wasn't in any way relevant to whatever he would do in the future. They have found some common interests in their weekend outings and time together. But they're still searching for something that will really inspire Seth and give him a real direction through his teen years, into college, and beyond. Since they're not going about it in the old hyperscheduled, militaristic way in which Andre was brought up, though, their explorations are bringing them closer, little by little.

Character Building

Everything discussed in this chapter contributes to one goal—raising a son with good character. There are few greater pleasures than looking at your son and feeling proud of the person he has become. The scope of your influence is directly related to the quality of your relationship with your son. How many teenage boys can you think of who follow the advice of a father whom they don't respect? Let's revisit three essential ingredients that you want to develop in your son—self-respect, values, and empathy.

Young people with genuine self-respect believe that they are decent, lovable, responsible, and competent. They are not easily swayed by others' influence and adhere strongly to their own beliefs. They acknowledge their shortcomings and don't feel a need to impress others with their achievements. One teacher summed it up perfectly: "These are the kind of kids you enjoy being around." Because they respect themselves, they also respect others.

In psychology, there's a controversy brewing around issues of self-esteem. Increasing numbers of educators and psychologists are suggesting that today's teens have too much self-esteem and that society has inflated their egos beyond what is good for them as individuals or for society's overall well-being. Kids are led to believe that they can do anything and become anything that they want, which makes them think they will do so without significant effort on their parts. Some teenagers don't understand that they have to earn what they want, and excessive self-esteem can grow into arrogance.

You can promote a balanced self-esteem, one based in self-efficacy, by pushing your kids when they need a boost and bringing them gently down to earth when their egos inflate. A few years ago, a father approached me after a speech I gave about building self-confidence. He told me that he often praised his son and tried to help him to feel unique among his siblings. I asked how he did this. He said he had one child who had a good sense of humor, another who was a current events freak, and a third who was an athlete. "We value our kids for who they are and try not to compare apples and oranges," he told me. Both he and his wife did not have unrealistic expectations for their kids and thought that the key to building their self-esteem is to accept them for who they are.

He's exactly right. Most of the time kids don't need to be pushed too hard or reined in too much. They need to be encouraged wherever they are. A student getting B's or C's isn't going to become an Ivy League freshman because Dad sets up a stringent academic plan and wills his son's improvement. The son must want it badly enough to make the sustained effort necessary to be at the top of his class. Fathers need to be realistic and encourage a B or C student to work hard and challenge himself, but your son shouldn't feel trapped and hopeless in trying to please you.

An integral part of self-respect is a well-developed value system. You model the actions that express the beliefs you want your children to have. There's no better way to teach children than to live the life that you're trying to promote and to instill essential values such as honesty, respect, and generosity. Every Christmas, one family I know donates old toys to their local children's hospital to instill in their children generosity. A boy I know watched his dad return a ten-dollar bill to the cashier at McDonald's when she gave him the incorrect change. Another father intervened when his son's football coach was getting yelled at by a visiting teammate's dad and was able to calm everyone down.

Teaching teenagers respect requires repetition. Young people are frequently in a hurry and can forget to say "Thank you," "Please," and "I'm sorry." Don't let them off the hook. Remind them to be polite when they're young and continue to do so until they say these things on their own. Explain to your son that if he wants people to treat him with respect, he needs to extend others the same courtesy. It can take time and years for this message to sink in.

Some teenagers curse their parents. Dads often yell back or punish them, but that's not going to help much. If your son does this, I suggest you walk out of the room and tell him you won't deal with someone who treats you that way. One father tried it. "Not long after, he came to me and asked me for something. I said, 'No,' and reminded him that it was hard to be nice to someone who wasn't nice to me. It hasn't made him an angel but he is learning to hold back his foul language."

Compassionate people are more attuned to others' feelings. Help an elderly woman with her groceries or a disabled person along a city sidewalk blocked with garbage bags, deliveries, and people. Perhaps your son will turn out to be someone who shares his drink with a friend who doesn't have the money to buy one, or who makes an effort to defend a kid who is the victim of others' taunts, or steps in to rescue a stray dog or cat that someone has abused. He'll see the importance of caring for other people.

It's hard work being vigilant with your children and teaching them what they need to know. You get better and better at it the more you actively engage with the many emotions and stages your son is going through. Your son will listen to you. Your wife will appreciate you. Maybe you'll even sleep a little better. Remember—there's ample opportunity to correct mistakes, rebuild relationships, and become the father you would like to be.

CHAPTER FOUR

What Dads Won't Say

Fathers' Secret Fears and How to Face Them

I met Barry several years ago. He began our meeting with the usual platitudes, that "everything is fine." His wife was fine. His son was okay. But we both knew he was sitting with me because things weren't fine. His wife was angry with him and his son was depressed. This session had to be about his issues, not theirs. Barry slouched in his seat and wouldn't look me in the eye at first. Therapy felt strange to him, almost fake, and he was uncomfortable, as some men are in their first talks.

"You don't look happy," I said. "You must be under a lot of pressure at work." He nodded. The circles under Barry's eyes were purple. "Being here is really hard for me," he said. I understood and told him that I was glad he had come in. "You're going to need to get some of these things off your chest if you're going to get through this," I said.

Barry began slowly. "I am really trying, Doc," he said, "but I'm screwing up. My marriage sucks, and that's hard for me to face. It's been this way for months. I've been staying at the office later and later. When I'm home, my wife tunes me out and my son knows that something is wrong. He's really quiet when we're together, and I'm not sure what to tell him."

"Do you talk to any of your friends about this?" I asked.

"No," he said. "To tell you the truth, I'm a pretty private person."

"What are you afraid of, Barry?" It's a question that few people ask men directly. Barry's eyes welled up with tears.

"I'm afraid that I'll lose my wife and son," he whispered. "I'm afraid that they'll never forgive me for not being there enough."

Men aren't comfortable talking intimately. Barry is not the only man suffering in silence. Many fathers keep their innermost feelings to themselves, revealing them only to a select few in a closely guarded inner circle. Some manage to bottle their feelings entirely, shutting themselves off from those who could most help them. But under the right circumstances, with support and understanding, they'll "spill their guts," which can mark the beginning of a new chapter in their lives.

Fathers who may look fine on the surface or say they're fine are often not fine on the inside. Maybe you're one of them, a good man struggling to be the best you can be, all the while knowing that something is not right. Maybe you're angry, sad, resentful, or even feeling incompetent. But if you are to become the father you want to be and the father your son needs, you have to get to the bottom of these feelings, and tell your story.

There's often a moment when I'm talking to a father when he admits something big. It often just about kills him to say whatever it is that he's holding back because he senses that admitting this deeply guarded feeling will snowball into explorations of even more deeply guarded feelings and it all will lead to change. And he's right. Many men express similar fears, resentments, and longings. Some men admit these feelings to their wives. Some don't. Admitting these secret feelings will not only help you understand yourself better, it will help your wife or partner empathize with you and understand you better. For instance, many men actually are used to saying things that seem insensitive, when they're actually trying to say something encouraging or loving, but they're uncomfortable expressing that. When they become able to admit this to themselves, they can then reach out to their spouses or sons in ways that connect them rather than drive them away.

In the following pages, you'll find a road map of a father's heart, a complex tangle of emotions shielded by pride and restraint. Perhaps you'll recognize yourself or your own father in this picture, and discover that your dad wasn't who you thought he was, and find aspects of yourself that you'll understand better.

WHAT MEN SAY BEHIND CLOSED DOORS

"I'm more comfortable at work than I am at home."

Work is a safe place for men. There they can speak the language of facts instead of the language of feelings, something nearly all men prefer. Men often feel they can control their work environment more than their home lives. Their role at work is clearly defined. At home, that's less true. Homer Simpson and Al Bundy are so entertaining because men recognize themselves in these bunglers who can't seem to get things right at home. A patient named Arthur sums up what many men feel. "When I'm at home, I'm never quite sure what to do," he says. "At work, I feel like I'm king of the hill, and by evening, I'm walking around the house awaiting instructions from my wife about what to do next. I suppose a lot of it is my fault. I'm sure that I could learn to do most of the tasks around the house but I leave most of the work to my wife. I'm not proud of it but deep down inside I think I like it that way."

At work people rarely challenge men on what they're feeling, so they don't have to deal with emotions or feel uncomfortable about them. Because men have had much more training in their jobs than they have had in being a father, it's easier for them to iron out problems at work than at home. When I asked Arthur, father of three young boys, why he let his wife dictate his involvement at home, he shrugged. "I know it's not what the modern dad is supposed to do," he said, "but it's easy doing things how she wants them. Then I can retreat into my home office when I need to get stuff done and she'll keep everything going."

Home is an uncomfortable place for some men. They don't feel like they fit in, because they don't always know how to act, what to do, how to feel. They feel helpless, like a fish out of water. Some withdraw and do what's most comfortable—watch TV, finish work from the office, spend hours on the computer. Men who are uncomfortable at home are often driven to succeed more in the workplace, and believe that people judge them by how successful they are. Some are so concerned with what the rest of the world thinks about them that they fail to consider what their own wives and sons think. One father told me, "I was raised to believe that a man's worth is defined by what he achieves at work. I'm out there every day proving myself to everyone around me. Sometimes I feel better at work because I'm productive there. At home, I don't get much accomplished."

Some fathers will deny any discomfort at home and insist that the reason that they work hard is to give their family a good life. Sometimes that's true. More often, however, these men are blind to their sons' father hunger and have no idea how much their wives wish they were more involved at home. "People leave me alone at work," one father told me. "At work, there are fewer hassles. My wife isn't there nagging me. My son isn't tugging on my pants leg to get my attention. I get unconditional approval at work so it's easy to know if I'm doing something wrong."

I've met fathers who try to run their homes like offices. But these CEO dads' parenting style doesn't work very well. In fact, it fosters considerable resentment. Family members, especially wives and older boys, want to be treated as equals, not as employees with a schedule of tasks and obligations. CEO dads lack the emotional skills to blend in comfortably with their families, and often revert to what is most comfortable for them—"control." This type of dad often had a role model (his own father) who was distant and uninvolved and he can be lonely and angry. Highly stressed, they have great difficulty expressing inti-macy—and their sons suffer.

I worked with Dennis, a forty-eight-year-old father, and his son sev-eral years ago. Constantly at odds with his fifteen-year-old son, Devin, Dennis was not one of my success stories. Devin was angry, rebellious, and failing school. He spent more time in detention than in the class-room. On weekends, he sometimes didn't come home, causing his par-ents to stay up worrying. Devin didn't particularly like therapy until I asked about his father. He could spend entire sessions insulting his father. He saw his father as a hypocrite, always talking about family val-ues even though he rarely showed up at home for dinner. Dennis reluctantly joined his son in therapy because I insisted that he be there if I was going to work effectively to change his son. On several occasions Dennis reminded me that he had a very important job on Capitol Hill and was missing important meetings to meet with us. He often checked his watch. As soon as Devin's problems came up, Den-nis interjected. "This kid's got a terrible attitude," he said. "He needs to grow up." I asked Dennis if it was at all possible that some of Devin's problems stemmed from Dennis's inability to put family before work, but he was defensive. "I work hard to give my family a high lifestyle," he said. "He doesn't appreciate any of it." Devin fired back and told his father to shove his money up his ass. That was the last I saw of Dennis, who said that unless I learned to control Devin and make Devin respect him, he wasn't coming back. I explained that that was his job, not mine, but he wasn't interested.

Unfortunately, a good number of fathers are unable to see how their professional decisions affect their families. Other dads feel stretched so thin financially that they have to work long hours and skip family time just to stay afloat—and for many, that is true. But some stressed-out fathers really don't want to admit their preference for work over their family. Whether they admit it or not, their sons pay the price for this bind that dads are caught in. Many dads are good men caught between a rock and a hard place. But some do see the consequences and still won't change. For instance, Nathan told me that he felt ashamed that he had created a monster—his son was having problems in school—but he couldn't bear to make the financial sacrifices necessary to get his home in order. Instead he escaped to the office every day; his wife and son pulled further and further away.

"My son will be okay as long as he attends the best schools and I provide well for him."

This is a rationalization for not being adequately involved with your son. To these fathers, like those described above, work is clearly more important than family. Sometimes these men are simply uncomfortable at being a father and interacting with children. They haven't been involved parents and feel that, as long as they "set up" their sons for a good life, they'll turn out to have one. But material things rarely fill in for a father's lack of involvement. Sons may turn out "okay," but they still feel a big loss along the way. They don't have good role models, don't feel loved or emotionally connected to their dads. These boys can become spoiled, feel entitled to future success, and lack the capacity to establish intimate relationships in their own lives. They will probably carry anger at their fathers for not being there for them that can spill out in inappropriate ways in all kinds of situations.

On some level, many fathers know that they're rationalizing their time away from home and they do a lot of denial. A forty-two-year-old stockbroker, Derek, came to see me with his wife, Lorraine, at her insistence. Upset because she believed Derek had a superficial relationship with their twelve-year-old son, Richie, Lorraine felt that all Derek cared about was his career and his image in their neighborhood. She swore that he looked forward to driving his Porsche convertible more than he did going to his son's piano recital. Derek laughed. "Not true," he said. Then he winked at me. "But I do love that car."

Lorraine didn't think he was funny. She looked him square in the eye and said, "Richie needs a real father." Derek knew what she meant. He had admitted that he always tried to make a brief showing at his son's recitals and basketball games just so "my wife will think I'm a good father," and now realized that Lorraine saw right through him. Derek explained that he had been really busy lately—he'd recently been promoted. "I've been sending Richie to a good private school for six years now," he told me. "He's a great kid. He's doing well in school and he's very involved. I'm so proud of him."

I asked if Derek thought that Richie wanted him around more. "Nah," he said. "He's so busy that sometimes I just get in the way of his activities. I'm doing my part, providing him a good life. He's doing his part by making me proud."

Clearly, Derek didn't think there was much of a problem, but I explained that just because his son was doing well didn't mean that he didn't long for a closer relationship with his father. Lorraine sensed that Richie wanted his father involved in his life but it didn't occur to him to ask his father for attention, and she didn't want to wait for Richie to pull away from the family in his later teens or begin resenting his father. It took a couple of months for Derek to realize how distant he was from his son. On my and Lorraine's urging, he began taking his son out twice a week and promised to be home for dinner three nights a week. Derek didn't see a huge change in his son—Richie was already a good kid—but he did find himself getting to know his son better and also admitted one day that cutting back at work was bringing the entire family closer together. And Lorraine had stopped snapping at him.

After Richie's latest piano recital, he had thanked his dad for coming. Then Richie took his dad around and introduced him to his teachers. He seemed to love "showing his dad off" in the same way that Derek had loved showing off his Porsche. When Derek saw that his son was happy simply because his father had shown up, that his presence had meant the world to Richie, Derek felt his eyes grow moist. He told me he had had an epiphany. "He really wanted me in his life," Derek said. "I know it sounds silly. Of course, your son wants his father in his life. But I'd convinced myself that he had so much support from Lorraine and from teachers at school that he was fine if I was busy. I saw that night that that wasn't true."

Fight the Fear: The previous chapters contain a lot of ways you can become more comfortable with your son at home. Spending time with him is key. You have to make the time to combat this fear. And the time you spend might be uncomfortable and awkward for you at first. But the only way over this fear is through it.

"I'll never be good enough."

My heart goes out to men who are doing the best they can but feel burdened with self-doubt. Unlike the dads who rationalize their lack of involvement, these men are painfully aware of their shortcomings as fathers. Some of them set extremely high standards for themselves that are difficult, if not impossible to achieve. They're their own worst enemies. Some also have highly critical wives who make them believe they're inadequate fathers. Others had highly critical fathers who made them feel unimportant as children. And some are prone to depression and negative thinking, which don't help them raise their sons in an emotionally healthy environment.

These fathers have a hard time believing that they're doing enough, caring enough, or having any sort of effect on their sons at all. Often they're doing just fine and don't need to be better fathers. They need to be more accepting of themselves. One forty-four-year-old dad named Saul came to see me because he was concerned that he was spending too much time in the office and wasn't around his son as much as he should be. Saul listed his fears one after another: "I should be playing with my son and trying to engage him in conversation. Sometimes I'm too strict with him. I get angry when he leaves his clothing all over the house and I reprimand him. Then I feel like I'm too hard on him and stay up half the night worrying."

Saul was so obsessed with being a better father that he didn't trust himself anymore. But Saul's wife was supportive. "She always says that I'm doing a good job," he said. "But my father made so many mistakes with me. I don't want to make any mistakes with my son." I told Saul that that was an unrealistic goal. Every father is going to make mistakes. Saul had turned out okay. I asked if he was trying his best. "I think so," he said. I reassured him that this was all he could do, and that he needed to try to let go of all his self-doubt. His son seemed normal, well adjusted, and happy, and Saul was striking a good balance between encouraging him and disciplining him. Over the next few months, I worked with Saul on trusting his fathering instincts, which strengthened his relationship with his son.

Discipline is not the same as bad fathering. Sons need to be punished and reprimanded when appropriate. They need toughness and tenderness—not one or the other. They certainly won't stop loving their dads because fathers correct them and teach them proper behavior.

Another father I worked with worried that he wasn't a good role model for his kids. A sports agent with a few big-name clients, Jackson loved his work. One week he would be in a small town in Nebraska recruiting an eighteen-year-old basketball sensation and the next he was in Los Angeles accompanying a Raiders player to a fund-raiser. Since he traveled so much, Jackson went out of his way to spend quality alone time with his ten-year-old twin sons when he returned home. "Sometimes I'm stressed when I get home and I have a few drinks and tell the kids that I need to relax a bit before I play with them or read them stories," he says. "But I feel really guilty that I'm not gung-ho, chasing them around the house, or breaking out the video games." I asked Jackson how much time he typically spent with the boys before bedtime. "An hour or two," he said. "I'm not sure that's enough, though. They always beg for a few more minutes each night." All kids beg their parents to play longer or stay up longer. It doesn't mean that they're hurting. He was doing fine. When they become teenagers, he'd be lucky to get ten minutes with his boys.

Fight the Fear: Saul and Jackson both practice too much negative thinking. They are extremely hard on themselves and need to look at their fathering more objectively. If you fit their profile, try the following:

- *Get feedback from those you trust.* Ask your wife how well you are fathering. You may be surprised to learn that she's happier than you think. If she expresses concerns, listen carefully, and do your best to address them. Don't hesitate to ask your son if he wants to spend more time with you. If he reacts enthusiastically, you can rest easy, and if he hesitates, don't be discouraged. Encourage him to tell you what else he'd like from you. You'll feel better when you see that your efforts aren't going unnoticed.

- *Challenge your negative thoughts.* If you often find yourself saying that you're not good enough, not around enough, or too critical, try countering these thoughts with more objective, positive statements. For example, if you're telling yourself you're not good enough, ask yourself, Says who? And try not to dwell on your mistakes. You've probably done just as many things that deserve a pat on the back.

- *Measure yourself against realistic expectations.* If you're talking to your son regularly, even when you're traveling for work, if you're attending many of his school or sports or other events, you're probably doing just fine. Remember that sons allow a reasonable margin of error. They don't expect perfection from us any more than we do from them.

"I don't want my son to be like me."

Several thousand years ago, Sophocles remarked, "My son, may you be happier than your father." Today's men echo this theme. Using all the courage they can muster, fathers admit to me that they frequently say this secret prayer: "Please don't let my son turn out like me." Every father's reason is different. Sometimes he doesn't believe he's successful enough and he wants his son to be more fortunate and have more options than he had. Others know they're too hard on their kids and want them to be better, kinder, more resilient. The bottom line is, these men are unhappy with themselves and they want their sons to have different life experiences from theirs. One fifty-three-year-old dad told me that he hated when he saw himself in his son. "I jump all over him if he's acting stubborn in a discussion," he told me. "When I think about it, my stomach churns. I'm just as stubborn. Remember that old Harry Chapin song, 'Cat's in the Cradle'? That singer sadly concludes, 'My boy was just like me.' For some reason, that's my fear. That my boy will be just like me."

It's difficult for men to divulge these feelings. To do so, they have to admit to an overall dissatisfaction with their lives. Many of them grew up swearing that they'd never act like their fathers—and then they see their fathers coming out in their own thoughts and actions. They grow ashamed and don't believe that they're very good role models, but, instead of changing their own behaviors, they put pressure on their sons to be different, which causes their relationships to become strained.

A businessman who built a multimillion-dollar construction company, Louie employed over one hundred men to build hotels and shopping malls. At forty-nine, by anyone's definition he was successful—big house, nice car, great family. Best of all, his eighteen-year-old son, Tanner, loved going to work with Louie and over the years they had developed a very close relationship. When young, Tanner had shadowed his dad at the office and tagged along with him to construction sites. In high school, Tanner began filling notebooks with drawings of famous buildings and trying his hand at carpentry. He even had installed a brick walkway through his parent's backyard garden. Tanner loved everything about construction and dreamed about buying an old house and restoring it from the ground up.

Early in his senior year, Tanner came to see me because he and his father had started to fight a lot. "Everyone is applying to college and he wants me to, too," Tanner told me. "But what if I don't want to go?" Tanner explained that he had told his dad that he wanted to work for him; he would start by fetching the foreman coffee if he had to. Louie was horrified by his son's interest. He wanted his son to go to medical school. "Dad's constantly online ordering brochures from different colleges' premed programs. Then he drops them on my desk, on my bed. I have no interest in being a doctor but these stupid catalogs are everywhere. He told me that I have to go to college. I told him that I just want to do what he does. I don't get what's wrong with that."

When I saw Louie, he explained that it was important to him that Tanner attend college. "He'd be the first in the family," he said. "I didn't bust my ass all these years so he could end up driving a crane around." As we got talking, it became clear that he was proud of the company he built but he didn't see it as "good enough" for his son. No matter how successful he was or how talented his crewmen, Louie still saw himself as a guy with a hammer hustling for work. He wanted his son to have the luxury of putting on a suit every day, slapping aftershave on his neck each morning. In essence, Louie wanted his son to be nothing like him. We worked on finding a compromise for father and son—Tanner would go to college but he would major in engineering or architecture or a subject that would help him know more about his dad's business. Then we spent months getting Louie to practice a little appreciation for himself and why his life could be good enough for Tanner.

It's difficult for men to be good fathers when they don't respect themselves. Sons learn many lessons by watching their fathers. If a dad constantly puts himself down, stirs with discontent or unhappiness, or tries to be someone he's not, his son will pick up on it. Sometimes the boy will begin to look at his dad with disrespect, but sometimes the son will incorporate these low feelings into his own view of himself, and suffer a lack of self-confidence. The effects of negative thinking can be subtle, which Hank realized when he came in to see me, saying that he was often depressed. "There are times when I feel my life lacks meaning," he said. "I try to hide it from the kids but they can sense something is wrong. They're always saying, 'What's wrong, Daddy?' Then I feel guilty because I know I'm making them anxious. I don't want them to ever feel the way I do." Hank feared that his sons would inherit his doomsday outlook. I asked if he had any reason to think that his mood was affecting them in a big way. He said he didn't, so far, but he worried about the future. Children of depressed parents can suffer from various insecurities and anxiety, and depression can be inherited, so Hank worked with both me and a psychiatrist who helped him find the right medical treatment for his mood disorder. As a parent, you don't want your low mood, sadness, or anxiety to wear on your children or worry them, which can set them up for their own mood disorder.

Fight the Fear: I've known many dads who worry that their sons will turn out like them, and still they manage to be good fathers. If this is your concern, try the following:

- *You may not want your son to be like you—but you're worrying about something that may not even happen, especially if you recognize and work on some of your faults.* I keep a quote from Mark Twain on my desk: "I've known a great many worries in my life but most of them never happened." Chances are that your son is going to turn out just fine, taking the best of what you can teach him and leaving the negative behind. Stop worrying!
- *Make a list of the traits that you hope your son does inherit from you.* You

have more to offer than you're giving yourself credit for. This simple exercise can serve as a reminder.

- *Pinpoint your fear.* What is it about your life or personality that you want your son to avoid? If you know what you want to change, it's easier to make changes. For example, if you have a bad temper, and you worry that your son will develop one, focus on controlling your anger, and talk to your son about what you did right and wrong in specific situations. This can be difficult because you need to be willing to admit your weaknesses and faults to your son, but it will give you more awareness about your need to change and more motivation.

"I'll never forgive myself for what I put my kids through."

This is among the most moving confessions a father can make. There's nothing more painful than watching your son screw up and knowing that you had a direct part in creating the situation. It makes a father feel he failed his son, let his family down, or wasn't "enough of a man" to deal properly with the problem. The pain is worse when there is a serious problem—a son's major depression or his running around with the wrong crowd—or a tragic ending—if a son dies of a drug overdose, drunken driving accident, or a suicide. Some problems can be resolved when fathers face a problem squarely and change the way they parent. Some can't, but you have to be involved and connected enough to your son to know the difference.

Often this confession of self-blame comes from men who have moved frequently, drunk too much, gone through painful divorces, or made poor financial decisions that hurt their family's lifestyle. One man told me about a bad business decision that had lost him thousands of dollars, forcing him to sell his home, and move his children to a less desirable neighborhood where they hated their new school. He was so ashamed of what happened that he pulled away from his kids. He couldn't look himself in the eye each morning, let alone his son. Another father told me that he had squandered his children's college funds on a bad technology investment. He was so stressed about the need to tell them that he came to see me for months just to prepare. He hated himself for having been so greedy that he gambled money he had been saving for decades. But neither of these men should be disparaging themselves quite so much. They meant well; they were trying to improve their families' lives. They didn't intentionally hurt their children, who most likely will be resilient enough to rebound from their diminished financial situations. And they certainly will have learned valuable lessons about work, career, money, and the market.

Some men can't help their situations. Wes was an army colonel whose work sometimes took him to whatever part of the world was making CNN Headline News. His family had lived on military bases from Guam to Germany. His children—two boys and a girl—would cry their eyes out every time that they had to move again. In his latest post in Virginia, his children loved the deer that wandered into their backyard and the mountains they saw in the distance. They had made friends with all the kids on their block. Wes's eldest son, Coburn, was twelve. One night, Wes tucked Coburn into bed. "Promise me that we'll never leave," Coburn said. There was something so desperate in his boy's eyes that Wes said, "I promise." But a few weeks later, Wes was in my office, his head in his hands, feeling tremendous guilt about having made a promise that he couldn't keep. He knew that his children were being denied the stability of putting down roots. He often apologized to them but he would remind them of all the things that their classmates in Virginia hadn't seen—how many kids can say they had ridden on the backs of elephants in the Philippines? But in his heart, Wes knew that Coburn craved permanency, a sense of place, a set of friends to whom he could get close that Wes couldn't promise him. So before his next reassignment Wes knew he had to have a frank talk with Coburn and confess to him that he had made a promise he likely couldn't keep.

Men also blame themselves when they see the negative effects of being heavy-handed, such as forcing a child to attend a certain school, play a sport he doesn't like, or make friends with the kids Dad likes. Sometimes the pressure is necessary—to change to a better or private school, for instance—but it can still damage your relationship with your son. If the decision was right for the kid's health, education, or future—and not an expression of your ego or desire to manipulate him—then you should be able eventually, as your son matures, to repair the relationship.

There are times, of course, when a boy's misbehavior becomes intransigent and intolerable and you have to take action to protect the whole family, such as when the boy displays extreme defiance, aggression, drug use, or a pattern of antisocial behavior. In these instances, an imposed placement in a residential therapeutic program may be helpful and necessary. Your son may not forgive you at first, but over time, as he changes and matures, he'll come to realize that this, too, was an act of love, not rejection.

Here's an example of pressure on a son that was not for the son's good: I met a twenty-year-old college student named Caleb who was so angry with his father that he refused to attend therapy with him. His relationship with his father changed when he announced that he was going to quit varsity football, which he had played all through high school, to join the lacrosse team during his senior year. "No biggie, right?" he asked me. I nodded. "Wrong," he said.

Caleb loved lacrosse and had been a founding member of his school's club team a few years before. During his senior year the high school recognized lacrosse as an official school sport, earning the team an intramural schedule, uniforms, and a paid coach, so Caleb decided he would quit football and join lacrosse since the game times frequently conflicted. His father flipped out. "There was cursing and yelling," he told me. "I couldn't take him anymore so I ended up staying on the football team. But every week I'd stand on the sidelines of the lacrosse games I could catch and my anger toward him just built. When I got to college, he couldn't tell me what to do really. So I joined lacrosse. You know he hasn't come to one game? Two years on the team—and he wonders why I don't talk to him when I visit home."

Divorce immediately changes the nature of a father-and-son relationship. Men find it particularly difficult to live with the pain they've caused their children in divorce when they know that they could have prevented it. On one hand, they divorce because they believe they'll be happier and that their children might be, too, if the marriage is fraught with arguments and discord. On the other, they feel it's a selfish act that will hurt the children. After a divorce time with Dad often becomes scheduled, which can draw fathers closer to their sons but also can drive them apart. When a father remarries and has stepchildren or newborns, his son has to compete with others for his attention.

One father I counseled came to see me about his ten-year-old. We ended up talking about his divorce fifteen years before and the relationship he had had with his first son, who was now twenty. He feared he was failing his preteen son the way he had failed his son from his first marriage. "It was the most difficult decision I had to make in my life," he told me. "I knew that I would cause my son the single greatest pain he'd ever feel. Now I tiptoe around him and his younger stepbrother. I'm so scared of hurting them." Gradually, this father came to see that he could not protect his sons from life's inevitable transitions, but he could help them deal with change. He apologized for the hurt he caused his first son, learned to communicate openly, and grew increasingly involved with his family. He included his first son in all of his new family's activities and encouraged the half-brothers to be close in every way he could.

I see a lot of divorced fathers in therapy. Some are remorseful, some vengeful; others are just plain scared. Terry, forty-one, and his wife, Sandy, divorced after Terry had an affair. "I can barely look my son in the eye," he told me. "He's nine years old and I don't know if he has any idea what I did but it doesn't matter. The thought that I did this drives me crazy. I wish I could take it all back." Sometimes the impact of a failed marriage influences the way we parent. Harris admitted that he bought his sons more things after he and his wife divorced. "It's hard to say no," he says, "because I feel so guilty. As much as I hate to admit it, I'm really trying to outdo my ex-wife. I'm not proud of it and I know it doesn't do the kids any good but I can't help it. I want them to love me more."

Fight the Fear: Guilt-ridden fathers must understand that material gifts and permissiveness do not heal old wounds, and they do not buy love and respect. You earn your son's love and respect by being involved and available consistently over time. If you take the trouble to sit down and talk regularly about painful moments, if you take your son's feelings into account, and if you adjust your actions accordingly, you'll have a stronger relationship with your son.

"My son is closer to my wife than he is to me."

Simon, father of eight-year-old Luke, told me, "I feel like Luke just always wants his mom. We play a lot and we have fun. But our conversations are always limited to whatever activity we're doing. When a boy bullied him on the playground last week, he told his mom about it, not me. I was so hurt by that. Much as I hate to admit it, I feel kind of awkward around him, like he'd prefer to be with my wife. Am I crazy to think that way?"

The truth is that sons are often closer to their mothers when they're young. Mothers are typically more nurturing, more available, and more tuned in to children's emotional needs. This dynamic often shifts during preadolescence and puberty, when the boy begins to identify strongly with his father. Still, fathers struggle in the early years because they don't understand why their sons are drawn to their mothers. When fathers become aware that their sons continually seek out their moms when they're hurting or when they need help with something, some fathers feel it's a slap to the ego, whereas it's simply a natural phase kids go through. Some feel left out, and grow angry and resentful, calling their sons "mama's boys."

As the father of a young son, remind yourself that this maternal "gravitational pull" does not mean that you're a bad father. As your son grows older, his bond with you will strengthen and he will begin to identify with you, if you're available and involved in his life. If you're not, you need to gently assert—or reassert—yourself in his life. For example, if your son runs to his mother with a scraped knee, or for help with homework, tell them both that you would like to handle it, and step in. They'll welcome your entrance sooner than you think.

Sons who are sensitive and artistic tend to be closer to their mothers, because women typically provide the acceptance and understanding these boys need. Fathers don't always know what to do with this kind of boy. "I just don't understand how this kid could be my son and not love football," one dad told me. "How are we even related?" Ethan, forty-three, started seeing me because he and his twelve-year-old son weren't connecting. Ethan had always figured he would connect with his son the way that his father had connected with him—through sports. But Gabe didn't like sports. He preferred designing computer games or reading books. "I know it's not politically correct to put down unathletic boys," Ethan told me. "But I can't shake the feeling that my son and I are just different, like we're unequal as men because he can't tell me who won last week's basketball game."

Men who have difficulty accepting sons who are different from them are typically more rigid, less flexible, and rely on stereotypical definitions of masculinity. Gabe had sensed this judgmental attitude in his dad so he had withdrawn and didn't talk to him much. But he could spend hours talking with his mother. Gabe and his dad did not have a high conflict relationship—they had no relationship at all. Because of this, Ethan was jealous of his wife and had begun arguing with her and criticizing her. "Stop coddling him so much," he told her. "You hover over that boy so much that he doesn't even know what it means to be a man." When he got upset with his son, he would tell him to "run to Mommy." Ethan didn't want to admit that he was pushing his son even further away from him with his verbal abuse and didn't believe his wife when she told him this. He did finally come to my office at her insistence, however, and we began to look at his own role in the problems he was having with his son. It wasn't until Ethan began to respect that his son was wired differently than Ethan was that he developed a relationship with Gabe. He worked at seeing the world through Gabe's eyes and accepting his son for who he was, which meant talking to Gabe about his interests, beliefs, and personality. Ethan had to realize what was more important to him: Gabe's happiness and their relationship, or molding his son to his vision of how a boy should act? It was a hard pill to swallow, but Ethan eventually took it and father and son began spending more time together.

In a May 2007 article in *Best Life* magazine, a father writes about what he would do differently if he could raise his son all over again. Number three on the list: I wouldn't have taught him "such a narrow-minded ideal of what it means to be a man." He tells readers to check their assumptions: "Go easier on the hyper-masculine mythology—the-whole-boys-are-strong-and-self-reliant ethos that gets its footing the first time we shame our 1-year-old for crying and is henceforth the 24-hour soundtrack to boys' lives. Sure, the gender model of the strong, silent type is the engine of three quarters of the stylish behavior in the history of our species, but it's tough to argue with its emotional downside. If a real man is supposed to be tough and sure, then a boy feels ashamed when he is weak and uncertain (which is, if memory serves, most of the time). We deal with that shame by retreating into anger or silence, both of which are reasonable facsimiles of the masculine strength we're supposed to have. It's not a formula for good relationships, and it's a recipe for risk-taking behavior."

When young sons are drawn to Mommy, be objective, not resentful. Think about whether he is naturally going to his mother for comfort, or if you're playing a part in pushing him toward her. Are you trying to be closer to him? Do you inadvertently react harshly when he does come to you or if he doesn't choose you first? Little boys—eight and under—rarely benefit from tough love. They may like to play rough, throw a football, and compete over who can swim the fastest, but their egos are fragile—and they may still be figuring out their place in your heart. Mothers rarely prescribe ideas about manhood for their sons but fathers often do. If a boy scrapes his knee and comes in the house crying, a father may tell him, "Suck it up," or "Stop crying." A mother is likely to pull the boy into her arms, rock him, and tell him it will be okay. Little boys need this kind of coddling. Fathers who "rewire" themselves to project a more loving and understanding side often become closer to their young sons. Again, I'm not saying you should act like his mother, but your relationship will benefit when you incorporate some of Mom's tender tricks.

Fight the Fear: A little nurturing can go a long way. Hug your son when you can, comfort him when he's hurt, and show him that you understand how he feels. Sons, like daughters, respond to tender gestures and soothing words. Your masculinity is not on the line here when you show affection to a child. In fact, your son will be pleased to get that affection from you—boys are sometimes jealous of their sisters' loving relationship with their dads—and your son will probably run to Mom less.

"I'm a closet chauvinist and don't know if I can change."

I'm afraid that men top the secrecy charts when it comes to expressing their feelings about their marriage and how it colors their parenting—and the quietest of them all are the chauvinists. Men are rarely overt about these feelings, especially with their wives. It's no longer politically correct for them to think women should take care of the home, and modern fathers know that it's a selfish outlook. But even the fathers who see themselves as equal partners to their wives sometimes make assumptions about child rearing and housework. I hear them in my office. "I'm not the 'babysitter,'" one father told me. "I make the money so we can hire a babysitter." "I help her as much as I can," another dad said, "but it's not really my job to give the kids baths and make them dinner, is it?" Today's fathers are more than willing to "help out" around the house but it's typically only after their wives request their help. Said one father: "I know how mothers and fathers are supposed to be—equal partners, sharing responsibilities of parenting. I try to play the role as best I can. But deep down inside, there's this feeling that I should not have to help with the dishes, the laundry, or the car pools. I work so much harder than her and I'm exhausted when I get home—but it's politically incorrect for me to say that to her. So I don't."

These dads are the "cavemen dads," the throwbacks we talked about earlier in the book. Their underlying attitudes are steeped in the "male tradition" and many have little genuine desire to change. They're not bad men—in fact, they care for their families. But they are quite content with the status quo. And they're missing out on one of life's most precious gifts—the feeling of comfort, security, and inner peace that comes from being emotionally open to one's kids in all kinds of situations. Many of these men had fathers who functioned in a similarly remote way, and so they're parenting in the only way they know how. But these fathers are not very good role models for their sons. They don't encourage their sons to express their feelings and vulnerability, or when their sons do, they make light of it. They'll talk about sports and attend games with their sons but they'll avoid "mothers'" activities—feeding the family, cleaning up, PTA meetings, car pools, etc.

Gene, a forty-four-year-old airline pilot, got a wake-up call during a talk with his wife, Carolyn. He was rattling off his usual platitudes about his job and explaining that he often left the rest to Carolyn "to do her part." The problem was that her part included raising the children, taking care of the house, working a part-time job, and making constant excuses for his peripheral family involvement. They were polarized in their roles and Carolyn was angry and frustrated. I asked Gene if he felt that he and Carolyn were partners. "I think so," he said. "I make more money than she does and she evens things out by picking up the slack around the house. She's better at this stuff than I am."

"Let me tell you something, Gene," she yelled. "I work a hell of a lot harder than you think, and if it weren't for me our kids probably wouldn't even speak to you. As it is, you barely know them. Just last week you asked how Mike's soccer game went. He'd played in a *baseball* game, Gene. *Baseball!*"

Carolyn looked at me. "I'm tired of this act we put on," she said. "I do the work and he thinks he can gallivant in and out of our lives. I can't take it anymore." Carolyn was seriously considering divorcing Gene.

This was a potentially explosive mix—an angry, resentful wife paired with a complacent husband set in his ways who feels little desire to change. Gene's reluctance to be an active participant in family life was obvious. His wife had been on to him for a while and now his kids were, too. Worst of all, Gene was passing on an untenable view of men's and women's roles to his sons—that men focus on work and mothers focus on family. Gene actually wanted his sons to view men's and women's roles as equal, but realized that he was modeling an outdated stereotype. Still, it was one that was deeply embedded in his psyche and behavior.

Men are often ashamed when they realize their chauvinistic tendencies, but it's more helpful for them to admit to these feelings and try to change than it is to deny them. Gene and Carolyn remained in therapy for several months. Gene would promise to take on an equal amount of responsibility and then break his promises. As I continued to work with Gene on finding things to do with his sons, however, Carolyn saw that Gene's relationship with the boys was improving, so she stopped nagging her husband about his share of the chores. "I can handle the laundry," she told me. "I can't handle watching my boys be disappointed by their dad time and again."

Fight the Fear: Even cavemen can change. You can change. Once you realize that you love your family and are hurting them and yourself with your outdated attitudes, you have to make some adjustments to ensure that you are sharing responsibility and parenting.

- *Take steps to get involved in your son's life and in running the house.* Offer to pick him up from drama practice or the orthodontist's. Run the vacuum through the living room—don't wait for your wife to ask. Do some laundry or pick up dinner.
- *Don't tell your son and wife that they can count on you—show them.* If you say you're going to attend your son's basketball game or take the family ice skating, follow through. Don't make promises that you can't keep. And do make promises.
- *If your career takes you away from the home, accept that you won't always be there and that a fifty-fifty split of running a household may be unrealistic.* But when you are home, help out as much as you can. It will improve your relationship with your wife, and show your son that fathers are responsible for more than their careers.

"I've hurt my son more than I've helped him."

Some fathers of troubled teenagers are remorseful in confessing their role in the problem, but some fail to take any responsibility. Those who do, ask, "Where did I go wrong?" A boy who once made his father proud takes a wayward path, gets in trouble with the law or drugs, or is continually at odds with his family. In response, fathers can grow depressed, worn down, or hopeless. They'll ask where they went wrong when they're about to give up, even though they don't want to, as well as when they want to justify to themselves that they're planning to write off their sons and that their sons deserve it. "I really don't like who he's become," one father told me, "and for that reason I'm not really sure that I want him in my life anymore."

I met Sam and Rita shortly after their nineteen-year-old son had been killed in a car accident. He had left a party drunk and wrapped his car around a tree in a sad and senseless ending to his life, but that wasn't why they had come to see me. Their sixteen-year-old son, Charles, was arrested for driving under the influence of alcohol a few months after his brother's funeral. He had begun blowing off school and was rarely making curfew. His parents worried that they might lose him, too. "It's like he's following in his brother's footsteps," Sam told me. I asked him and his wife why they thought Charles was acting that way. "He tells us we're trying to control his life," Sam said. "He complains that I'm too strict and I don't understand him. We have a lot of arguments that don't get resolved. I'm just not sure where I've gone wrong. I know I failed him." Sam was staring at his knuckles. His lip began to quiver. Rita put her arm around him and gave him a squeeze.

I asked Sam if he had been close to Charles before their other son's death. He inhaled and sighed, "Not really. I was never really close with either of them. I wanted to be but there was always something to argue about—they weren't doing their schoolwork or they weren't listening to their mother. I'd wind up hollering at them and punishing both of them. But it never seemed to work."

Sam was caught in the punishment cycle and didn't know how to relate to his son or talk to him. He acted out of desperation and constantly sent Charles to his room, which only made things worse. Charles felt misunderstood and Sam felt angry when Charles thumbed his nose at his father's authority. "It wasn't always like this," Rita reassured me. "After we adopted them as babies, we were very happy. We'd do things as a family. But toward the end of elementary school, things started to get more difficult. There were behavior problems and calls from teachers—"

"And I started losing my patience," admitted Sam. "A lot of it is my fault, I think. I pulled away and let my wife deal with things."

Sam came to see that he had substituted punishment for other roles as a father. We worked on changing the limits and consequences that he set for Charles and on finding ways to reconnect with his son. And I worked with Charles to uncover some of his own fears and guilt about his brother's death. All three recommitted to being a family together.

We all make mistakes as fathers. But if we don't acknowledge them we can push our sons away from us. Asking yourself "Where did I go wrong?" takes courage. When you own up to things that you're not particularly proud of, it forces you to show your true feelings. And that opens the door to change.

Fight the punishment cycle:

- When you set rules and meaningful consequences, discuss them with your teenager first. Explain why you need them and ask for your teenager's input.
- If possible, offer the opportunity to negotiate. Teens are more likely to accept rules when they've had a say in the process.
- If a rule is broken, don't scream, criticize, or put your son down. It only makes matters worse. State your position calmly, explain your reasoning, and listen carefully to your son's explanation.
- When you impose a punishment, make certain that it is fair, relatively short-lived, and effective so it teaches your son why he should not do what he did (e.g., drinking, breaking curfew).
- Always discuss the rule violation after the punishment is over to make sure your teenager understands what you expect of him and what the consequences will be if there is a repeated offense.

CHAPTER FIVE

Sons Speak Out

When Dads Hurt and Disappoint Them

Ten-year-old Calvin came to see me one afternoon after school, referred because he was an underachiever and disruptive in class. I liked him as soon as I met him. He had a broad smile, a sweet freckled face, was quick with a joke, and loved talking about his passion for tae kwon do. Calvin couldn't understand why his parents had sent him to my office but he hadn't protested. "My grandpa says I'm a pleasure," he said, brightly.

I didn't ask him why he was doing so poorly in school, which made him relax. I was more interested in how he spent his time and who his friends were. How did he get along with his parents? Calvin said he had tons of friends and cheerfully described his love of funny movies. He said he was addicted to video games such as Madden's NFL, a virtual football game.

I changed the subject and asked about his family. I wanted to know if he was close to his mother. Calvin's tone changed. "She's fine," he said. "She nags me sometimes but other than that . . ." I chuckled because most boys complain that their mothers are nags. Then I asked about his dad. "He's okay," Calvin said with a hint of sadness and resignation.

"Sometimes boys get angry at their fathers and they don't like to talk about it," I told him. Calvin looked up.

"Why?" he asked.

"Sometimes they're upset that their fathers aren't around much or that they yell a lot or they feel like their dads don't understand them."

Calvin was nodding. I leaned forward in my chair.

"What you feel is really important, Calvin," I said. "I'm guessing you hardly ever talk about this but I'd like to. Maybe I can even help."

Calvin remained quiet.

"I bet you've got some pretty good reasons to be angry at your dad, like those other kids I mentioned."

Calvin nodded again. And then he really opened up, saying his father wasn't always around. He was often working at the office or at the marina, where he was restoring an antique Bristol sailboat. Calvin often felt as if he was bothering his dad if he asked him for anything. "Does he come to watch you at tae kwon do exhibitions?" I asked. Calvin rolled his eyes.

"He says he's coming but then he gets tied up at the office or he comes thirty minutes late," he said. "It makes me so mad."

"I'd be angry, too," I said.

"My dad is always complaining about my grades in school," he says. "But you know what? He doesn't know anything about my grades. Mom is the one who goes to all the meetings and reads over my homework."

Calvin hadn't told his dad how he felt and hadn't even realized how upset he was until he and I got talking. Still, he didn't want to talk to his dad about his feelings. "It's a waste of time," he said. "He'd just find a way to blame everything on me. He'd say I'm lucky to have what I have and I should appreciate him more."

Sons are astute observers of their fathers' behaviors. They keep score of what is or isn't done for them. They carry grudges even as they worship and criticize their dads. Fathers are the men that boys love to hate and hate to love.

Numerous youngsters like Calvin yearn for their father's attention and approval but fail to get it. Their lives are not terrible. Like Calvin, these boys have nice homes, attend good schools, and are enrolled in many extracurricular activities. But something essential—their father's presence—is missing from their lives. Calvin's frustration with his dad is only the surface of his pain. Deep within lies a longing for an emotional connection with his father.

Too many boys make do in their everyday lives with little involvement from their fathers. They want their fathers' attention, guidance, approval, and love but don't know how to ask for it directly when they don't get it. Sons grow more and more distant from their dads after each disappointment, each criticism, each dismissal of their feelings. Eventually these boys are unlikely to want to spend time with their fathers at all. They learn to settle for dads who are half there and conclude that it's a father's nature to be unavailable. To cope the boy learns that, when he expects less from his dad, he'll hurt less. Over time, father and son fall into a pattern—Dad assumes everything is okay since there are no complaints, and his son assumes that his father doesn't want to know him.

A younger boy tends to give his father the benefit of the doubt more than an older child. A young boy overlooks disappointment and forgives easily. Grant, a six-year-old, told me that he's never sure where his father is at dinnertime but still looks forward to his arrival. "I tell Mom to have supper ready for him, too, in case he gets home early from work," he says. Jacob, a thirteen-year-old, had little patience when his father didn't show up for dinner. "My dad does what he wants to do," Jacob said.

Men can often admit that, in father-and-son relationships, what you see can be misleading. A father who loves his son to death may never show it directly. A son who yearns for his father's presence may act as though he could not care less about his dad. Why? Fathers and sons rarely express their feelings. It's no wonder that so many boys are bursting at the seams when I ask them to tell their stories. They follow the "male code." *Don't show weakness. Assume others will read your mind. Keep your wimpy complaints to yourself.* With each school recess, sporting event, and outing with friends, sons learn the social mores of manhood, which include hiding their innermost feelings for fear of being labeled a "wuss" or a "wimp." Even with their fathers, boys feel they should project strength and toughness since some fathers do label their sons sissies at any show of weakness.

Sons want to talk to their fathers, but don't always know how. This yearning reminds me of a scene in the '80s teen movie *The Breakfast Club*. In the film, Emilio Estevez's character is in detention for bullying another boy. He feels really bad for what he did—his admission to the other kids in detention nearly brings him to tears. When a classmate asks why he bullied the boy at all, he replies, "I did it just to please my old man." Estevez's father was always pushing him to be tough, to win, to be number one, so he assumed his father would be proud of his son's machismo, even though his behavior lacked integrity. Estevez later admits how angry he is at his dad and, clearly, years of built-up resentment are behind his statement.

Many boys feel anger toward their fathers, but few reveal it because they fear their fathers' rejection or blame. This is particularly true for preadolescent boys. Evan, nine years old, spent months in therapy unraveling the complex love-hate relationship he had with his father. Evan said his dad treated him like "a stupid kid" and often lost patience with him. Evan liked to dawdle; his father valued efficiency. "I don't know what my dad would do if I told him that he was always mean to me," Evan told me. "He'd probably tell me it was my fault that he was mean and then he'd punish me." My heart breaks when I hear boys talk like this. In nine years, this boy had already learned that he couldn't express himself freely with his father, that being truthful about his feelings might inspire his father to criticize him or pull away from him. Twelve-year-old Alfie told me that it hurt every time his father broke the promises that he'd made him. The week before, his dad was supposed to take him to a baseball card show and he had canceled at the last minute because he was tired. I asked Alfie why he didn't tell his dad how upset he was. "He would have just told me to stop acting like a little girl," Alfie said.

Boys receive rigorous training in withholding their feelings from "experts"—their fathers and other men. When fathers make light of their own feelings or someone else's—or never express their feelings— a boy concludes that feelings are strange, unmanly, and unimportant. Frankie, a thirteen-year-old, asked me this very question: "How can anyone expect me to tell my father what bothers me? He'd never do that with me or anyone else and my grandpa is just like him." To Frankie, expressing feelings seemed like something only an alien from another planet would do. I couldn't blame him. In his household, no emotions were shared.

These days men no longer score points with women for being stoic and their sons certainly don't applaud the behavior, but it continues. Most fathers would acknowledge that their sons would be better off talking about what's on their mind, yet they are threatened by the notion. Sometimes our habituated response of clamming up in the face of messy emotions prevails over the acquired conventional wisdom that it's best to talk about them. We know it's better but aren't comfortable acting on it.

Nevertheless, I hope that you will want to change after hearing boys reveal their innermost thoughts and stories. Here are the "Enlightening Eight"—the greatest complaints sons have about their fathers.

THE ENLIGHTENING EIGHT

1. "Dad's always busy and never around."

This one heads up the list. Throughout the book, you've heard it echoed again and again by sons of all ages: Dad is always at the office. He travels constantly. He brings his work home. There's always something he has to do. He breaks his promises to take me places, can never find the time to be "there," or worst of all, can't be counted on when I need him. The message a father sends to his son when he's unavailable is "You're not that important to me." Many boys carry this terrible hurt with them every day—it lingers and colors all aspects of their lives. When sons are little, they'll often ask, "Where's Daddy?" But what they're really asking is, "Why isn't Daddy with me?" As boys grow up, they begin to comment on how busy Dad is, asking things such as, "Why does Dad always have to work?" They want to know what could be more important than spending time with them. By adolescence, however, boys begin to write off their fathers when they don't feel loved or cared about.

Teenagers can be particularly vocal about preoccupied fathers, even openly angry and insulting. Some sons will attack their fathers' faults—he's judgmental, selfish, materialistic—but most of their anger can be traced back to their childhoods when they felt cast aside, even by "provider" dads with the best intentions. Fifteen-year-old Max told me, "My father always has an excuse for why he's not around—things are overwhelming at the office, there are bills to pay, or there's stuff he needs to do around the house. He'll always say he'll join me as soon as he finishes his latest project. But who's he kidding? He's been telling me this shit for years. I don't even listen anymore when he comes up with his latest story. If I told him how I felt, I'm sure he'd turn it around and talk about all the good things we have because he works so hard. He's saving for our education, for our nice vacations, to get us cars when we turn sixteen, and anything else he can come up with to justify his stupid behavior. He won't take the blame for anything and the whole family knows that he'll only do things his way."

Are you an unavailable dad? To find out, ask yourself,

- Does your job always come first?
- Do you often break promises to your son (e.g., "I'll see you at your game Thursday night")?
- When your son talks to you, do you try to do something else at the same time?

- Are you truly aware of what's going on in your son's day-to-day life?
- Do you make your son feel like he's important to you?

2. "Dad never listens."

Many boys tell me that their dads are zoned out, they don't pay attention, or they're forgetful. These are common mistakes of dads. You may not be purposely forgetful or distracted, but overworked and stretched. Still, sons hate—yes, hate—spending time with their dads unless they have their full attention. It's hurtful to him if you show up at a soccer game and then talk on your cell phone on the sidelines. A few years ago, fourteen-year-old Seth was complaining that his dad would spend time with him but sometimes type on a BlackBerry and answer his cell phone during their outings. "It's like he's an ADD dad," Seth told me.

I haven't forgotten that term. Many fathers, including myself at times, are guilty of juggling so many things in their minds that we never fully enjoy whatever we're doing. We're preoccupied with thoughts about work and upcoming sports events, the repairs the car needs or whether we can take a family vacation this summer. What we're not thinking about is the present moment. And that's where our sons need us. They want us fully immersed in the exhibit at the zoo or laughing heartily with them while watching the latest Will Ferrell comedy. If a boy mentions to his dad that he has a golf tournament the following week, he wants his dad to ask what the course is like and what's his predicted handicap. Lots of boys report that their dads will ask these kinds of questions but seem distracted, like they're on automatic—asking all the right questions but not really listening to the answers. All of us know what it feels like to be "tuned out" by someone. It's obvious when someone isn't really listening to you. Men are often the culprits—so much so that mothers and sons often joke with me about a father's "dizzy" and "forgetful nature."

When talking with their sons, men often say, "Get to the point," which makes them feel unimportant, like Dad is in a hurry. This is devastating and the sons begin to believe their dads don't want to listen to them at all. Davie, a thirteen-year-old, came to see me two years ago, not because he was having problems with his dad, with whom he had a good relationship, but because David said his dad was "spacey," and it sometimes got to him. "I'm just never sure if he's really listening when I'm talking," he told me. "Last week, I was telling him about the school play when right in the middle of it he asks me where I'd like to go to dinner that night. I said, 'Dad! I was just talking about the school play.'" His father apologized but he didn't stop. Davie said he interrupted him again later at dinner when Davie was talking about his fish. Davie said it bothered him, even though he didn't think his father did it on purpose. His dad seemed to want to know what was going on in his life, but just couldn't concentrate. And there he is, the well-meaning, hardworking, distracted ADD Dad.

Are you a dad who has trouble listening? To find out, ask yourself,

- During conversations, does your son often yell "Dad!" because he notices you're not tuned in?
- Do you often forget things that your son tells you? Is it because you don't remember hearing them in the first place?
- Do significant others (wife, family, close friends) comment that you're not paying attention when they talk?
- Do you ever pretend to listen (knowing that you're not)?

3. "Dad demands respect but he doesn't give it back."

In a January 2007 episode of the TV show *Friday Night Lights*, star quarterback Matt Saracen's father returns from Iraq for a two-week visit. Matt is extremely proud of his father and considers him his hero, so he's thrilled when his father shows up to watch him practice for an upcoming game. Matt runs harder than usual, tackles harder, and throws with the strength of a cannon, just to impress his dad. After practice, Matt introduces his father to Coach Taylor. Taylor gushes about Matt's football skills. His father looks surprised. He doesn't smile and says, "I didn't know he had it in him. Just hope he keeps doing okay under pressure." Matt is crushed, having expected his dad to gush right back. Coach says, "Oh he has plenty in him," and the viewer watches Matt look at his dad like he's seeing him for the first time. It's as though he's trying to understand why a man he regards as a hero doesn't respect him when, at that moment, the quarterback has the admiration of everyone on the field, except his own father.

Growing up in a schoolyard culture of domination, boys are pretty sensitive about earning respect. Sometimes they're noticed for sports, their acting chops, or charismatic personality. But if they fail to gain any recognition, they often struggle. They long to belong, but feel like they're struck. But none of this disappointment compares with the damage wrought by a father who fails to make his son feel as if he has his respect and appreciation. It cuts to the very core of a boy's sense of identity.

Younger boys find it hard to identify these feelings and describe their anxiety instead, saying something like "Dad doesn't like my Lego castles," or "Dad says that I don't try hard enough in baseball." But older boys put their anger right out on the table. Jay, twelve, an artsy kid who loved to draw cartoon characters, complained that his father always belittled his interests and treated his drawings dismissively. "Don't you have anything better to do with your time?" But Jay kept drawing, encouraged by his mother and a teacher at school. By high school, Jay was the best caricaturist in school. He stopped showing his work to his father and he didn't invite him when his drawings were exhibited in the school's gallery. "I'm not going to beg him," Jay told me.

Luckily Jay thrived despite his father's lack of respect, but some sons internalize it. Sixteen-year-old Dante told me that he didn't get along with his dad because, ever since Dante could remember, his dad would make wisecracks about him, even in front of his friends. It embarrassed and angered Dante but he never said anything. Now Dante couldn't stand being in the same room with his father. Teddy, also sixteen, stopped expressing his opinions around his dad. "Whether we're talking about politics, sports, or a movie," Teddy says, "Dad always has to have the last word. I don't even bother telling him what I think anymore." Another high school senior named Pete turned to alcohol. Said Pete about his father: "He's always preaching about how he wants me to respect him but he never gives it back. I know how damn insecure he is. He tries to make himself look better by putting everyone else down. When I was a kid, I'd disagree with him and sometimes rather than listen to me, he'd counter with how I was being disrespectful. Well, I got sick and tired of hearing his crap and decided to start doing what I felt like."

It's hard to undo the damage caused by disrespect, although it's possible. It takes a son willing to talk, a father willing to listen, and a family willing to admit their mistakes. It can be difficult to convince fathers that they're being disrespectful toward their sons, perhaps because they see themselves as well intentioned and genuinely concerned about their son's best interests. Often they don't want to admit it to themselves or their sons, even in the face of the evidence—their sons grow distant or react strongly to their comments. They also fail to see the effect of their disrespect on their sons. Healing from these hurts requires serious reconstruction of attitudes, actions, and relationships. A father must learn to take his son's feelings more seriously, whether or not he agrees with them, and stop saying and doing things he now knows to be hurtful. A son must acknowledge his part in fanning the flames of disagreement, despite his temptation to blame the whole thing on his dad. Both must learn to forgive and forget, and live with what they can't forget. It's difficult but it's possible to end up with mutual respect and closeness.

A little respect goes a long way. Pay it now and reap the benefits as your son gets older.

Do you demand more respect than you give? Ask yourself:

- When your son talks, do you take his thoughts, opinions, and feelings seriously?

- Can you admit when you're wrong?
- Do you ever put your son down for his interests?
- Do you insist that your way is the right way or the only way?

4. "Dad has no patience. He always blows up."

My friends and I play tennis on weekends at a school near my house. While I'm on the courts I often enjoy watching little boys playing with their fathers. It warms my heart to see a father gently showing his son how to hold a baseball bat or to shoot a basketball on the adjacent fields. There's physical contact, laughter, and high-fives, moments that are among the great joys of fatherhood.

Sometimes things can get ugly, however. Father and son start their outing innocently and enthusiastically, but before long there's a shouting match between them, the father angry and son tearful. One day a boy of about five years old and his father arrived at the park with their baseball gloves and began throwing the ball back and forth. After a few rounds, it was obvious that the boy wasn't too good at catching, and when he threw the ball back, it was often too short. "Didn't I tell you to pull your arm back and throw the ball up?" his father started screaming. The boy said he was trying. "Well, try harder," the father yelled. The boy pulled back his arm and thrust it upward with as much force as his small frame could muster. The ball traveled only a few feet. The father went ballistic. "Watch me and copy," he shouted impatiently. The boy tried again. No luck. I tried not to stare but it was an awful, riveting scene, with the boy practically in tears. A part of me wanted to intervene but I knew it was none of my business. After five minutes, the father gave up and they left. I never again saw them at the park.

I often hear stories of impatient fathers and have seen fathers yell at their young sons for not properly following their directions, for not doing their homework fast enough, for not immediately obeying their orders. Why is it so important to some fathers that their sons get it just right? Often their sons are doing the best they can. Todd, who was eight when I first started seeing him, was trying his hardest in math. He told me that he would work hard on his homework and his dad often offered to help. The problem was that Dad didn't help Todd, he hurt him. "I hate when Dad helps me," Todd said, "because all he does is scream at me. I tell him that I don't get it but he insists that I should and we keep going over the same thing again and again. He says I should do it his way and I say that's not the way the teacher showed us in class. He says he doesn't care. Then I refuse to do any more work. I usually wind up calling Mom and she breaks us up." I later learned that these failed attempts at tutoring ruined his father's evenings, too, and the hurtful effects reached into other aspects of their lives. Todd avoided anything that required his dad to teach him something, fearing his father's blow-ups. He often cried afterward, just as he cried talking about it in my office.

As impatient fathers and their sons grow older, their interactions may not change. It's especially sad to watch a teenage son and his father argue about something trivial, such as how long to microwave a dish of food or how to build a fire. Both have lost patience with the other.

This cycle can be broken. Fathers must learn when to talk and when to keep their mouths shut. Boys must tell their fathers that they won't tolerate angry overreactions. In Chapter Eight, I'll talk about how fathers and sons can learn to express themselves to each other. The key is to think about what you're going to say before you say it. If it's likely to be hurtful, do as Archie Bunker suggested: "Stifle yourself."

5. "My dad's a control freak."

Anyone who has spent time around a teenager knows this line and many parents are accused of being one. Sometimes teens are simply angry at a parent's authority and setting of curfews or limits. Other times they're tapping into a truth. Some fathers want everything their way—no discussions, no negotiations. Sons should do as they say and everything will be fine. But it rarely is. Dads can get away with being controlling in a boy's younger years, but a few maintain their iron fist through their son's teenage years, believing that they're keeping their sons out of trouble and on track academically. But their heavy hands have the opposite effect, planting the seeds of rebellion rather than preventing it.

Younger boys often complain that there's not much they can do to change their dads, so they rebel in small ways, such as failing to follow a teacher's direction or arguing with a soccer coach or even passively protesting rules in silence. One boy I counseled said "Yes" when his parents asked him to do something but rarely followed through. As boys grow into adolescents, their comments become less charitable and sometimes downright hostile, mostly because the game remains the same—father is determined to stay in charge, and son rebels against his efforts.

By the time I met Gil, he was fifteen and had been arguing with his father for years. Gil wasn't a model son but he wasn't a bad kid. He often pushed the envelope, sometimes ignoring his curfew or cutting a class. He'd get punished, which didn't faze him. "I get punished for everything," he told me. If Gil forgot to take out the trash, he'd lose TV for a week. If he talked on the phone too long, his father would grab it out of his hand, hang it up, and forbid him to use it for the rest of the night. His father took him and his friends to the mall, but when Gil arrived five minutes late to the agreed meeting place, his father's veins bulged in anger and Gil wouldn't be allowed back to the mall for a month.

Gil told me he wanted more freedom and for his dad to treat him like a man, not a child. So he often argued with his father. "He's always interrogating me," Gil told me. "No matter what I'm doing or where I'm going, he puts me on the witness stand. 'Why are you wearing that shirt?' 'Why are you on the computer when you should be doing your homework?' I get a knot in my stomach whenever we're in the same room. He thinks he knows everything."

I asked Gil if he thought that his dad kept close tabs on him because of his irresponsible behaviors. Gil buried his head in his hands. "But it doesn't matter if I do good or bad. Now he just punishes me for everything. I figure if he's going to do that I might as well do what I want," he said.

There is no easy fix in situations like this. Gil's father was rigid and inflexible, Gil defiant and rebellious. When fathers and sons are locked in battle, there is little room for a meaningful dialogue and relationship. They need to step back, take an honest look at what's going on, and try to reinvent their relationship. It can take months for "controlling fathers" to see and admit that their behavior backfired and has gotten them the opposite result. But once everyone in the family agrees that they're unhappy with the status quo, they have a foundation for change. If there's a "control freak" inside you, I'd advise you to address the issue as early as possible.

We spoke earlier about how to break the teen control/rebellion cycle and still exercise influence—but here are a few more tips to help you move away from "control freak" status:

- Ask yourself why it's so important for you to be in charge at all times.
- How would you feel if someone were constantly telling you what to do?
- Do you want your son to be able to think for himself and make his own decisions? If so, you'll need to teach him how to question authority respectfully and speak his mind. That means engaging in a two-way dialogue, not "my way or the highway." Remember that you're a role model for your son.

6. "Dad's a couch potato."

If a controlling dad is hyperinvolved in his son's life, a passive father is underinvolved. Traditional guys, couch potatoes and cavemen, are passive dads. They are not angry or imprisoned by their careers. These guys love their families. They're just not very involved fathers. A boy with a passive dad often complains that his dad doesn't want to do anything with him. One seven-year-old told me how he had to bug his dad just to give him a ride somewhere, let alone spend time with him. A nine-year-old said his father was always planted in one place—in front of the television. When I asked a fourteen-year-old why he and his dad weren't close, the boy quipped, "Dad has no life."

These sons often feel sad about their fathers and angry at them, but more often than not, they accept their dads' lack of involvement in their lives as a given. Still, they yearn for them to get involved. Many boys' dream day would be spent with their fathers on a trip to the local science museum, ballpark, or movie. Without a steady, involved dad, boys often fantasize about what their fathers could be. Sid, a ten-year-old, wished that his father would stand up for him. "My father picked me up after a soccer game and when he got there, two boys were pushing me around," he told me. "I know he saw it but he didn't say a word about it. Why couldn't he tell them, 'Leave my son alone or I'll break your neck and call your parents.'" Sid said his father let him down a lot. He often went to his mom for help with things. Other times his mom would get mad at him, yell at him, and punish him. His dad was sitting right there, watching TV. "It's like he never even notices and even if he does he doesn't do anything," Sid said.

The good news is that passive dads are often the easiest to change and are particularly responsive to pressure from their loved ones. They simply fail to understand—until they're told—that their family needs them. You'd be surprised by the number of dads who are unaware of how deeply and negatively their behavior affects their family. Some do want to be more involved but they're uncertain how to be. I once taught Joey, a twelve-year-old, to use reverse psychology on his father. Tired of his dad choosing time in his woodworking shop over time with him, Joey wanted his dad to start coming to his basketball games. "First I told dad that everyone else's father was coming to the game that week because it was a really big game," said Joey. "When he resisted, I said what you told me to, Dr. B. 'Why don't you just admit that you don't love me and you don't want me around?' That got dad out of his chair." Joey was laughing. His dad came to the game.

I know, I know. It's not always going to be that easy to read your son. Get involved.

Are you a couch potato dad? To find out, ask yourself,

- Do you ever do things without being asked or nagged?
- Would you rather sit around watching TV, surfing the Net, or puttering in your study, than spend time with your son?
- Does your family ever make comments like, "Can't you ever help?" Or worse yet, do they ignore you completely?

7. "Dad never tells me what's really going on."

I've heard it from younger and older boys alike but the message is the same: "Dad doesn't tell me things. He doesn't think I can handle the truth." "Sometimes Dad will pretend that everything is fine when he knows that it's not." Like mothers, fathers have a protective instinct to try to shield sons from harm. And fathers can be pretty private. Despite this, there are situations—impending divorce, a parent's illness—when your son needs you to explain what's going on. When a son learns of a painful secret from another source, your relationship will suffer—trust is eroded, feelings are bruised, and sons feel betrayed.

Oscar, a sixteen-year-old honor roll student, whom I began seeing when his parents divorced, was angry and devastated that they were splitting up, but he was even angrier that his father never sat him down and explained what was happening. "Mom mentioned it to me a few times," he told me. "She apologized for what my brother and I were going through, but Dad acted like nothing was happening." Oscar said that he and his dad went out to a movie the weekend before. Afterward they stopped at a diner and ordered cheesesteak sandwiches. Over dinner, they discussed the Nets, then the Giants. "He was moving out in a week," Oscar said. "I knew that. He knew that. But he didn't say anything to me about it. It felt weird." On the day that his father packed up his things, he waved to Oscar as he carried out the last box. "Don't worry. I'll see you soon," his dad told him. It seemed to Oscar that his father didn't care about leaving or about hurting Oscar. "I don't get how he could do that to me," he said. "He just left. He didn't say anything else. How could he not realize how upset I was?"

I told Oscar that I would have felt just as angry, and asked him if his dad had ever done anything like that before—had he kept other secrets or purposely withheld information? Oscar thought about it for a second. "Now that you mention it," he said, "Dad lost his job four or five years ago. What he told me was that he was taking some vacation time off before he started a new job. But it was months before he went back to work. I remember always asking him why he was home. He insisted that he was on vacation." I understood where Oscar's father was coming from. He didn't want his sons to worry about finances or think that he was lazy or unmotivated. But most boys, including Oscar, prefer knowing the truth. When boys complain that their fathers won't tell them anything, I often ask them to see that their fathers want to protect them and keep them from worrying—still, they say they'd rather know the truth. Then their dads would be treating them like equals.

It took months for Oscar to get his point across to his dad. We invited his father to join us in therapy and we talked about it in several meetings. His dad acknowledged the problem, but was slow to come around. With some probing, I discovered that Oscar's dad's own father had protected him in the same way he was protecting Oscar. I asked Oscar's dad if he had liked being kept out of the loop.

"No," the father answered quickly.

"Then why did you do it to me?" Oscar asked his dad.

His dad said he didn't want to hurt Oscar and didn't want him to worry, but, "Mostly, I do it because it's easier for me," his dad admitted. "It's hard for me to explain to you what's going on. Sometimes I get a lump in my throat just thinking about it." Oscar nodded his head. He understood.

"But it would be nice if you could try sometimes," Oscar said quietly.

When fathers try to shield their sons from reality and real feelings, they often hurt them more than help them. If you find yourself doing this, ask why you do it. Is it simply because you're protecting your son, or is it too hard for you to disclose the truth and talk about it? Most likely, it's a little of both, but you have to go out of your way to fill in your son on life's "secrets." Start by revealing smaller things, such as a fight you had with your boss or the reason why you lost your temper. Then you will be ready to explain the bigger problems that come up.

I feel I can't say it enough—sons want to hear explanations from their fathers more than from their mothers. It's a respect thing. Most likely, your son already knows that you're keeping something from him. So he's waiting for you to come to him. He wants an explanation. Remember—treating your son like a man helps him to become one.

8. "Dad doesn't know me."

I hear this from many adolescent boys I counsel—Dad knows nothing about me but he thinks he knows everything. This is sometimes true. Dads may think they know everything because for a long time they did. Many tracked their sons' development from potty training to algebra, but they don't always track emotional development. Fathers can be shocked by their sons' mature line of thinking, as if they're surprised that their boys think coherently at all.

Feeling like their dads don't know them leaves boys angry, disappointed, and estranged. Boys want their fathers to know more than what grades they earned on a report card or their baseball team's record. They want their fathers to understand who they are inside—what drives them, what they believe in, what they're sensitive about, and what they're not. Many dads come up short when asked to describe the thoughts and experiences, interests and dreams that make their sons who they are. They often know one aspect of their son well. They'll complain about a boy's bad memory or praise his academic successes. Many assume that their boys think like they do or that they think like "most boys." But fewer can recognize what makes their son unique.

When fifteen-year-old Kurt came to see me, I spent the first session trying to understand why his parents thought he needed therapy.

President of his sophomore class and a star forward on his high school's basketball team, he was fascinated by classic rock legends and dabbled in guitar. He had a girlfriend, a tight circle of friends, and seemed confident when he sat down opposite me, looking me in the eye and smiling. But his parents thought he was depressed. He didn't talk to them much and often locked himself in his bedroom for hours blasting music.

Unlike many teenagers, Kurt didn't fight his parents about coming to our sessions. He admitted early on that he rarely spoke to adults. He thought it was nice to have someone to bounce ideas off of. His mom was okay, he said, but she overreacted too much so he never told her anything. "Dad's another story," he said. Kurt said his dad often "checked in" with him and had done so for as long as Kurt could remember. His dad would get home and ask him how he was doing, how his grades were, if his teacher liked his oral history report. He didn't ask about anything else so Kurt didn't share much else. Occasionally his dad would ask about student government or take him to the batting cages, but Kurt said he always felt distant from his dad on those outings—he knew that he was lucky to be spending time with his dad but was disappointed by how little his dad asked about him.

As I got to know Kurt, I realized that he wasn't depressed. He was lonely. When he went into his room, locked the door, and blasted music, he was trying to drown out his father hunger. Over time, Kurt also realized that he was angry at his father and had been trying to avoid him so that he didn't keep getting disappointed in his dad and hurt by him. I asked Kurt if he really believed his father didn't care about him. "If he does," he told me, "he certainly doesn't show it."

Your son needs to feel understood by you. Even if you ask your son questions and he seems irritated, don't let that fool you. He wants you to ask and know about his life, but he does not want you to nag him about it. Think about what you wish someone would ask you. Then ask your son similar questions.

WHAT'S A SON TO DO?

Now that you've heard the voices of many different sons—some angry, some fearful, and some uncertain about where they stand with their fathers—you can hear the common yearning for their fathers' respect. They need to feel empowered in their relationship with you. They can express their concerns and get you to listen, but you both have to learn to speak what you've largely left unspoken. You can do it through an e-mail, face-to-face contact, or with the help of a therapist.

But it's not easy for many sons to speak to their fathers. Often, I remind them that their feelings are important, that their father wants to hear them, and they have nothing to lose and everything to gain. Whether it's saying, "I wish you were around more," "You always yell at me," or "You never listen," a son's need is the same. He wants you to listen to him and treat him with respect, and he wants to feel as if he matters. With encouragement and support, most boys are able to express themselves to their fathers directly and respectfully—but not all fathers make it easy. Try to make it easy for your son to share his feelings. Encourage him. If you do, your son will feel validated, and he'll begin to respect you more.

William Weaver, chairman of surgery at Atlanta's Morehouse School of Medicine, told a story about his father on National Public Radio in 2006. His dad worked as a janitor and chauffeur when Weaver was growing up. Now fifty-seven, Weaver said that his father knew him so well that Weaver called him for advice on every decision he ever made. He learned this after an incident in high school. He was struggling to learn algebra and couldn't seem to grasp the concepts. As the night went on, he grew more and more frustrated. His dad offered to help, but Weaver told him, "They didn't even have algebra in your day." Weaver said he went off to bed. His dad opened his son's algebra book. At 4 A.M. that night, he woke Weaver up. "What he had done,"

Weaver told NPR, "was sit up all night and read the algebra book. And then he explained the problems to me so I could do them, and understand them . . . To this day, I live my life trying to be half the man my father was, just half the man. And I would be a success, if my children loved me half as much as I loved my father."

CHAPTER SIX

Boys and
Their Tech Toys

Supposedly, Danny had been writing a paper on symbolism in J. D. Salinger's novel *The Catcher in the Rye*, for three hours. The book was on his desk but the seventeen-year-old was typing to his friends over IM. He didn't feel like finishing his lit paper, and didn't see what Holden Caulfield had to do with him anyway. His cell phone beeped. Danny flipped it open, read a text message, and typed one back. Then he clicked on his Facebook.com profile and changed his "status"—an entry that sets a user's mood—from "keeping it real" to "procrastinating." His cell phone beeped again. He flipped it open, glanced at the message, and snapped the phone shut. Spotting an icon on his computer screen flashing—he'd received another IM, or instant message—he read, "Did u see what Z added to his profile?" Danny clicked back on Facebook and found a picture of his best friend Zane hanging upside down on a set of monkey bars, two pretty girls standing in low-cut tops next to him.

Danny's parents were lying in bed with their door open. Just after midnight, they saw that their son's light was still on and heard the clicking of the computer's mouse. "Should I tell him to go to bed?" Tony asked his wife. "He should have finished that paper hours ago." No answer. Tony reluctantly pushed off the covers, knocked softly on his son's door, and asked "Can I come in for a minute?" Danny clicked out of Facebook and pulled his Word document back up on the screen so his father would see his paper, not his Internet conversations.

"I'm busy, Dad. Can you come back later?"

"Later? It's twelve o'clock! You need to go to bed."

Danny rolled his eyes and moaned, "I got to finish my paper."

"But you've been working on it since nine o'clock. You're not focused. Get offline and finish it."

"I'm talking with friends *about* the paper."

"Get offline, Danny—NOW," Tony says.

"You just don't get it, Dad. This is when everybody talks. I'll have the paper done in an hour anyway. Don't worry about it," Danny says.

"Fine," Tony said. "But lights off in an hour. You finish that paper or I'm gonna take away your Internet privileges for a week."

Danny watched his dad close his bedroom door, then pulled his IM conversation with his buddy back up, writing his message in code: "Sorry—PIR, KPC." *Translation:* "Sorry—Parent In Room, Keeping Parent Clueless."

Sons are living in a world vastly different from the ones that we fathers grew up in. They have unlimited access to information on just about everything. Need to do research for a school project? Forget the encyclopedia—go to Wikipedia.com. Struggling with a paper? Forget reading the book—head to SparkNotes.com and download detailed summaries of novels, plays, and historical moments. They "Google" everything from their own names to their favorite singer's concert schedule. Every one of their thoughts—Is it normal to masturbate so much? Who was voted off American Idol last night?—can be answered or validated with a click of the mouse in the world of the high-stimulation generation where laptops, camera phones, PS3s, and iPods rule. The Kaiser Family Foundation reported that, in 2005, 86 percent of American homes with children ages eight to eighteen had computers and 39 percent of children in this age group had cell phones—and these numbers rise each year.

Sons live the bulk of their existence in cyberspace—and their parents know very little of what they do. Yet these days fathers cannot really understand their sons if they don't understand what they're doing online. According to the Pew Internet & American Life Project, 55 percent of kids today have online profiles on social networking sites such as Facebook.com and MySpace.com. Of those individuals, 66 percent use passwords to control who reads their profiles, meaning these "online diaries" are often under lock and key, even to parents. Much of their behavior online is innocent: they post pictures of themselves, let friends in on boring details of their days, such as when they're taking a shower, walking the dog, or writing a paper. But kids sometimes also use their profiles to post inappropriate material such as suggestive photographs, leave explicit notes on one another's Web pages, and spread hurtful gossip. In 2007, *USA Today* reported on the prevalence of "cyberbullies" among kids ages nine to fourteen years old who use the anonymity of the Web to "unleash put-downs, nasty rumors and humiliating pictures in e-mail and blogs that can strike victims at home and at any time." According to the article, students at an elementary school in Fairfax, Virginia, conducted an online survey of who was their ugliest classmate.

When children get information about a subject online rather than from books in a library, something is almost always lost in the translation, details are left out by the superficiality of the description, and they do not learn the context from which ideas have evolved. Most kids today communicate through a string of cryptic sound bites—*Do U no wat I mean?* They fall in love after exchanging a few IMs and e-mails. They scroll through pornographic websites before they've reached the sixth grade. This accelerated pace of emotional life makes a father's role more important than ever and you need to be involved in your son's Internet activities and limit them just as you're involved in other aspects of his life. If you're not, your son will set his own limits. Says one seventeen-year-old student: "As long as my grades are up, Dad doesn't ask any questions."

BONDING ON BLACKBERRIES

It's not just boys who are fascinated with technology and gadgets. Grown men tap into their Treos with the same zeal as their fourteen-year-olds on PlayStation. Walk into an Apple Store on any given Saturday and there are dozens of men trying out the sample computers. For fathers and sons, taking a trip to Best Buy has become a rite of passage. Technology has opened lines of communication between fathers and sons, offering them alternative means of expression and an entire collection of goods to bond over. According to the Entertainment Software Association, 43 percent of video gamers are between the ages of eighteen and forty-three. This supports what I see in my practice—a lot of fathers and sons are playing Madden Football together.

Many wives roll their eyes when their husbands mention a love of video games. I'll admit that it is boring to be around someone who's playing video games unless you're taking turns and playing yourself. But unless their men are addicted to gaming, women can rest easy that it is a comfortable way for fathers to bond with their sons. Video games give fathers an avenue within which they can compete, laugh, and teach their sons. Since men connect through doing, rather than talking, it's easy for them to spend time with their sons when they're busy slaying assassins. Gaming should be in the same category as playing catch or building a tree house—a way to bond.

Technology can bring together even disparate father-and-son pairs. Fathers can use the subject as an excuse to talk to their sons and even ask their more savvy sons for technology tutorials. Inquire about how to make a document graphically interesting, how to find some obscure information, or even which Internet provider you should sign up for as a family. Your son will have plenty to say. Afterward you can thank your son and tell him that he's your "computer man." You won't learn your son's intimate secrets by doing this, but you'll convey the message that our son's thoughts and opinions matter. Moments like this build trust and might even inspire regular give-and-take. The boy may ask for his dad's advice on something down the road.

Darren didn't have much in common with his son so he made a point of asking eleven-year-old Mason for advice on anything that he found technologically challenging. When Darren bought his first iPod, Mason showed him how to download songs. Then Darren came home with a new cell phone. Mason showed him how to change his ringtones. Over time, Mason felt as if his dad trusted him and he learned to trust his dad. The boy asked his father to edit his school papers, help with his campaign for student government, and come up with an excuse for getting him out of gym class the day his classmates ran a mile. When I asked Darren about his proudest moment as a father, he recalled their interaction after his son had been caught shoplifting a candy bar. "The store yelled at him and let him go," Darren said. "But my son still came to me and told me. That was so important to me. I would have *never* told my father that when I was a kid. It made me feel like I must have done something right along the way." Trust is built upon years of honest interaction, but if you are having trouble finding neutral interests to bond over, technology is a good subject to fall back on. Sons love when their fathers ask them for help. It makes them feel special, that their fathers look up to them in the same way that they look up to their fathers.

Become familiar with Facebook.com and MySpace.com, which are like a cyberspace billboard and communication network—cheat sheets into your son's inner sanctum. They're second nature to him but a little intimidating to parents. Emily Yoffe's March 2007 article in Slate.com, titled "Facebook for Fifty-Somethings," provides an entertaining account of the generational gaps. She writes: "You know how in *The Tipping Point* Malcolm Gladwell describes the person he calls a 'connector'—the charming, gregarious individual who knows everyone and makes things happen? I'm the opposite of that person. Even within my small circle, I'm always falling out of touch, and I never know what's going on. But finally, there seemed to be a solution to my isolation that didn't require me to actually go out and see people. Facebook, the three-year-old, 17-million-member social-networking site once the exclusive province of students, recently opened to anyone. The site has so addictively insinuated itself into the daily lives of those under the age of about 24 that academics are studying how it is changing the very nature of their social interactions. I decided to see if someone old enough to remember when answering machines were a radical communication breakthrough could find someone, anyone, among those 17 million willing to connect with me . . ."

Kids post everything on their Facebook profiles these days—high school football players have been suspended from games because their principal saw photos of them drinking on a classmate's online profile. Parents can scan their son's page for early warning signs of potentially deadly behaviors. A March 2007 article in the *Chicago Tribune* told the story of a teenager who loved to drive fast and another who boasted about his drug use. Both kids posted details of their exploits on MySpace.com. One died when he wrecked his sports car while driving a hundred miles per hour. The second was found dead after overdosing on opiates and antidepressants. "Such seemingly inevitable tragedies have some experts urging parents to use social networking sites as an early warning system to alert them to problems from substance abuse to eating disorders to violent fantasies," says the article. Amanda Lenhart, a research specialist with the Pew Internet & American Life Project, adds, "It's not a panacea, going through your child's profile . . . but it can be a window into their life. It can be a conversation starter."

So to know your son, there's no better place to go than to his online profile. I'm not saying spy. You might ask your son if he'd be willing to share his profile. Bryce, a forty-four-year-old father, didn't know anything about MySpace, but knew that his son was on it all the time. So he decided to follow my advice and ask if he could see Ian's profile. He approached fifteen-year-old Ian one night after he finished practicing the trumpet. Ian was defensive at first. "Why do you want to see it?"

he asked. Bryce explained that he was curious. A lot of the fathers at work were talking about it. They said that it helped them get to know their sons. "What do you want to know?" Ian snapped. After several minutes, Bryce convinced his son that this wasn't an inquisition. He reassured him that he had nothing to worry about.

"Swear that you won't tell Mom what you read," Ian said.

"I swear," he said. Bryce swallowed hard. He wasn't sure what he was getting into. What if he couldn't keep his promise? When his son pulled up his profile, he was shocked by what he saw. There was a photo of his "shy" son with his shirt off, muscles flexed, and a caption saying, "ready for action." His profile described a fun-loving kid into rap music, "hooking up" with girls, and IM'ing late into the night. There were details about his friends, his exploits, his fantasies. His son quickly scrolled past those. At the bottom of the page, there were large letters that read "Girls Aint Nothing But Ho's and Tricks." Ian started cracking up when he saw his dad's eyes widen. "It's a private joke, Dad," his son said. "That's not how I see girls. Girls think it's hilarious, too."

Bryce forced a smile. He didn't know what to say to his son. Then he heard my voice in his head. I had told him, "Don't put your son on the witness stand. Just be curious, look, listen, and learn." So Bryce sat there an hour longer and his son continued to open up to him. Ian showed him a couple of his friends' profiles. He explained how fun MySpace was to use.

A couple of weeks later, Bryce came back to see me. He told me what happened. "At first, I felt like I hardly knew him. He seemed so different online. I admitted that I was a bit shocked by it all but that it must take guts to post so many details about his life. I don't think that was the reaction he expected, and he was clearly encouraged by it. He went on and explained a lot more to me about what the different entries meant. A few of them ruffled my feathers a bit, but any discomfort was outweighed by the newfound closeness I was feeling toward him." There would be time later to talk more about safe sex and his other exploits.

The prevalence of social networking sites raises these two fathering dilemmas:

1. *How much time should a son spend online?* This depends on how responsible kids are when it comes to finishing their school-work and meeting responsibilities. Generally speaking, one to two hours a day is reasonable. However, many kids spend much more time online. It's very difficult to monitor when you don't insist on keeping computer use to the kitchen or family or other common room, so you should seriously consider making that a rule. You can't always be sure what they're doing online, otherwise. They have codes they send to friends before they switch activities to avoid detection—like POS, or Parent Over Shoulder. But if a child is doing well in all aspects of his life and pulling it off while spending a few hours online then it's probably okay. If they're spending four or more hours a day online in non-school-related activities, it's probably time to intervene. That means limiting the time, checking on him often, using parental controls if necessary, or even canceling the Internet service.

2. *Should you be a cybersnoop?* I don't recommend going into a kid's profile without his knowledge. It erodes goodwill, trust, and only makes a boy more secretive, which is not your goal. It's more effective to take the time to discuss a profile. If you do go into a son's profile, you should explain to your son what you did and why you did it. Yelling at him because you disapprove of something he did online will only anger him. I once did a story for *20/20* about this topic that included some nightmarish stories of parents who hid cameras in their kids' rooms and tapped into their computers to spy on their online exploits. When the kids found out, they were enraged and alienated from their parents. As one kid put it, "If they spy on us, we may as well spy on them." Their relationship turned adversarial. Look, you're a parent, not the FBI. If fathers start eavesdropping on their sons' conversations and

monitoring their e-mails, they're not giving their sons the freedom to come of age. Most of us did a few things wrong along the way and we turned out just fine. It's different, of course, when parents catch their children in serious crimes such as dealing drugs, cheating, or harming someone. But those kids are the exception, not the rule.

E-MAILING IT IN

Boys often tell me that they love going online because in cyberspace they can be anything or anyone they want. They can be more aggressive or more mysterious. Anonymity drapes a cloak over their insecurities and they say all the things that they have wanted to say but typically hold back. "When I'm in a chat room or IM'ing," one twelve-year-old told me, "I feel like I'm a master of the universe. I can say what I want, do what I want, and control everything." This disinhibition is also true for fathers who can use the Internet to reinvent themselves to their children and reconnect. A seventy-two-year-old father told me that he didn't really know his kids before e-mail. On e-mail, he was comfortable revealing more about himself and sharing his emotions. He could ask his kids questions that he didn't have the courage to ask in person.

On the computer, men can escape the traps of masculinity, speak from the heart, and feel as though they're being intimate. But sometimes they're not being intimate at all, and feel betrayed when subjects discussed online are talked about in person. It's as though fathers and sons—and everyone else in this country—are developing dual personas; we're not always the same in person as we are online. Phillip, a thirty-seven-year-old magazine writer, was shocked to receive an e-mail last Christmas from his aging dad. His father had recently learned how to use the computer at the local senior center so he'd signed up for a Gmail account. Phillip laughed when his father asked him for his e-mail address. Then he got the e-mail. His father wrote about how much he was looking forward to Phillip's visit, where they were going to play golf, and asked for suggestions for what he should get Phillip's mother for Christmas. Phillip sensed a sweetness in his father's tone. At the end of the e-mail, he mentioned how proud he was of Phillip's last article. "That would never happen in person," Phillip told me. "I'm lucky to get ten words out of my dad when I'm visiting. It's odd how much more comfortable and communicative he is on the computer. I feel like I'm actually hearing his voice."

Fathers are willing to share more of themselves online. It's easier for them to explain their actions and feel heard. All of us enjoy the blank slate that an e-mail provides. We can vent our frustrations to someone else without interruption. One father I was seeing had trouble expressing himself to his son, and his frustration would often translate into anger. During one session, he and his son actually came to blows and I had to pull them off each other. A few days later, the father sent me a copy of an e-mail message he had sent to his son. It was probably the first time that his son had heard him speak from the heart: "I'm sorry I have such a bad temper. What you don't know is that my father had a temper, too—and he'd often take his anger out on me. He'd find whatever he could to beat me with. It was humiliating. And after that, I swore that I'd never lay a hand on my own son. But I did the other day and I haven't been able to sleep. I can barely eat. I'm sorry. I'm sorry that I'm not always the perfect father." I was so touched by the letter but even more impressed by the power of the Internet. This father would have never said any of that in person.

E-mail or text messages can also be used to keep up with each other throughout the day. Stan, a partner in a large law firm, relies on e-mail to chat with his son during the business day. "I'm often tied up in meetings and can't get to the phone," he says. "But my son knows that if he wants to reach me, I'm on e-mail and I'll always respond immediately. Last week, he sent me an e-mail after his basketball try-outs to tell me he'd made the JV team. I shot back a quick response on my BlackBerry saying that I was excited for him. He shot back a note saying that he was going to start his math homework. I told him that I'd help him when I got home. He shot back a smiley face. The whole time we were e-mailing I was in a legal deposition and I could have never picked up the phone."

While fathers enjoy connecting to their sons online, boys like the Internet because it keeps their fathers off their backs. An eleven-year-old I was seeing told me, "I like that my dad and I can e-mail back and forth because we can talk about almost anything without arguing. He doesn't bug me as much as when he's at home. His e-mails are always shorter and I don't have to listen to that long lecture that he likes to give. I guess we both get to the point quicker and can think about things a moment before we say them. We don't waste any time that way." I laughed at my young patient's insight. He had a point. While e-mail opens up opportunities for father-and-son dialogue, it can also short-circuit the process of emotional bonding. Excessive reliance on e-mails and text messaging can become a cheap substitute for physical affection, eye contact, and the type of disclosures that evolve in another's presence.

Bottom line: the Internet should help fathers and sons talk—but not replace the talking.

WHAT'S TOO CONNECTED?

Unfortunately, the Internet is keeping many families from spending much time together at all. In a recent survey conducted by the Pew Internet & American Life Project, 64 percent of teenagers admitted that the Internet reduces the amount of time they spend with their families. I imagine that that percentage would be even higher if parents were surveyed about the same issue. Indeed the array of available tech toys combined with excessive computer use can keep young people locked in their rooms for hours on end. I often think of these kids as high-wired and mighty tired. Some spend entire Saturdays in chat rooms while others spend their weekends absorbed in video games. All the while they're fiddling with their iPods, cell phones, and BlackBerries. And once kids get started, it's hard for them to let go. God forbid they miss out on the latest gossip or text message. (Our generation was the same way about telephone calls.) So why would a boy spend time with his parents when his bedroom is a virtual entertainment center with a constant buzz of activity?

That's what I helped one family figure out. Julia and Doug came to see me because their sixteen-year-old son, Cameron, spent a lot of time online. I asked them how often and Doug said, "I don't even know anymore." His wife, Julia, shrugged. "We're lucky to get him downstairs for dinner." Cameron lived in a virtual world filled with friends he had never met or talked to over the telephone. He played fantasy games for several hours on school nights. I asked if he ever talked to his parents.

"Rarely," they responded in unison.

"And you allow him to stay in his room for as long as he wants?" I asked.

Doug looked despondent. "What are we going to do about it? When we force him to get off of his computer, he gets irritable and angry and still doesn't want to talk to us. Before we know it, he's back in his room again." Cameron was barely getting passing grades in school. I sensed that Cameron was addicted to computer games.

Parents who have children who spend more than three to four hours a day (particularly on school nights) online may have a serious problem and need to find a way to regulate their sons' time online. You can come up with a "user schedule" for your son or insist that he spend several hours a day away from the computer in an activity that connects him to other kids. When I told Cameron's parents this, they were incredulous. "We don't know what Cameron will do if we do that," Doug told me. I told them I know what would happen if they didn't: the problem would get more serious.

Cameron fought them tooth and nail at first, but he eventually realized that his parents were sticking to their guns. They enforced time limits and insisted that he sign up for several after-school activities. After four months, Cameron returned to a more reasonable pattern of use. He was still playing his games a few hours a day, but kept more time for homework, and even made a few friends to spend time with on the weekend.

If you have concerns about your son's pattern of online behavior, I strongly suggest that you err on the side of caution and begin supervising his activity. Better yet, supervise it from the beginning. There will be plenty of opportunity to increase his computer time gradually as he demonstrates responsible behavior. Remember—your involvement and awareness are your most effective weapons.

The more stimulation boys get, the more that they want. Many are so used to being entertained by their tech toys that they actually don't know how else to spend their time. A year ago I was talking to a ninety-year-old woman and asked her what she did as a child when she got bored. She chuckled and said, "Darling, we used to go to our mother and complain about that and she would tell us to go outside and 'twiddle our thumbs.'" I got her point. Figuring out what to do when you're bored is one of life's essential skills. It requires some independence, a dash of creativity, and an ability to feel comfortable being alone. Young boys must learn to manage downtime, and the Internet isn't always the best default. You are the best person to teach your son how to entertain himself. If your son comes to you and says, "Dad, I'm bored," don't send him off to the family room to watch the new plasma TV. Help him find something to do—together.

Forty-six-year-old Mel decided he would solve the problem by spending a tech-free afternoon with his ten-year-old son Owen every Sunday. When he told Owen his plan, the boy was shocked. "What'll we do?" he asked. Mel said they'd do something different every weekend. Owen shrugged. "Don't expect me to leave my iPod at home," he said. Mel said they'd leave behind the BlackBerries, the Game Boys, and the iPods. "We're not even going to listen to the radio," he told his son. "We're going to entertain ourselves."

The silence was awkward on their first Sunday together. There were no beeps alerting Mel he had a voice mail and there was no click-click of a Game Boy. Without the radio, Mel and his son talked more. Mel realized early on that there were so many things he had never done with his son. One weekend they rented a canoe at a local boathouse. Another day they headed to the batting cages. They tried rock climbing. Tech-free Sundays began to feel like worry-free Sundays. As the school week drew to a close, Owen began asking his dad, "What are we doing this weekend?" On their most recent trip, they went to the beach and collected seashells. Owen thought it was "lame" at first, but he went along with it when he saw how many different kinds there were and when they identified them in a guidebook. Collecting shells is a simple act, but Owen was learning to see the world differently. Said Mel: "He keeps the shells we collected in a little jar on his desk."

THE NEW PSEUDO-INTIMACY

A year ago I listened to teens talking online in a chat room. I was shocked to see some of the screen names that the kids were using. "Babyboy69" was engrossed in a seductive dialogue with "ho4u." "Dgenerate" was trying to find someone to talk to and "Ibadass" had just signed off. Many boys go into chat rooms to meet girls. Some genuinely believe that they can talk to someone online for a few hours and develop an intimate relationship. Boys and girls will spend late nights IM'ing their "secrets" to one another, fantasizing (or actually arranging) clandestine encounters, and even declaring their love for one another—usually before they have met. Teens are trusting and often assume that the people they're talking to are who they say they are. Stories abound about teens getting into serious trouble as a direct result of cyberspace deceptions. It's why *Dateline NBC*'s "To Catch A Predator" is so popular; it illustrates how easily teenagers can be targeted.

Many boys tell me that they love the feeling of anonymity when they're talking to girls online. One teen explained that it's much easier for him to say stuff when he doesn't have to look the girl in the eye. I asked him why. "It's less embarrassing and I don't feel uncomfortable," he said. Another boy told me that he isn't always honest with girls when he's IM'ing because "it's a game—you try to impress the other person, make them think you're cool, try to get with them." Boys today don't always understand that relationships are not "sport," but that's what the Internet has reduced some of them to. They can carry on Internet conversations with three different girls at once. They can have a girlfriend at school and then a few more secret "virtual" girlfriends who live in the next town—or in the next state.

It's important that fathers make it clear to their sons what's right and what's wrong, explain why this is so, and insist that they be respectful of girls and women. You need to talk frequently with your son to help him understand intimacy. In the past, a father could rely on societal norms to shape a boy's outlook, but boys who grow up in the tech age may have no idea that love isn't talking in a chat room for a few weeks. You must demonstrate to your son that love is built upon honest exchanges and mutual trust.

Preston's story drives home my point. He met Melissa one night in a teen chat room. Their conversation began innocently. They were bored high school juniors living several towns apart. Within minutes, they learned each other's basic bio and found things in common. They loved the Dave Matthews Band and had attended the same concert the previous summer. They'd gone to sleepaway camp in the mountains. He hated jocks; so did she. Within a week, their online courtship blossomed. They talked nightly on IM, shared their experiences with drinking, sexual experimentation, and failed relationships. They visited each other's Facebook and MySpace profiles. One night they chatted about what they wanted out of their relationship. Both agreed that it was really great when you could hook up with someone you're into and not worry about things getting weird. Then Melissa wrote: "I think we're right for each other, Preston." Months later, Preston would tell me that that was the moment when he fell in love with her. But that night, he only asked her if she would meet him at the mall the next Saturday night at eight o'clock. The week couldn't pass fast enough. Preston told his friends about her. "You got to see this girl," he said. "She looks super hot in her pictures."

Preston is always late but on Saturday night he arrived at the mall ten minutes early. He waited patiently by the movie theater for fifteen minutes. Then another fifteen minutes passed. Preston suddenly felt uneasy. He kept checking his watch. Another fifteen minutes went by. *Where was she?* He called her cell phone—she'd given it to him in case they had trouble finding each other. Her voice mail picked up. He reluctantly walked over to Sbarro and grabbed a slice of pizza. *Maybe she was running late . . .* He went back to the movie theater half expecting to see her there, a smile on her face and a funny story about how she'd finally made it. He waited until ten o'clock before he reluctantly headed out.

When Preston got home that night, he immediately checked his e-mail. There was no note from Melissa. Then he checked her MySpace profile. His heart dropped when her page flashed onto his screen. She had taken a picture of Preston that he had sent to her and drawn a red X over his face. Under his picture, she'd typed: "Another boy who pretends that he's hotter than he is. I saw this one in person and he is grade A super cheesy. Send real pictures, people!" Preston couldn't believe it. She'd been there and seen him—and left. A wave of humiliation washed over him. He pulled up his Facebook.com profile and began posting nasty notes about Melissa. As he typed, he bit back tears. *Boys don't cry, you idiot.*

Preston heard a knock on his bedroom door. It was his dad. *"What?"* Preston shouted. His dad let himself in and told him to hush. His sisters were sleeping. He thought it was odd that Preston was home so early on a Saturday night. He sensed that something was wrong. "What's the matter, son?" he asked. Preston said nothing. His dad tried to peer over his shoulder at what he was typing. Preston minimized the window. "This isn't a good time," he said. "Can't you just leave me alone?"

His dad sat on his bed. "What did you do tonight?" he asked. Preston sighed and shook his head. "You might feel better if you talk about it," his dad said.

Something loosened inside Preston's chest. "I was supposed to meet this girl that I really liked but she didn't show up," he told his dad. "I met her online and we'd talked for days. I was in love with her."

"You're that upset about someone you've never even met? I don't get it," his dad said.

"We were really close, Dad," he said. "We talked constantly and planned this in advance. And I just found out that she did show up but she didn't think I was good looking so she left."

His father bit his tongue. How could a girl you meet online mean anything? But he could see his son was hurting. He'd played out a fantasy that hadn't had a happy ending. "This online stuff can be very confusing, even to someone like you who knows everything about it," his dad said. "I can see how important this girl was to you but you were almost strangers. Your whole relationship was based on IM—"

"We talked a few times on the phone," Preston said.

"Well, I'm sorry this happened. I am. But it's not that easy to develop a relationship. It takes time and patience. You have to really get to know somebody."

His father was about to launch into a lecture about the dangers of meeting people online but he caught himself. Preston didn't need a lecture but his father was at a loss of what to say next.

If I had had a chance to counsel him before this conversation, I would have told him to talk about his own relationships. Fathers can teach intimacy through stories. Kids don't respond to the all-knowing sage, but they do to men who've made similar mistakes and learned from them. A father might talk about his own forays into dating, how much time passed before he told his girlfriends, "I love you," how he coped with heartbreak, and why he fell in love with his wife.

Preston needed those lessons because he didn't understand intimacy. His mind-set had been shaped entirely by short-lived, but intense online relationships. He'd had twelve girlfriends in the last few years and only met three in person. Many of the relationships ended once the love affair jumped offline. Preston had actually had friendships with these girls, not romantic relationships, but he counted them all as "girlfriends." I understood his confusion. When you're that intimate with someone online, you can mistake the closeness for love. But talking about holding hands isn't the same as doing it.

"I never thought she was the kind of person who could be so nasty," Preston told me.

"That's because you didn't really know her," I said, gently.

THE PORN PROBLEM

Wally was surprised when he got a call at work from the father of one of his son's friends. "Let me guess?" Wally asked him. "You need me to car pool this weekend." Wally's ten-year-old played in a soccer league and all the dads took turns driving the boys to and from practice.

"I'm afraid it's a little more serious than that," the father said. "I caught the boys looking at porn on my computer yesterday. They switched it off in a panic when I walked in but I saw a list of the last four websites they were on. A little bit of it wouldn't worry me, but you don't even want to know what they were looking at. It was some pretty hard-core stuff."

Wally gulped. He remembered how he'd steal his father's *Playboy* magazines out of his closet and read them with a flashlight under his covers. But he'd been fourteen, a freshman in high school—not in the fifth grade. Wally hadn't even had a chance to deliver to his son the dreaded speech about "the birds and the bees." His son was still . . . a little boy. Wally shuddered. He didn't want to tell his wife, who would be distraught.

"I didn't say anything to them," the father told Wally. "I'm going to buy those computer programs that block certain websites. But I'd talk to him about looking at that stuff. Who knows what they think sex even is . . ."

When *New York* magazine called porn "the raunchy wallpaper" of respectable lives, they weren't referring to young boys, but they may as well have been. Type "porn" into Google and over 900 million hits pop up. In their e-mail accounts, boys find spam sent from sex sites, making it easy for them to click on a link and visit a virtual orgy. Teenage girls sometimes post revealing photographs of themselves on their personal profiles—*American Idol*'s Antonella Barba caused a row when suggestive pictures she took for her boyfriend showed up on every laptop in America. And I can guarantee that every little boy took a peek. Young kids come across porn by accident. Pop-up boxes entice viewers to visit their sites. Sometimes even seemingly innocent websites have ads touting hot girls. According to a study by the University of New Hampshire, 42 percent of Internet users ages ten to seventeen have looked at porn; 66 percent have come across it accidentally.

Jerry was livid when he noticed a sixty-dollar charge from an adult entertainment site on his credit card statement. When he first approached his son about it, Kenny insisted that he knew nothing about it. Then he admitted that his friend Jimmy had looked at it the other night when he'd slept over. "He was looking at a dumb ad and he might have clicked on the button by accident," his son said.

"Oh, and he accidentally came across my credit card, too," Jerry snapped.

Kenny's cheeks turned crimson. "I'll pay you back, Dad," he said. "But please don't tell Mom."

Jerry could see that his son was humiliated. "I understand why you'd be curious and think it's fun," he said. "But the fact is it's for adults only. What upsets me most is that you used my credit card. I get another bill like this and you can kiss your sixty-gig iPod good-bye."

I don't think dads should be the porn police. Boys will be boys—and they always will be. The temptation of porn is irresistible and it's impossible to control all access to it. Even if you restrict a boy's access at home, he can see it at a friend's. But it is important for you to talk to your son about it and help him put what he's seeing in perspective. And you can even give him permission and encouragement to walk away from it at a friend's house, just as you would want him to leave if his friends were drinking or doing drugs.

Although an occasional visit to an adult site is probably normal, the danger increases exponentially with increased exposure. The same article I cited in *New York* magazine earlier used anecdotes to demonstrate that men who visit porn sites regularly are developing unrealistic views of women. Dr. Ursula Ofman, a Manhattan-based sex therapist, is quoted as saying that porn "is so accessible, and now, with things like streaming video and Webcams, guys are getting sucked into a compulsive behavior. What's most regrettable is that it can really affect relationships with women. I've seen some young men lately who can't get aroused with women but have no problem interacting with the Internet. I think a big danger is that young men who are constantly exposed to these fake, always-willing women start to have unreal expectations from real women, which makes them phobic about relationships." The article was referring to men in their twenties, but if young boys grow up with these same images, consider the long-term effects. Boys may become physically disappointed by the real thing and learn to objectify and devalue women.

This is where dads can help. You can be the voice of reason, the purveyor of moral standards, and the enforcer of reasonable limits. Let your son know when you're concerned and tell him that you'll check his computer if anything seems suspicious. When done respectfully and discussed openly, your questions and rule-setting can actually improve the bond between you and your son. Educating him is an opportunity to understand him better, and show him that you were a boy once, too. The younger the boys are during these conversations the better because, like it or not, they can begin finding explicit material as soon as they know how to work a computer.

When Joe caught his fifteen-year-old son looking at porn for the second time, he knew that he had to talk to him. Joe didn't have any idea where to begin and many other fathers don't, either. Here are five themes to discuss with your son.

1. *Acknowledge the temptation.* Fathers don't want to make their sons feel like perverts. We all know masturbation is normal and it's important that sons realize the same. A father may tell his son that he knows that it's exciting to look at the images. He may share examples of his own youthful ventures to make his son feel normal. Joe began compassionately. "I understand why you want to visit these sites," he said. "It's pretty cool to see naked women and all kinds of sexy things you hear about." His son nodded. Then Joe told his son about how he used to look at *Penthouse* magazines with his older brother. "I couldn't believe that girls would pose that way," he said. "I guess you probably feel the same way." His son nodded again. He wasn't made to feel dirty or humiliated. If boys feel they can go to their fathers with their most intimate secrets, they'll probably go to them for other things, too.

2. *Pornography is a distortion of reality.* Tell your son that women with huge breasts and men with big penises are not the norm—both are often digitally enhanced online. People don't have sex all over the place in all different positions with people they barely know. If that sounds like an obvious statement, it's not: that's the picture of sexuality painted by online porn. It gives kids the wrong idea about sex and leads them to believe that women always

want to have sex, that sex is a sport, and that sadism or sado-masochism is typical. You need to deconstruct these assumptions for your boys.

Joe told his son these very things, but his son was still confused. "I just don't know what I did wrong. We're not hurting anyone," his son said. Joe acknowledged that they weren't hurting anyone but the ideas that they were absorbing online might hurt them or someone else down the road. "What you're seeing is not realistic," he said. "Things don't happen like that and you might expect them to. I want you to know that many adults laugh at some of the porn out there. It can be silly." In letting his son know that some of the stuff is "laughable," Joe's letting his son know that what he's seeing isn't real. It's a subtle, important step.

3. *Sex is a serious act.* It's important that you make it clear that sons should take sex seriously. You want to define for him not only what constitutes sex, but what role it plays in men's lives, why it's important in relationships, and the emotional link it gives men and women. You also want to give an idea of the risks that unprotected sex carries, including disease and unwanted pregnancy.

"People who have sex usually respect one another, and are often in love," Joe told his son. "It's an act of closeness between two consenting adults. The sites you're looking at make sex look like a game."

"How so?" his son asked.

"It makes you think that you can take sex lightly and that you don't have to care about the woman you're having sex with," Joe said.

Joe explained that men and women feel connected to the person that they have sex with. It's not an act that you share with a stranger. Joe talked about the first time he had sex—how he'd been in love with his girlfriend for a year before he did it. "Your first time should mean just as much to you," he told him.

4. *Respect women*. This is a natural time for men to talk to their sons about the fact that girls and women are equal to boys and men, and should be treated with respect—as you would want your son to treat everyone. Porn can make it seem like women welcome every sexual advance that comes their way. Fathers should make it clear that if boys approach girlfriends in this way they'll strike out every time. Talk about women by referring to a girl that's important to your son—his mother, his sister, a close female cousin. Boys could be challenged to think about how bad they would feel if one of those women was in some of the images he's looked at. Fathers can ask their sons how it makes them feel to imagine his sister being treated that way. Usually, reality hits a boy fast. "I'd kill anyone if they treated my sister that way," a typical boy might say. A father can say, "Then you shouldn't treat anyone's sister like that, should you?"

5. *Pornography isn't for kids.* Fathers often ask me, How much porn is too much? It's best to discourage their viewing of any pornography knowing that they'll probably cheat once in a while. If a father tells his son that "once in a while is okay," then his son will surely take that as subtle permission to visit these sites more often.

"I don't want you watching this porn stuff until you're older," Joe told his son.

"What, like sixteen?" he asked.

"No, at least eighteen, because that's when you're considered an adult," Joe said. "That's my final answer and I'll impose consequences if it happens again."

"All right, don't get so bent out of shape, Dad," his son said. "I'll try not to."

"I don't want to have to watch you constantly," Joe said. "Be responsible and make smart decisions. You hear me?"

"I hear you, Dad."

CHAPTER SEVEN

The Father-Son Competition

Basketball practice was getting a little boring for my son and me. I'd been coaching my son's team for five seasons. He was fourteen, full of beans, and ready to prove it, as were his teammates. I was running out of drills and the boys were losing interest. "We're tired of shooting practice," my son whined. I put on my psychologist cap for a moment. How could I rekindle their spark? How could I inspire them to practice harder?

The idea came to me instantly—a father versus son basketball game. The boys loved the idea. They couldn't wait to play against "the old guys." "We'll kill them," yelled one. Another boy said he wasn't so sure. "They're bigger than us," he said. I wondered how many fathers would show up. Typically, there were more mothers at the games than fathers.

On the day of the basketball game, eight of ten fathers walked in the door of the gym. They came decked out in old college shirts, gleaming athletic shoes, and warm-ups. They practiced intensely before the game. The boys were equally pumped up. There was a spirit of excitement in the air. When I threw up the jump ball, the fathers lunged for it. I thought that they might "take it easy" on the boys. Instead they approached it like an NBA playoff game. These men were playing with a ferocity that few of them had displayed on the sidelines. They were pushing, shoving—and the boys pushed and shoved right back. We weren't five minutes into the game before one boy took an elbow to the head. His father helped him up. "You'll be fine," he told him. A couple of minutes later a father twisted his ankle coming down from a layup. A parent who was a doctor checked it out. Then the injured warrior jumped up and ran down the court.

The heated rivalry was striking. Fathers and sons were out to prove themselves. They fought for position and rebounds. When the fathers won the game, the boys immediately demanded a rematch the following week.

I tell this story because what played out on the court is exactly what plays out in everyday life. Fathers and sons are men, and men can't help but compete. My son's teammates loved showing their fathers their skills on the court, and in doing so they felt as if they were earning their fathers' respect. The same could be said for the dads. One father winked at his son every time the dad nailed a three-point shot. Then his son would run faster down the court to show his strength.

Competition is ingrained in the male psyche—Who is faster? Who is smarter? Who is taller? Men are drawn to films like *Gladiator, Braveheart, The Godfather* because the main characters fight to the death, and win. In many hit television shows about survival, viewers watch male characters battle for domination every week, a match of the minds to determine how the rest of the survivors should live. Some reality shows are interesting only because there are so many contests.

Men are competing even when they don't think they're competing. One thirty-five-year-old coach I interviewed often spars with his assistant coach about who had the toughest father growing up. Imagine two dads competing about parenting? "My father had me up at five A.M. chopping wood," the coach boasted. "It made me who I am today and I'll have my kid do the same. Yesterday, he was outside watching me mow the lawn. He's two years old. I said to myself, 'Don't worry little guy. Your turn will come soon enough.'"

Some fathers like to fashion themselves kings when it comes to their sons, and there is an unspoken narrative that often connects them. Sons hope that one day they'll be worthy of the king's crown and are always out to prove themselves to their fathers. They want their fathers to see them as equals, as men worth competing against. Men who are less successful than their fathers may develop feelings of inferiority in many spheres—everywhere from a trivia game to chess to fishing.

Men compete in order to interact with one another because it doesn't involve the direct expression of feelings. Debating who won the 1982 World Series makes a boy and his dad feel close without being "touchy-feely." A son is connecting intimately with his dad on a subject that they're both passionate about. They may be posturing but they're also expressing love. I could say the same for the coach that I mentioned earlier. In talking about how tough his father was, the coach is really expressing his love for his dad. He's simply using an argument with his assistant coach to demonstrate it.

With competition driving many father-and-son relationships, it's important that we reflect on its implications. In what ways can a father harness a competitive spirit and strengthen the bond he has with his son? In what ways can rivalry pull fathers and sons apart? Young boys idolize their dads. They want to dress like them, walk like them, and talk like them. It's not unusual to see a father and son wearing the same baseball cap and rooting passionately for the same team. Look a little closer—they're probably arguing about which player is better. The seeds of competition are planted early and remain firmly rooted throughout the life cycle, and there will be plenty of battlegrounds for these feelings to play themselves out. Whether it's comparing sports knowledge, playing Ping-Pong, video games, or checkers, boys thrive on competition with their dads—and fathers welcome the challenge.

COMPETITION THROUGHOUT YOUR LIFE

In the first grade, boys jockey for position at school during recess. *I'll bet you can't beat me to the water fountain.*

Can too!

In the lunchroom, their egos are at work.

My sandwich is bigger than yours.

So what? My juice box is bigger.

They come face-to-face with their first competitor at home—their father. Competition is a rite of passage, and it permeates the childhood years. Ever watch a little boy wrestle with his dad? You would think it's a matter of life and death. They're laughing hysterically and screaming, but there is an underlying battle for domination. After the battle of the century, there's the obligatory animated discussion about who gets the bragging rights. Fortunately, it's all in good fun—or at least it should be.

You couldn't even pin my left arm, Dad. I'm half your size and twice as strong.

Twice as strong? I had every one of your limbs in my grip!

Competition between father and son is often a boy's first lesson in being a good winner and a good loser. Wrestling matches are fantastic teaching moments. Remember—sons have hawk eyes. If a father can't admit that he lost or that he's wrong about who won the 1982 World Series, his son will probably pick up the same obstinate behaviors. If a father fails to congratulate his son on a good game after the boy's soccer team loses, then he's telling him he'll never be good enough. It's the same way with good sportsmanship. Cheer on your son even if he drops a pass. Compliment his curveball even if you knock it out of the park.

Dads don't realize how easy it is to create a son who is an unhealthy competitor. It's important that fathers work carefully with their sons to foster the spirit of "Daniel" in the film *The Karate Kid,* and not his nemesis, Johnny, a boy willing to win at any costs. "When do I learn how to punch?" an impatient Daniel asks Mr. Miyagi in the 1984 film. Answers Miyagi: "Better learn balance. Balance is key. Balance good, karate good. Everything good. Balance bad, better pack up, go home. Understand?"

Balance is the key to good fathering, too. Sometimes fathers ask me,

The Father-Son Competition

"When I play a game with my son, should I let him win?" There's some confusion about when a father is building his son's self-esteem, and when he's pummeling it. Seek balance here, too. At a young age, letting your son win once in a while is a good idea. It makes competition between father and son more fun. If a father purposely throws the game too often, though, his son will lose interest. There's no reason for him to compete. Keeping a one-on-one basketball game close encourages your son's best efforts. If you win 22–0, your son will lose interest just as quickly. Some fathers like winning so much that they use their sons to feed their ego. If they're playing baseball, they might hit the ball harder, giving their son little possibility of catching it or practicing his fielding. Sure, it makes Dad feel good, but no one else. It takes the fun out of the game. Sons walk away from a potential bonding moment feeling bad. Over time these overzealous behaviors will hurt a boy's self-esteem.

Henry, a pilot, came to see me at his wife's insistence. Worried about Henry and their twelve-year-old son, Dylan, she thought that their rivalry was a little "too much." As soon as he walked in, I noticed that Henry is the kind of guy who measures you up, and then gives you plenty not to measure up to. "Have you ever flown a plane, Doc?" he asked me. *No.* "You got a boat?" *No.* Apparently, he was also trying to "one-up" his son. He and Dylan always argued at the dinner table. It didn't matter if it was about the latest movie or the upcoming presidential election. It could be about who would get in the shower first or who would eat the last banana. Each had to have the last word. Henry chuckled. "Boys just like to get their way," he told me. Dylan had complained to his mother that his father never gave an inch. He was starting to feel that his dad didn't care what he thought. So as his dad made light of the situation, Dylan was growing frustrated. Yes, fathers and sons can be a little immature. Again, the trick is balance. Says Henry's wife: "I know he loves Dylan but he can be a big baby. I've asked him, 'Who's the one in sixth grade? Dylan or *you*?'"

A funny thing happens on the way to adolescence. Suddenly our sons remove us from the pedestal, begin to question our beliefs, and distance themselves from us. This only heightens the father-son competition. Arguments grow more heated and each is more determined than ever to prove his point. When they play a sport together, it's often a real contest. After all, there's a lot at stake here. I call it the "locker room thing." Boys and men love to talk about who is better at what. They compare, they boast, and they tease. It's a playful sort of interaction, but one that they feel compelled to engage in. It's as natural as breathing.

We continue to compete with our sons when they're young adults. But the physical differences between us increase with the passing of each year. Dads grow old. They carry canes rather than briefcases. So we find other ways to compete—some subtle, others more obvious. An architect I know went out and bought a Porsche a month after his thirty-four-year old son did. The architect had always wanted a Porsche, but had never considered buying one. He and his son often went to car shows and ogled the car's sleek shape. But when his son pulled up in one, he had to have one, too, to level the playing field between them.

My son and I started playing tennis when he was eight. At first, it was a teacher-student thing. I'd hit the ball gently to him and try to keep it in play as he learned the various strokes. When he turned ten, we started playing games. It wasn't a heated contest, but we simulated the real thing. As he approached adolescence, the going got tougher. He'd run full speed and shout at me to hit the ball harder. I did. He still wasn't good enough for me to completely level the playing field.

I kept on winning—until he got to college. By then, I had salt-and-pepper hair and although I was in good shape, I didn't have the stamina of an eighteen-year-old. I huffed and puffed while he tirelessly weaved back and forth across the court. My son was determined to finally beat me and I could sense that my winning spree might soon end. Still, I didn't let him win. That would have made him mad. And he knew the importance of persistence.

He was visiting home during his sophomore year when he finally beat me. It was a close match but he won fair and square and strutted off the court with a grin on his face and my arm on his shoulder. We were beginning a new era. He had proved to me that he could take me and it made me seem to him a tiny bit vulnerable. Somehow that drew us closer. Now the court belongs to him. We still play when we can. He knows that he can wear me down, and he often does. The torch has been passed.

MANAGING THE FATHER-SON COMPETITION

Sometimes competition is deliberate and sometimes it is unconscious. In an earlier chapter, I talked about the ways that fathers inherit the parenting patterns of their own fathers. Fathers who compete with their sons might think about why they do that. That's what Liam did. Whenever he and his son, Isaac, discussed their favorite shows, *The Simpsons* and *The Bernie Mac Show,* they would disagree about what was funny and what wasn't. Sometimes the discussions were fun, but sometimes they would get a little heated. Liam thought their contention was strange until he remembered that he'd done the same thing with his own father: they spent hours debating the top ten movies of all time. He remembered that it was in good fun—neither walked away feeling upset. So he decided that his and his boy's contests must be okay, too.

It's important to be able to look at a situation and see what's fueling the competition. Is it a compulsive need to compete with your son, a residual from your own childhood, or an incessant demand for perfection? Perhaps it's self-imposed and stems from your son's natural desire to prove himself to you, his father. At its best, competition can energize your relationship, draw you together, and serve as a teaching tool that prepares him for the many challenges ahead—succeeding in school, dealing with his peers, mastering new skills, and finding his place in society.

Neal came to me because he and sixteen-year-old Jesse weren't connecting. Neal was an accountant who played the violin with a local orchestra. Jesse loved to swim and spent more time in the pool than he did at home. They had little in common, so I suggested that Neal and his son take up a new activity together, something where they could engage in some healthy competition. Neal gave Jesse three choices. They could join a darts team, enroll in archery lessons, or train for a marathon. "Darts," Jesse said. Yes, it was nerdy but father and son enjoyed it. They'd see who could hit the bull's-eye most often. If one did, they'd high-five—the male version of the hug. Their healthy competition allowed father and son to bond.

Sometimes, however, a young man's competitive urges can become unhealthy. Christian, a senior waiting for results from his college applications, was stressed about school. He couldn't relax. If he had downtime, he'd act anxious: he'd tap his leg obsessively while watching TV, pick on his mother, and get into fights with his brother. His mother asked him to come see me, and after a few sessions it was clear to me what was wrong. His father, Steven, was a successful newscaster. A good dad, he asked only that his son do the best he could in school. He didn't pressure him to follow in his footsteps but encouraged him to try many hobbies. He wanted his son to be as fortunate as he was and find his passion. Despite this, Christian felt as if he had to "keep up" with his dad or his dad wouldn't respect him. "I'll never measure up to him," Christian told me.

"Who says you have to?" I said.

"No one—I just feel like people expect that of me."

"You mean you expect that of yourself?"

Christian smiled. We talked for several more months before he realized that he didn't have to compete with his father, that his father was proud of him for who he was. Before we met, he'd convinced himself that his father resented his "failures," and he'd pulled away from his dad. But the contest and disappointment were all in his own head. Today, their relationship is on the mend.

Father-son competitions can become downright destructive, even violent. One father-and-son pair even competed about "who treats who worse." The father told his son that he was a "loser," and his son called his dad a "hypocrite." They didn't stop until the mother and I got between them. Apologies don't come easily to these sorts of combatants. Wherever they go, whatever they do, each is determined to get the best of the other. Often these overly intense rivalries stem from a father's unhealed wounds inflicted by his own father. These dads often don't realize that they're replaying these old scripts with an unsuspecting son as the victim. Nonetheless, the pattern recurs.

Giles had been at odds with his son since he and his wife divorced, when Cole was ten. He hadn't wanted his parents to split up and was angry that his father had moved out; he felt as if his dad had abandoned him. But when Cole and Giles were together, they rarely talked of the divorce. Giles complained that Cole was stubborn and uncooperative. Cole thought that his father needed to win at everything he did. Their rivalry spilled over into all their activities. When Giles and Cole went out together, their interactions would go south after a few hours. One night, at an NBA game, Giles wanted to leave early and beat the traffic. Twelve-year-old Cole wanted to see the end of the game and refused to follow him out. They got into an argument about who was right, and didn't speak for the entire car ride home. So much for bonding.

Now Cole was fifteen, and his relationship with his dad was an ongoing contest. Who is better? Who is smarter? Who started the argument? Nothing was exempt. As I sat with them, I wondered how I could help. I started with the obvious: "It seems like everything you talk about turns into a debate. Do you guys actually enjoy this?" They were silent for a moment.

"I sure don't," said Giles, "but my son is always determined to prove me wrong."

"You're the one who always has to be right," his son yelled.

"Wait a minute, Cole," I interjected. "I asked if you enjoyed the arguing and you didn't answer me."

Cole sighed. He said that he didn't like it, either, but he didn't know how to stop doing it. That was my opening. "Look," I said. "You're both unhappy with your relationship and yet you keep doing the same thing over and over again. I can understand why you each want to defend yourself, but your lives have become a constant battle. Frankly, I think you're similar to each other in a lot of ways. You're both strong willed and like to win. But I know you wouldn't be sitting here with me if you wanted to continue with things the way they are."

"He made me come here today," Cole said.

"Yes—but someone had to blow the whistle or you two would be fighting till they buried you." Cole thought that was funny and settled down a bit.

Over time, I helped them realize that they had lost touch of any positive feelings for each other. Cole didn't even try to get his father's approval, and his pride kept him from asking his father for love and support, which he sorely needed. Giles was trapped, too. He wanted to be closer to his son, but he lacked the communication skills to do so. After a few weeks, we realized that Giles was treating Cole the way that his father had treated him, and he had been trying to win that contest since he'd lost it as a child. Many of our joint sessions focused on helping father and son to get more of what they needed from the other. Hurts were shared and apologies offered (at my insistence). Ultimately, Giles and Cole agreed to stop trying to one-up each other. Today, they're still working on their relationship, and things can still be awkward at times. They've needed to find entirely new ways of interacting. But the important thing is that the destructive behaviors are in check.

Fathers need to push and challenge their sons whether in school, at home, or on the athletic field. It's your job to prepare your sons for the real world. But there's more to life than competition. Boys must also learn to become team players, to offer help to others, and to be humble. Again, it's a question of balance. Should a boy treat every little challenge as if his life depends on it? *No.* How much competitive instinct should a father instill in his son? *There is a limit.* But that limit depends on the individual characteristics of the child. If he welcomes the challenge of competition, fine. But if he bows out of it then the father may have to temper his expectations.

Every father needs to search his soul and decide what lessons he wants to teach his son. Is life all about winning? Should you step on people to get ahead? Since competition is such an integral part of a growing boy's character, it affords many opportunities to build self-confidence—and to screw up a boy. Some fathers are so competitive that you'd think they themselves were on the field playing in their sons' soccer games. Forty-eight-year-old Dale didn't want to be like the other fathers at his ten-year-old son Ira's soccer games. Ira was an excellent player and his coach felt that he was destined to be a star in high school. But Ira was incredibly hard on himself. He would get worked up before every game and when his team lost, he'd insist that it was his fault. Dale assured him that he was a factor in the team's successes, but Ira only saw his mistakes. As the season wound down, Dale asked Ira if he wanted to sign up for a select league. Ira didn't answer right away. "It's not fun anymore, is it?" Dale asked him.

Ira nodded. "I feel like I'm always disappointing the coach."

"I don't want you to play soccer to please me," Dale told him. "Maybe you take a season off and think about things for a while."

Ira leaned against his dad's shoulder. He nodded again. Later, when he was thirteen, he told me that he valued this moment with his dad. It was clear that his dad understood him. He had friends whose fathers pushed so hard that the boys had become nasty competitors. "All they care about is winning," Ira said.

The moral of the story? Seize all opportunities to manage your son's competitive spirit. To help fathers along, I've outlined the most important things a man can say to his son to push him to be the best without pushing him away.

"Be a good sport."

As one wise father put it, "I'd rather my son be a gracious loser than a miserable winner." It's certainly easier to be a good sport when you're on the winning end of things. But disappointments have their value as well. When properly handled, they build character and determination—and with a father's support, boys can be encouraged to try again and work at improving themselves. In ninth grade, Kevin failed to get the lead role in the school play. His father found a drama camp and asked Kevin if he wanted to attend it the following summer—guess who got the lead in the tenth-grade play? I often tell fathers to tell the story of Andre Agassi's career. In his early days, he had burst onto the tennis scene as a brash, egotistical young star. After some years as a contender, his game started slipping and he devoted himself to retraining, emerging as a real force as others in their middle years waned. His contests are the stuff of tennis legend, and he departed as a mature, humble, and gracious champion. Teach your son that he shouldn't have to brag about his successes. People will recognize him for his accomplishments and appreciate his modesty.

Sherman's eight-year-old son, Chase, was athletic and popular in school. But Sherman had received several phone calls from the teacher telling him that Chase was "hard on the less athletic boys." He would tease them and purposely humiliate them. He'd pitch a curveball to a boy with a weak swing. One evening, Sherman talked to Chase about it. "I'd rather have you be an average kid than a star who takes advantage of other people," he said. Chase was defensive.

"But all the other kids tease and it's just for fun," he whined.

"Well, I don't like it and I want it to stop," his father said. "How would you feel if the other kids teased you, or if some older kids pushed you around?" Chase shrugged. His father went on: "I'm proud of you for being a great athlete, but I feel ashamed and angry when I get complaints from other people about you being a show-off. From now on I'll expect you to treat the other kids with respect. I know you can do it, Chase. Okay?"

Chase nodded. He stopped his bullying.

"Do the best you can."

Not everyone can be a superstar. The sooner that boys learn this lesson the better. Whether it's school, sports, or simply chores around the house, your expectations as his father should be the same: he should know that what's important is giving something his best shot. When young people come to believe that adults mean this, a great weight is lifted from their shoulders. They learn that a good-enough effort really is good enough. If they don't have to be perfect, they'll be freer to express themselves. The result is a more confident, less stressed young man. Of course, conveying this is easier said than done.

There are bound to be times when our sons disappoint us in their performances. You'll be tempted to criticize, push harder, and even threaten consequences if they don't raise the bar a little higher. That's certainly understandable but keep your son's capabilities in mind. After all, what's most important is how he feels about his performance, not how you feel. Ideally, you should get pleasure from seeing your son fulfill his own expectations. Competition is a good thing, but do not ram it down his throat. Different boys have different thresholds for how much competition they can tolerate.

Angelo can attest to this. At work, he was driven, one of the top computer salespeople in his large company. In his free time, he would go all out to win, whatever the sport of the moment was. He tried his hardest to sell his thirteen-year-old son Howie on his values, but Howie wasn't buying it. A laid-back kid, Howie wasn't that athletic but played on the lacrosse team. He had decent grades, but lacked the "killer instinct" that his father prided himself on. Overall, he seemed pretty happy, but at his mother Sally's urging, the family came in to talk about Howie's conflicts with his father.

"He never really 'goes for it,'" Angelo told me. "He's a good kid but he could be getting A's and playing a varsity sport."

I turned to Sally and asked how she felt about it. "I think he's doing fine," she said. "I just can't stand the arguing that goes on between them. Angelo's always pushing and Howie's always resisting."

I asked Howie how he felt about things. He turned to his dad. "This 'go-for-it' stuff is your thing, not mine," he said. "Why don't you just let it go?"

Wow, I thought, *this kid is doing my job.* Angelo tried his best to plead his case, but he couldn't convince any of us that Howie needed to do things his way. I asked Angelo what was more important—his relationship with his son or his own competitive spirit? He quietly acknowledged what we all knew: nothing was more important to him than his son's happiness, and he certainly wanted to have a good relationship with him. It took only a few meetings to help Angelo to reorganize his priorities. The turning point occurred when I asked him if he could say the words that his son needed to hear. He finally did. "Howie, I realize that I can't make you into who I am. I can see that you're happy the way you are, and you seem to be doing fine. So somehow I'm going to find a way to keep my big mouth shut."

I was touched and asked Angelo to go over and give his son a hug. He did and Howie hugged him back. Both were tearful.

Angelo and Howard had a nice ending to their story, which I wish for all fathers and sons.

Encourage your son to try his best, to compete when he needs to (or chooses to). Learn to accept his failures as well as his successes. Help your son face his fears, practice the skills that he needs to master, and put his best foot forward. When you play with him, play hard, but not as if your life depends on it. Whenever he says he's had enough, respect his wishes. Nothing has ever been gained by pushing children beyond limits. And whatever you do, don't try to make him a clone of yourself, or the person you wished you were and never became (sports star, academic prodigy, etc.). Even if you succeed, he may resent you for it in the long run. Let him be himself and take pleasure in knowing that you've been a good role model—not a slave driver. He'll thank you for it when he's older.

Competition is a fact of life. Not all boys are created equal. Some thrive on competition while others are burdened by it. Talk to him, play with him, and be his guide. Let him know that you're with him through childhood and adolescence, in body when you can be, and in spirit when you can't. Remind him that you want him to find his own way. If he winds up at Harvard or in the NFL, more power to him. But if he feels comfortable with his life and is close to his loved ones— whether he's a doctor, teacher, or craftsman—consider yourself a lucky man. You can rest assured that he feels the same way.

CHAPTER EIGHT

Love, Dad

Unlocking the Language of Feelings

What lies behind us, and what lies before us are tiny
matters compared to what lies within us.

—Ralph Waldo Emerson

I cried at my father's funeral. Crying wasn't something I typically did.
My mother had also died ten years before, and at Dad's funeral I felt as
if I was reexperiencing her loss as well. A week later, I was talking with
my son and daughter about how I felt the day I buried my father—how
hard it was see him in a coffin and say good-bye as I shoveled the first
mound of dirt on the oak box. My kids were young then. Dan was eight.
Julie was five. They had stood on either side of me.

"You cried, Dad," Dan said. I nodded. It was the first time they had
seen me do that.

Julie pointed at her brother. "You cried, too," she squealed.

"Did not!" he snapped back.

"Did too! You were rubbing your eyes."

"I just got something in them," he yelled back.

At eight, Dan was already schooled in denying his emotions. I
thought similarly about tears when I was his age, but I wanted my son
to be different. I wanted him to know that it was okay to be vulnerable sometimes. "Crying is okay," I told him. "If you're hurt and upset,

it can even make you feel better afterwards." But Dan wasn't convinced. He had watched boys at school make fun of one another if they cried, and boys on TV did the same.

Boys learn from messages all around us: Real boys don't act like girls. When boys show their feelings, others will think that they're weak and make fun of them. So it's safer to use words that don't reveal what they feel inside and don't let others know what's bothering them. Then no one can use those feelings against them. Many men will deny this, but we see it every day in their and their son's behavior. Indeed men are defined by the stereotypes perpetuated in pop culture. Think "The Rock," Vin Diesel, Jean-Claude Van Damme—all masters of machismo. Even when a man expresses his feelings, his friends will often make light of them and ask, "When did you become one of those 'touchy-feely,' sensitive New Age guys?"

But people are defined by feelings and emotions. That's problematic since most men rarely show those feelings to others so few people will ever know who they really are. Some men purge their feelings on their deathbeds—all the things that they wanted to express over their lifetimes suddenly pour out. Many men wait until they're dying to express themselves because it's considered culturally okay for men to be vulnerable when they're taking their last breath. But that's awful. The longer men keep their feelings locked inside, the less energy they have to devote to the pursuit of happiness—and a healthy relationship with their sons.

Feelings are the building blocks of intimacy. People who are out of touch with their feelings are often lonely and angry, unable to reach out to others and establish close relationships. Even some men who are happy and joke around with their families may not actually be communicating with them, either. They think that they're close because they eat breakfast together, attend church together as a family, and celebrate holidays together. But the intimacy is assumed, not lived. Their wives and children may feel distant from these dads, taken for granted. That's why I urge fathers to make their feelings known and to allow their sons to feel that their feelings are important.

Think of building intimacy like getting a new BMW with a stick shift and not knowing how to drive it. If you practice often, you'll master this new skill. It will become comfortable, even exhilarating. Before you know it, driving the car will be second nature. Admitting to your feelings is like mastering a stick shift—awkward at first, natural soon enough. When you give personal expression even half as much attention as other skills you've learned over the years, you can become closer to your son in a couple of months.

Marty, a fifty-three-year-old navy doctor, talked to his fifteen-year-old son Sam often but would get stuck anytime the conversation turned emotional. During one family meeting, Marty and his wife, Sara, were discussing Sam's declining grades. Sam offered little explanation and insisted that he would do better the next marking period. Marty retorted, "That's his standard answer—then it's déjà vu all over again."

"Maybe if you didn't bug me so much I would study more," the boy snapped.

I asked Marty why he nagged his son. "Because he won't get into a decent college if he keeps up at this rate."

"Yes, I will," Sam said. "B's and C's are fine as long as you don't want to go to Yale. Why is it so damn important to you, anyway?"

The discussion was deteriorating so I shifted the direction. I turned to Marty, and asked if there was any other reason he argued with Sam so much. He said he didn't want Sam to waste his life. I pushed a little further. "Isn't Sam important to you?" I said.

"Of course he is," Marty responded.

"How often do you tell him?"

"He knows it," Marty said with great conviction. I asked if he could look at Sam and say it right at this moment. Marty hesitated—the words didn't come easily. "You're so important to me, Sam, I just . . ." There "it" was, right before my eyes. This bright, verbal guy was getting stuck—actually melting down a bit. He was clearly uncomfortable with his feelings. I asked him if he was okay.

"Yeah," he responded. "I just got something in my eye." I thought of my son denying his tears at my father's funeral.

"Dad gets like this whenever he talks about something that's emotional," Sam said. "He's good at giving lectures but when things get too personal he fades out on us. He's good at expressing his anger, but it's hard for him to talk about his loving feelings about our family."

I turned to Marty, who was quiet. "I'll bet there are many feelings in you that Sam needs to hear," I said.

"It's hard to talk about this stuff."

"I know," I said gently, "but Sam needs this from you. Could you try to tell him why he's so important to you and how you feel about him? Do the best you can. The feelings are already there—try opening the door a little and letting Sam in."

Marty was quiet and his eyes grew watery. "I love you, Sam," he said. "I can't tell you how much you matter to me. When you were born it was one of the happiest moments of my life. I told myself that you and I would be great pals and have a good life together—"

Sara moved closer to him on the couch and took his hand. Although Sam was silent, he was watching the action closely and was visibly touched by his dad's softened reaction. I turned to him. "Any chance you could go over to Dad and give him a hug?" I said. "If it were me, I sure could use one."

Sam smiled. "Sometimes he hugs me after my soccer games, you know. But I guess this is a little different," he said.

"This is the real deal," I commented. "What do you say?" Sam went over and hugged his father tentatively—and Dad hugged back tightly. It was a powerful moment for everyone in the room—a new beginning for father and son. This new closeness would do more for Sam's school grades than any lecture, threat, or incentive his parents could make up.

Dads will talk about how important their sons are to them, but only in the abstract. When a dad says "Life is treating you well," he's really saying "I'm proud of you." Men have trouble talking about love, and often choose to show their love through action instead of words. For instance, a father might ask his son to go fishing, which, from his point of view, is proof of love for his son. He might put an arm around his son at his college graduation. For many men, there's no reason to say the words "I love you." They're implied. One father told me that he went ten years without telling his son that he loved him. "Well, I do sign my e-mails, 'Love, Dad.' Doesn't that count?" he asked. I shook my head. No.

Boys sit in my office and tell me that they're not sure their fathers love them because "he doesn't say it." Fathers assume their sons know that spending time together is showing love, but sons do crave to hear the actual words "I love you" from their dads. Many sons grow into fathers who aren't comfortable saying the words to their own sons, arrange a ski trip to express their affection instead, and the cycle starts all over again.

There's an old saying that goes "Love wasn't put in your heart to stay, love isn't love till you give it away." That's my advice to fathers and sons alike. Sure, expressing your love is uncomfortable at first, but you'll be surprised how quickly it becomes second nature once you've begun to say "I love you" directly. Mothers tell their sons all the time that they love them. It's natural for women. They've been reared to express their feelings freely and men know it. So take your cue from the experts: squeeze the words out, and let your sons know how you feel about them. Eventually they will get the message and emulate your actions. That's the most important thing: you as the father need to break the cycle of unspoken emotions.

Start by giving hugs to your son. Football players do it, soldiers do it, and dads should be doing it. Go home and hug your kid. That's what Hayden, a forty-five-year-old real estate broker, struggled with. I'd been seeing him a few months because he was concerned about his relationship with his nine-year-old son. At first he resisted my suggestions, claiming that it would make him uncomfortable. I asked why. "Because I've never done it, and my father never hugged me," he said.

"How would you have felt if he did?" I asked.

"Well, it would have been weird at first, but I probably would have gotten used to it."

"So will your son," I assured him. A few weeks later, I got a call. Hayden had started hugging his son every night before bed. He said he felt funny at first, but he noticed how much his nine-year-old liked it. He'd squeeze his dad right back.

Fathers aren't the only ones who need help expressing their feelings. Sometimes their young sons get stuck, too. Almost twenty years ago, a show on *Sesame Street* featured Richard Pryor talking to a group of small children about their feelings. He would pantomime a feeling such as sad or angry and ask them to identify it. It took a few minutes and a few giggles, but they quickly caught on. Then he asked them to play "kiddy charades." "Show me scared," he said to one little boy. The boy wrapped his arms around himself tightly and cowered. "Good," Pryor said. He pointed to a second boy. "And you show me silly." The boy made some animal noises and the group laughed. I've used this same exercise for years to help children of all ages learn to express their feelings. It's a wonderful way to help them read the facial expressions and feelings of others more accurately—while simultaneously learning to communicate what they themselves are feeling. It's also a perfect activity to practice with your son. If you say "Show me sad" or "Show me frustrated," your son will feel comfortable showing you those emotions. If you make a sad face back, you're showing your boy it's okay to make a sad face, to acknowledge this difficult emotion and very human vulnerability.

Sons need permission to express their feelings freely. To do so they need courage, a redefining of masculinity, and a receptive audience in you. There's a line I love from an old '70s song, "Tin Man," that goes: "Oz never did give nothing to the Tin Man, that he didn't . . . already have." In the film *The Wizard of Oz,* the Tin Man wanted a heart but found that everything he needed to be an open, loving person was already inside of him. Your feelings are already there inside of you—you just need to let yourself let them out.

It's trickier teaching older sons how to express themselves—which is one reason it's important that you start with your son at an early age. But even a sixteen-year-old oozing attitude is listening although he acts as if he's not. One thirty-one-year-old told me that his dad changed after he had a stroke. The son was fifteen at the time. Suddenly, his stoic father wanted to have heart-to-hearts. The son said his dad would force him to go on camping trips. On one trip, he told his son stories of his childhood, talked about women he had dated, and why he had fallen for the boy's mother. He told his son how proud he was of his hockey team's winning season. "I acted like a punk the whole time," the son, now thirty-one, said recently, "but I can remember every word he said to me on that trip. It meant so much but I felt weird the whole time. It was awkward talking to him like that."

Let your son know that he doesn't have to be strong all the time. "Macho is not mucho," and sometimes, as a father, you need to read between the lines. Your son's anger and bravado can mask feelings of hurt. Help him learn to express his feelings, to know that it's okay to be scared and it's okay not to have all the answers. To do this, you need to model these attitudes and help bring them out. Your son should be able to tell you when he won a game or failed a test, lost a job or got engaged. "Stop asking for your mom when you call," one father told his grown son. "I want to hear things from you, too."

A few ideas of what you can say to get the ball rolling with younger sons:

1. "I know how it feels when you bump your head. I can remember when I was eight and crashed into someone on the baseball field. I cried and cried and can still picture my dad running to get ice and then comforting me."
2. "When I tried out for the school play, I was scared stiff. It really helped to talk to my parents about it."

3. "Your feelings are really important to me. Whatever they are, good or bad, happy or sad, I'd like to hear them."

A few ideas of what you can say to get the ball rolling with older sons:

1. "When I was a teenager, I didn't tell my parents much. I used to wish that they could read my mind, but of course, they couldn't. When I got older, I realized that it felt better to talk things out. I think you'll feel the same when you try it."
2. "I had my share of screw-ups when I was growing up. I'm sure that you've had a few along the way, too. I just want you to know that you can always talk to me if you mess up at something. I'll do the best I can to help."
3. "I know you talk to your friends about a lot of stuff you don't tell me and I'm glad they're there for you. But sometimes it helps to get a grown-up's point of view. I really want to be in on your life and hope that you'll take me up on my offer. Believe me, it would be pretty hard to shock me. And even if you do—we'll deal with it."

MORE TALKING ZONES

Men can learn to express feelings often thwarted by the "male code" that still prevails in our culture. Lucas, ten, was never quite sure what to say to his father, Blake, when he was upset. Lucas knew that his dad loved to hear about his successes in school and on the soccer field, and knew that his dad cared about him. He idolized his father, but felt uncomfortable telling him when something had gone wrong. There was the time when his good friend had a small sleepover party and didn't invite him. Lucas was upset and worried that his friend didn't like him anymore, and didn't tell his dad, but told his mom. He feared that his dad would say it was no big deal and have him call someone else to play with. During one of our sessions, I told Lucas to try telling his father the sleep-over party story. He did. Sure enough his dad confirmed his thoughts by telling him, "Don't worry about it." Lucas came back to see me and said knowingly, "See, I told you so."

Yep, they had work to do. Lucas had to learn that it was okay to share vulnerable feelings, and his dad needed to be the one to make him feel okay with it. I told Lucas's dad that he was discouraging his son from opening up to him. When I first said it, he denied it vehemently, but in the next meeting, he confessed that it was difficult for him to deal with his son's feelings, because they made him uncomfortable. I asked Blake to think about what his son had said that made him feel that way. He was quiet for a moment and then acknowledged that he feared his son might reject him. When Blake was a kid, his friends would tease him about being overweight or yell "ditch him" and run—Blake's pride kept him from expressing his feelings to anyone as a kid, and he was still hiding them. I explained that Lucas needed to see those feelings sometimes. Then the boy might stop feeling as though he could only talk about his successes to gain his father's approval. "I think you have a lot more to talk about than you realize," I said. "You have plenty of experiences to share, and Lucas would be a good audience. Try opening the door a little and see what happens." Blake's first step was to iden-tify his feelings; the second was to practice expressing them. One afternoon he approached Lucas and told him he wanted to talk, then told him about the boys in fourth grade who teased him. "I hate bul-lies," Lucas said. "There's this bully at school . . ." Suddenly, father and son were talking.

Self-doubt can prevent you from expressing your feelings. When fathers and sons don't trust what they feel, they often keep it to them-selves. I've even seen this in the most innocent of circumstances. One father was angry at his thirteen-year-old son for forgetting his birthday, but he knew that he hadn't reminded him about the occasion and wasn't sure that his ex-wife had, either. He struggled with whether or not to bring it up. I told him that he should. How would his son learn about his feelings if he never told him? Two weeks later, he returned and told me that he had mentioned his disappointment to his son in an e-mail. The following weekend his son showed up with a birthday card and a surprise for him. He couldn't have been happier, but he had almost kept his feelings to himself, which would have allowed it to fester into a larger problem.

Theo, fifteen, confessed to me that he never told anyone what was going on inside of him. I asked him why. "Because I'm never sure if I should be feeling the way I do," he said.

"How will you ever know if you keep it a secret?" I queried. Theo admitted that he was scared to put it to the test. Over time, it came out that Theo was lonely. A sophomore in high school, he only had a couple of friends, and mostly played video games or Frisbee on his own. Expressionless, he was the kind of kid you could spend an entire afternoon with and not know much more than you did when you started the day.

"Don't your friends ever press you about how you feel about something?" I asked.

"No, they like it, I think. I never say anything personal so there's no drama. One friend calls me 'Spock'—you know, the Martian guy from *Star Trek*." I felt more sadness than amusement coming from him at this admission.

We talked about how feelings are a personal thing, and often there is no right and wrong to them. I explained that no one could ever really get to know him if he didn't express his feelings, that sooner or later he was going to have to take the risk and let someone in on them. He listened but remained skeptical. I was especially curious about his parents. It turned out that Theo's father was quite similar to him. "What about your mom?" I asked.

"Oh, she talks a lot," he said.

"About her feelings?"

He nodded. "Well, doesn't she ask you about yours?" I asked.

"Yeah, but she usually answers her own questions and then keeps on talking," he said.

"No wonder it's so hard for you," I commented. "You've got a dad who never shares anything and a mom who talks for both of you."

When Theo met a girlfriend at school, he started opening up. She pursued him. He liked her black eyeliner and interest in books. After they had been going together for two weeks (an eternity in the teen world), she began pressuring him to talk about himself. At first Theo was reluctant, but he slowly opened up on IM. When the relationship moved to the phone, he started sharing more of his feelings. Within a month he was sharing things with her that he had never spoken about before and, he told me, he liked the way it felt. "One night she asked me if I thought she was pretty," he told me. "I said yes. She wanted to know why. I didn't know what to say at first. I know what I wanted to say but it was hard. Then she told me why she thought I was cute. I don't know but I suddenly wanted to tell her everything. It was pretty embarrassing because I was shaking when I said, 'I like your black eyeliner and your blue eyes and your laugh and your red painted nails.' She laughed."

The experience helped Theo trust his feelings and express them more openly. I pointed out that he could try the same approach with his dad and see what happened. He was reluctant at first, but with my encouragement, he broke the ice and told his dad about his girlfriend. To his pleasant surprise, his dad asked a lot of questions. I reminded Theo that this was only the beginning. Perhaps he and his father could practice this type of sharing and develop a closer relationship. "Think of yourself as the coach for now," I told him. "Sons have a lot to teach dads, you know."

Men and boys won't share feelings unless they trust it's acceptable to do so, and so you may want to create "safe zones." Choose a place where he feels comfortable having an intimate conversation with you—at a ball game, at his bedside, in the car. Whenever you want to be sentimental or loving or have a deep conversation about life, you and he will know you can express yourselves in this place. Obviously, your goal is to be able to talk to your son anywhere, but that's not always realistic, so start off slowly. You and your son's safe zone will become a place to express yourselves freely. Think of it as your own private therapy: Boys come to me once a week and they're ready to talk, arriving in my office and willing to spill their guts. You can groom your son to do the same thing with you. Over time, your son will no doubt begin to bring up his own emotions or feelings to you. He'll trust that you are a receptive audience and that what he says will not be held against him.

IDENTIFYING YOUR FEELINGS

To learn how to express your feelings, you have to start by identifying them. Basically, listen to your own body. If you feel a knot in your stomach, stop and think about it a minute. Don't ignore it, push it away, and pretend it's not there. Maybe you're nervous about a project you need to turn in to your boss next week. Maybe you're anxious about your mother's recent heart attack. Maybe you've been snapping at everyone at home and are increasingly annoyed by little things. Name what you're feeling. Put your emotions into your own words. The first step in learning to communicate your feelings is accepting how you feel.

Fred, a thirty-seven-year-old divorce attorney, came to see me because his family was tired of him blowing up at them. Fred said he was exhausted when got home from work and wanted to relax, but his kids would get noisy and rambunctious. He would yell at his wife for not straightening up the house. She'd yell back and suddenly they'd be in a fight. I challenged Fred to think about what was really bothering him. Was it the screaming kids or the fact that they didn't focus their attention on him? Was it the messy house or the fact that his wife didn't look up from washing the dishes when he walked in the door?

Fred thought about it. He wasn't sure. "The whole scene just gets to me," he said. "But I guess there's more to it. I don't really think about it much. I just walk in and react to what I see." It had happened as recently as the night before. Had Fred tried to talk to his wife about what was bothering him? "Nah, I just went on the computer," he said. "I hate talking to her. She always makes a bigger deal of things than they are."

"But maybe you're feeling more than you're willing to let on," I suggested. Fred laughed. "You might know more than I do, Doc," he said. I had hit this wall before with many men. We're so used to crumpling up our feelings into a ball and throwing them into a wastebasket that we men often don't know how to acknowledge what's really going on inside of us. Fred and I talked for a few more sessions and, after some probing, we realized that Fred resented his wife for having so much time home with the kids. Since she was home, he expected her to have everything in its place when he walked in the door, and was annoyed by the kids and the clutter because he didn't think he should have to deal with anything after working all day.

Fred had to go right to the source of his irritation—his wife. It was time for him to talk. Over a glass of wine, Fred told her about his frustrations. She was defensive. She was busy all day long with the kids. She wasn't going to have everything perfect just because it was six o'clock. Then he launched into the emotional stuff, and his wife's tone softened. "I feel like you're so busy when I get home," he said. "I want to talk or hug you or make love and you're just wrapped up in the kids. I want to feel close to you again."

Okay, okay—I'll stop. It's mushy. But all men have to go there to fully work out what they're feeling. After our sessions, Fred stopped snapping when he got home from work. He felt such a relief telling his wife that he still needed her. He was pleasantly surprised at how much more effective he was when he switched from grouchy mode to feelings mode. Sure, there was a risk in expressing his feelings. Often men are unsure what their wives or sons will do with their emotions. Will their family members resent how they feel? Will they understand? Will their feelings come out right?

One thirty-nine-year-old father I interviewed said, "I love my son.

I really do. But I never feel comfortable when I'm around him. It's hard to explain this uneasiness, but I know it relates to my difficulty finding the words to say during difficult moments. Whether it's his sadness over a lost baseball game or his disappointment over a broken play date, my reaction is the same. I feel sorry for him and I want to fix it and make his pain go away. But I never get to say the words he needs to hear—'I know how upset you are.' I'm sure he could do without my long-winded rationalizations about why the event occurred in the first place. I guess that sometimes less is more."

Try to become more comfortable with the "I" word when you talk to your son. It's the doorway to expressing your feelings. It ensures that your statements are personal and come from the heart. Start out small. Say anything nice, even something like "I like your running shoes." As you practice, you'll find it easier to say the more difficult things, like "I was hurt when you ignored me at the mall," or, on a more serious note, "I still feel sad about Grandpa's death, too. It'll get easier to deal with, I promise you." Most important, your son will see you practicing what you preach.

To help identify and express your emotions, here's an exercise you can try: Ask your wife—or even your son—to identify moments when you're not being honest with yourself about your feelings. Let's say your friend is in the hospital for back surgery. Your wife asks how he's doing and you shrug it off and say "fine." But if pressed, you might be forced to put into words how you really feel—scared because your back has acted up in the past and you're worried that you might need surgery some day. Once you start this exercise, you may be surprised how transparent you are to your wife. Fred practiced and became better and better at identifying his feelings until it had become second nature to him. "I retrained myself," he said. "When I get ticked off, I don't just yell at everyone. I stop to think, What's really bothering me? My relationship with my wife is stronger now. She'd always complain before that getting me to talk was like pulling teeth. It was so hard for me to share."

MANAGING ANGER, HURT, AND FEAR

Too many men inadvertently squelch their sons' feelings when they themselves are uncomfortable with those feelings. Twelve-year-old Ricky told me that his father would tickle him whenever he got angry. It made it impossible for Ricky to express his feelings, which was exactly why his father did it. Harris, his father, had been short-circuiting Ricky's anger since he was a little boy. When I asked Harris why, he told me that his own father had tickled him when he got angry. "I think it's how we all got along," Harris said. "Everything was smoothed over with tickling." Harris felt that he was making it easier on his son by not letting the anger turn into a shouting match or the "airing of dirty laundry."

But, of course, this dad wasn't doing his son a favor. In fact, his own discomfort with anger prevented him from teaching his son that it was okay to express anger respectfully. Without a healthy outlet for his anger, Ricky was ready to explode. In time, Harris came to understand why he was avoiding emotional expression. His own father had controlled the family by acting aloof and masking his private misery with public smiles. Problems were swept under the rug. After several sessions, Harris's fear of his own anger diminished and he learned to express his feelings, but he would need to work on that for the rest of his life, given the heavy conditioning he had been through for forty-some years. His efforts did improve his relationship with the entire family and his son also became more conscious of his feelings. Ricky is now an articulate, gracious young man.

Anger is one of the most complicated emotions to manage. When we express anger appropriately, calmly sharing our feelings, another person can better understand us. The other person may change his behavior so he won't hurt us again. Think of healthy anger as letting the air out of a balloon a little at a time. Unfortunately, we often express destructive anger, which is more like letting go of the balloon and having it spin out of control.

From early on, teach your son that it's okay to feel angry and show it in the right way. When Julian's son, Jared, was little, he would sometimes break his toys when he grew frustrated with them. Julian, a forty-five-year-old securities trader, was patient, sat his son down, and told him that he understood how upset he was when he couldn't get his toys to work properly. "But breaking them is not the answer," Julian explained. "The next time that happens, I'd like you to come to your mother or me and tell us why you're so angry. We'll try to help you in any way we can, and if we can't, we'll take time to try to figure out how to solve the problem." Some fathers would yell at their sons if they broke a toy. Other fathers would just take the toy away. Each one is teaching a different lesson. Julian is teaching his son patience. To yell at Jared would teach the boy to get even angrier when he's frustrated. To take the toy away only breeds frustration—without an explanation, the boy doesn't understand what he did wrong.

Julian continued his lessons into his son's boyhood. When eleven-year-old Jared came home with a black eye, Julian asked what happened. "I got in a fight," he answered.

"I'm not interested in who started it or who won," Julian said. "But are you still angry?"

"Yeah," Jared said. Julian told his son he needed to call the boy that night and talk about it. "Or you and I can call his parents together and straighten it out. It's your choice." Jared squirmed. He didn't want to talk to this boy on the phone. But he understood his father's point. Over the years, he and his dad had argued and his dad always insisted that they finish the discussion—no slamming the door and walking out, no subjects closed, no bickering. They always talked until they worked out their anger. Julian would listen attentively to his son's side of the story and his feelings and then tell his. Usually, neither won nor lost, but Jared always felt better off afterward. He knew what he needed to do with his school rival and told his dad he'd call him that night.

Hurt often lies at the root of anger. It's harder to express than anger because hurt implies vulnerability, and boys are not groomed to show it. Difficult as it is to fail at something or be disappointed by someone close to you, it's much worse to pretend that nothing is wrong, because you're cheating yourself of the opportunity to be consoled by those who care for you. It takes more energy to feign indifference than it does to "fess up." That's where dads come in. You can share your own vulnerabilities with your son so that he'll feel safe acting open. It's one thing to tell a boy that his feelings are important and you want to hear about them. It speaks volumes when you practice what you preach.

Hurt

Every March, seniors wait anxiously for e-mails from their college of choice. Tommy didn't get in to his and was devastated. His father tried to reach out. "They're making a big mistake," he said. "Don't worry. There are thick envelopes on the way." Tommy didn't want to talk about it, but his dad didn't give up, knowing that sometimes you need to push your son to talk. "Tommy, do you remember when I switched law firms about five years ago?" he said. He put his arm around his son's shoulders. "I don't think I ever told you why." Tommy shrugged. "Well, to tell you the truth, they passed over me when it was time to choose their new partners. I was crushed. I had busted my butt for almost ten years and that was how they repaid me. I was angry, hurt, and ashamed to face my colleagues who made partner. For weeks, I was walking around like a zombie."

Tommy looked up. "What did you do?"

"Well, I talked to Mom about it a lot. She was supportive and reminded me that I'd bounced back from other hurts before—like when I lost the election for the school board, and when a real estate investment went bad. Eventually, she asked me, 'Are you going to stay there and be miserable?' That's when I started looking for another law firm."

Tommy was listening attentively. His dad said he found a better job within a few months. Two years later, he made partner. "So you rebounded, huh, dad?"

"I did," said his father. "But it still hurts when I think about it and that helps me to understand how you must be feeling. I wish I could make your pain go away but I can't. So just try and hang in there, okay? I know there are good things ahead of you."

"What if no one accepts me?" Tommy said.

"I thought the same thing. What if there's not another law firm? But there was a better one. You're going to find a better school." Tommy sighed.

"I guess," he said.

"Trust me," Dad said. "Tommy, you mean the world to me. The right school is out there waiting for you."

Fear

Boys have trouble showing fear just as much as they do showing hurt and anger. I'll always remember April 17, 2007, the day after thirty-two students and faculty were murdered by a psychotic student on a rampage at Virginia Tech. I was walking around the campus as I waited to do a segment for the *Today* show, and trying to understand the senseless killings. It was a cold, windy day and the chill penetrated my bones. Students milled around aimlessly, still in shock. A few were alone, most were in groups—all struggling to grasp the enormity of the catastrophic event and somehow console one another. I could feel their sorrow and fear and thought of how fathers would talk to their sons about what happened. It would be difficult to discuss the unthinkable, acknowledge their fear, and express sorrow. But that was exactly what their sons needed—encouragement to speak about the tragic event from a father who himself could do so.

Talking to your son about his fears is one of the most important things you can do. Whether it's thunder and lightning, falling off a swing, boarding an airplane, or an impending terrorist attack, it's your job to talk and listen, offer explanation and comfort. A father who tells his son to "suck it up" or "be a man" is pushing away his son and discouraging him from expressing any emotion at all. Be open with your own fears with him. If the nation's terror alert goes up, there's no reason for you to deny your own anxiety. Don't smother your family with your worries—particularly when your son is young. You can be frank and calm, striking a balance.

When my kids and I were vacationing in Jamaica fifteen years ago, we climbed a lush waterfall in Ocho Rios where we had to hold ropes for supports. Somehow I slipped, lost my balance, and began sliding down the waterfall. "Dad!" my son screamed. Thank goodness, I broke my fall and was able to climb back toward him. Dan jumped into my arms and hugged me hard. I comforted him but my heart was still pounding. When we discussed it afterward, I realized how important it was for him to talk about his fear and be reassured over and over again that nothing terrible could have happened to me. When I told my son that I was scared, too, he was so relieved. He liked knowing that he wasn't alone in his fears.

Even benign fears should be treated seriously. One ten-year-old boy I worked with had begged his parents to go to sleepaway summer camp. The night before Jamie left, he asked his dad, "Can kids go home if they don't like camp?" His dad realized Jamie was getting cold feet. "You must be a little scared to leave home, huh?" his dad asked. Jamie nodded and said he wouldn't know any of the kids. What if he didn't like the activities? Rather than dismiss his worries, his dad softened.

"I can remember fearing some of the same things that you do," his dad said.

"What did you do?"

"I told my parents that I was scared and they told me that I had nothing to worry about," said Jamie's father. "To tell you the truth, it didn't help much, but I went to camp anyway. It turned out to be one of the best summers of my childhood." His dad launched into tales of the pranks they pulled late at night. One time they balanced a bottle of talcum powder over the door and it fell on the counselor when he walked in. Everyone was hysterical and no one ever confessed who did it. Jamie giggled. "I understand why you're a little nervous about camp," his dad said. "Let's talk about some of your worries and figure out how to make you feel better. But I also want you to think about how much fun you're going to have."

"Sure, Dad, but did you make that story up about the powder?" Jamie asked.

"It really happened. I was the guy who thought of the idea!"

This same moment could have gone differently. When Jamie said he was scared, his father could have told him everything was going to be okay, tapped him twice on the back, and left him to ponder his thoughts in his bedroom. To many dads, that's a sufficient amount of comfort. But Jamie's dad took his reassurance a step further, attempted to talk out Jamie's feelings, and Jamie immediately perked up and relaxed in the face of this new experience, prepared to enjoy it rather than look for confirmations of his fears.

Unspoken feelings are a barrier to closeness. Hide them and you'll be a hostage to your own discomfort. Express them and you'll feel relieved, understood, and probably loved a little more by those who matter to you most. Remember Kevin Spacey's character Lester Burnham, in the 1999 hit film *American Beauty?* Lester's life is boring and ho-hum. He lives in a suburb where every house looks the same. He's bored by work. He rarely lets anyone know how he feels. Then he sees a gorgeous high school cheerleader at his daughter's basketball game and experiences an awakening. He's not going to keep his feelings in anymore—he's going to live life to its fullest, which for him involves smoking pot, working out, and divorcing his wife. Only after he completely loses it does he start expressing himself. The movie should have been called *American Male Awakening* because Lester begins to say aloud whatever he's feeling or thinking—and it's liberating to him. The film captures just how much men keep simmering under the surface and how it feels to let it all out.

Fathers today need to learn to let it all out, too. It feels good when you let your son see what you're thinking and feeling. Once he sees that you are open to personal expression, he'll be open right back. As a father today, you can break the negative emotional cycle of previous generations.

CHAPTER NINE

The Father Project

A Mother's Role

It's not easy raising a father these days.
—forty-year-old mother

I was sitting in a Wendy's thinking about how to begin this chapter when I noticed a father and son sitting next to me. Three or four years old, the boy was playing with his food, not eating it. His father's patience was wearing thin. "Come on, buddy, eat your nuggets," he pleaded. When that didn't work, he turned to threats: "You better eat or else!" Or else what? He didn't say. Suddenly, he picked up his cell phone and made a call. I assume to his wife. "He's refusing to eat again," the father said in an exasperated tone. Dad listened briefly, smiled, and said, "All right, I'll try it." Looking at his son, he picked up a chicken nugget, and pretended it could talk. "Please don't eat me," said the terrified nugget in a Mickey Mouse voice. The toddler perked up and laughed. Suddenly, the food was prey. The child grabbed it and bit into it with a smile. When he was finished, Dad picked up a second nugget: "You better not eat my brother!" Sure enough, his brother— the second nugget—was headed down the hatch. Now father and son were laughing together. The man picked up his cell phone and again called his wife: "It worked! He ate them. Thanks, babe. I'll see you later."

And there it was. Mom the coach and Dad the player. They were working in tandem, playing for the same team.

If only it were always that simple. Over the years, many mothers have told me that it gives them great pleasure to see their sons in sync with their fathers, and fathers are equally pleased to be in on the action. So how come it doesn't always happen? You've heard a book full of explanations already, but now it's time to put the last piece of the puzzle in place. That's you, Mom.

SAVVY MOMS PROMOTE GOOD FATHERS

Aimee and Bob got married twelve years ago. Aimee knew that her husband had been raised by a traditional caveman dad, but Bob had promised he would never be like him. After they had Wyatt, however, she realized he was a chip off the old block. Following the only parenting style he knew, Bob assumed his wife would change Wyatt's diapers, warm the bottle, and get up in the middle of the night to soothe the baby's cries. Aimee joked with friends that Bob handled their infant son like a watermelon.

But she was frustrated. Aimee had grown up with a hands-on dad, and wanted Bob to get his hands dirty as much as she did. So she decided to become her husband's ally, not his adversary. Having seen too many couples at odds over their division of responsibilities, she was determined to avoid the single-parenting trap. She didn't want to pick at him, which would drive him away, but it wasn't easy. Bob would goof up the simplest of tasks. He'd drop off their two-year-old at day care without a change of diaper. He'd promise to put the baby to bed by eight, but Aimee would get home at nine with Wyatt still awake.

Aimee decided to cultivate her husband in what she called "the father project." She made a point of telling Bob how excited Wyatt was when he played with him as a preschooler. Sometimes she would excuse herself from the room so her husband and son were left alone to interact.

When Wyatt got to elementary school, and a schedule or study issue arose, she would press Bob about what he thought. She assigned Bob tasks—check Wyatt's homework, walk him to the bus. Pretty soon, Bob was doing both out of habit. When Wyatt's fifth-grade baseball team needed a coach, Bob volunteered. It wasn't his sport, but Aimee had convinced him. She also went out of her way to handle all the phone calls for him, set up the car pools, and pick up the team's equipment, acting as co-coach, since it was a time commitment for both of them as parents with careers.

Some mothers might resent having to "set up" fathering moments. "He should just take it upon himself to do things for the kids," one mother told me. "He should know when they need something, just like I do." But you have to be proactive with some men because they just won't know what to do, otherwise. Focus on the dos instead of the don'ts. After all, good fathers, like good mothers, are made, not born. They're men who have worked to balance careers and family.

About twenty-five years ago, on the night before my wedding, my father had a talk with me. My mother had died a year earlier and he himself was getting up in years. My dad hated being alone and missed her terribly. We both wished that my mom could have been there for that special moment. "Perhaps she will be," I told him. It was one of those bittersweet occasions in life when sadness meets joy. "You know, kid, your mother and I had a pretty good life together," my dad told me. "Things weren't always easy, but we got through it. The only advice I have for you is: 'Remember, marriage is two, not one.'" It took me the better part of a lifetime to digest his words.

We all believe on some level that if our partner did things our way, life would be so much easier. But that's not how marriage works. It's compromise in motion. It's learning to accept another person for who they are. It's about understanding that there will always be a few bumps in the road. Like it or not, the state of your marriage has every-thing to do with the kind of parent you are. Your happiness or sadness filters right through to your son. The effort you put into your relationship sends a compelling message to your spouse and children, one of cooperative problem solving or protracted combat. If you as a mother are going to make Dad a better, happier camper, you'd better go back to basics first—your own marriage. Aimee's "father project" was successful only because she spent time helping her husband. If she had expected him to get it right immediately, she would have grown frustrated each time he disappointed her. Many wives resent this extra work, but it's worth it. It can improve your marriage and your family. So use this chapter as inspiration for your own father project.

The first way to help improve your husband's fathering skills is to organize him. Often fathers need help setting priorities. They want to be a dad for all seasons. They don't want to slack off when it's back-to-school season and there are a ton of errands, for instance, but too many feel pressed for time. Moms know that feeling well, and many manage only because they're extremely organized. If your husband has trouble breaking away from the office or managing his stress or knowing how to spend time with his son, you need to figure out how to make it easier for him to do. I've had mothers create parenting "schedules" for their husbands—they hand their husbands tickets, directions, and times for that weekend's father-son whitewater rafting trip, for example. Some men grow to rely on this and sit back and continue to be cavemen, rather than pick up the responsibility for creating time with their sons. But I'm just being realistic and you'll have to be, too, and adapt your methods to your husband's schedule and attitudes. Setting up fathering moments helps your marriage because you won't be constantly disappointed when your husband doesn't do it himself. And, in the end, what counts is that father and son are bonding, right? Men typically enjoy father-and-son time so much that, ultimately, they do begin to set up trips of their own. You're just greasing the wheels, getting the relationship started.

Sometimes mothers are the only reason that fathers and sons have a close relationship at all. Bruce, a vice president at a public relations firm, knows he can't do everything he wants to do as a father. His work schedule doesn't permit it. His wife, Aileen, is often just as busy running her own boutique business, but Bruce says she's the portrait of efficiency—and the family survives because of it. "Aileen keeps the schedules of the kids and tells me when I have to be there for them. I depend on her to help organize my life. To be honest, I'm often so stretched at the office that I lose track of time. Sometimes Aileen has to call me and remind me that I promised the kids I'd be home early that night. It's not that I don't care. I'm involved with our family and I get home for dinner when I can. She's just a better traffic manager than I am." Bruce says he repays Aileen for her hard work by managing other aspects of the household—handling home repairs, yard work, paying the bills. He drives car pool on weekends and does the laundry Sunday nights. Aileen said the setup works for them and she's not resentful. She feels like she's just orchestrating up the fathering, rather than trying to do his job.

To this day the brunt of organizing family life often falls on your shoulders as a mother. Sometimes this works for a family, provided it's done by mutual consent. Sometimes it doesn't. You have to work something out so there's no lingering resentment in your adult relationship that spills over to children, as well. Children don't benefit from arguments about why Dad wasn't at the ball game. When you willingly help your husband be a better father, you'll be happier yourself. I understand why women get frustrated and stuck on their husband's lax attitudes, but these feelings can destroy a marriage. So I encourage women to accept that their lives might run more smoothly if they "set up" their husband's fathering.

THE BIG, FAT COMMUNICATION DIVIDE

Men think differently than women. They're more interested in solutions than analysis, hate feeling controlled, and have trouble admitting when they need help. Bottom line—don't expect your husband to come to you if he's struggling. Intervene, but plan your approach. Going in with guns blazing is only going to anger your husband. Instead, make him feel that he's needed. He wants his son's approval and your approval.

Popularity of books such as John Gray's *Men Are from Mars, Women Are from Venus* and linguist Deborah Tannen's *You Just Don't Understand* are evidence of widespread marital communication gaps. Often it's not what we say that matters, it's how we say it. The same could be said for mothers and fathers who are knee-deep in parenting. One of my patients, Larry, told me that his wife rambles on and on when they talk about their children. He's thankful because his wife is catching him up, but after a long day, he'd be happy with the CliffsNotes version of the epic film that's produced by his wife. "I stop listening to her after a while," he says. "I want to know what the kids are up to but she's so long-winded." I asked Larry if he ever told his wife how he felt. "Yes, I have, but she gets upset and says, 'Never mind,'" he said. "I tell her that I can't handle the information overload. She thinks that means I don't care at all."

I hate to say it—women might think I'm being sexist—but most men I've met with do prefer it when you get to the point quickly. "When I talk to him, I try to think of it as a news headline," Peggy said, another client's wife. "First, I grab his attention. Then I fill in the details. He'll ask more questions and naturally get more involved. Last week, he got home from work and I told him, 'Brady's in trouble again.' Naturally, he wanted to know what happened. That was my cue. I told him that his teacher had e-mailed me that our son wasn't turning in his homework assignments. My husband talked to Brady himself. I didn't even have to ask him." Let's say Peggy's husband got home and she had said, "I can't take Brady anymore. He's not doing his homework and I talked to his teacher and she's not happy and . . ." Peggy's husband would have probably tuned her out. Men respond better to summaries and bullets. When women talk to their husbands as if they're their girl-friends, they're spinning their wheels. Men are capable of these conversations. They just don't enjoy them. As *Washington Post* columnist Richard Cohen once wrote, "Men fake listening, women fake orgasms."

Certainly, there will be times when you will need to challenge your husband. He may be too detached from the family, or one of those passive guys who always needs pushing. Maybe he acts like an army officer and orders everyone around. Either way, I recommend that you first try tickling him with a feather, rather than hitting him over the head with a sledgehammer. A wife is in for a battle if she starts a conversation with "I'm sick and tired of the way you treat our son." It's a provocative statement and offers no opportunity for a resolution. Your husband will feel defensive, blame you for catering to his son, and suddenly you'll be fighting. Men like to feel needed. An easy way for you to get your husband's attention is to ask for help. I call it the "ego massage." Let's say that a twelve-year-old boy is caught sneaking out while his father is out of town on business. Rather than complaining about how lax your husband is or how he doesn't pay attention to Johnny, you might say, "We've got a problem here and you're usually pretty good at solving things. I'm hoping you can help." Men respond to this kind of plea. It makes them want to think of a solution. Suddenly, they're on board.

Avoid saying things like "You'd better take your son out to play this afternoon." It'll get a man's dander up. He'll feel like you're telling him to do something, and men hate that. You might try saying, "Johnny's been looking forward to showing you the new basketball move he learned." Dad will get the point and probably head outside to find his son. One more suggestion: make a point to express your appreciation of your husband, even if it's just about taking out the trash. Women don't realize how often they're recapping what their husbands don't do without ever giving credit to them for what they actually do.

In order to master "creative father change," it's important that you think about who your husband is. What are his roots? Did he have an overbearing mother and a passive father? What types of behaviors does he bring into your relationship? Does he crave more affection or does he need more space? What motivates him? Does he have a fathering role model? What is that model? Wives who can see from their husbands' perspective often have an easier time inspiring them to change. When you understand what's behind an attitude or behavior, you can alter the way you respond and change the outcome to something more to your liking and your son's benefit.

That's what Stephanie did. She came in to see me about her son but we got talking about her marriage. "My husband talks a better game than he plays," she told me. "Whenever I ask him to do something, his response is 'No problem.' He's so cheerful that it makes me want to believe him. But all too often, he doesn't come through." Over the years, she learned that she needed to question him further after he made a commitment. "Are you sure you want to do this?" she'll ask. If he hesitates, she'll either drop her request or emphasize that it's particularly important to her. "It works especially well where our son is concerned," she says. "He does the same thing with his father." Rather than his father not showing up and disappointing his son, the boy will inquire a second time, "Are you sure you want to drive me to that track meet an hour and a half away? I can get a ride, if you can't." Don't confuse this with laying guilt on Dad. Both mother and son have simply adopted a more straightforward style. It gives Dad an option out and does not accumulate the emotional baggage it would if he were to make a promise and not show up. And it works for that family.

Think about your own husband's conversational styles. What kind of cues does he send? How does he respond to you? How might you adjust your own reactions or behaviors to change his? For example, if your husband says that he's really pressed with work this weekend, and you yell at him for never being available, the conversation may end before it ever gets started. He'll retort that you're always criticizing him and don't understand how much pressure he's under. Instead, try saying, "I know how difficult things are for you right now, and let me know if there's anything I can do to help, but our son would be really heartbroken if you missed his playoff game Saturday morning so please try to set aside a few hours so you can be there with us."

Gerard was a real screamer. He would lose his temper easily and blame other family members when something went wrong at home, even something as simple as the washing machine breaking. At first, his wife, Lea, would yell right back at him and they would end up arguing, which invariably led to a stalemate. With practice, she learned to approach it differently. Gerard would come home from work and say, "This house is such a mess." Rather than get defensive, as she usually did, she said, "You're right, Gerard. We've got to do something about it. Let's sit down and figure out what each of us can do." Gerard didn't get angry, and although reluctant, he sat down for a discussion, realizing, as the old saying goes, "If you're not part of the solution, then you're part of the problem."

Many wives don't realize how well husbands respond to nurturing. Moms know that their boys crave it, especially in their early years. And men usually respond to their own mothers' indulgences, which their wives take amiss and perceive as an interfering "mother-in-law." But I've had many men confess that they miss the "warm fuzzies"—yes, a few men have used that word—and unconditional acceptance that they got from their mothers when they were growing up. Few men ask for nurturing directly. They're not programmed that way. Yet, they welcome the coddling with open arms and greatly appreciate it when it's given freely. I'm sure that many women reading this are thinking, What? Me? Act like his mother? No way! But you'll have to trust me on this one—a little nurturing goes a long way with men.

Susan explained this as well as any mother I've spoken to. "I learned to stop keeping score a long time ago," she told me. "My parents bickered a lot and I was determined to not follow in their footsteps. Franklin's far from perfect, but then again so am I. I try to encourage him to ask for help when he needs it, especially with our son Mark. If I treat him the way I want him to treat me—he's likely to be more responsive. So I try to be affectionate and remember what he likes. He listens to me and I listen to him. We disagree, we fight, we make up, we make love. I try to be as loving to him as possible. Early on, I realized that encouraging him to be a better man made him into one."

One caveat. Be careful about confusing nurturing with smothering. Nurturing feels good, not overbearing. Many men need some space and usually don't want hovering wives. You can tell the difference between attention and intrusion and you'll reap the benefits of a more responsive husband and better father.

If you want to maximize your influence, show your husband that he is loved, supported, and can feel safe expressing himself. In the last chapter, I discussed how a father can learn to express himself more openly and feel a little safer in the process, particularly with his son. But as his wife, you can make it a point to speak the unspoken with your husband: "I know how upset you are about your mom's recurrent cancer." "I'd like to wring your boss's neck for not giving you the credit for that big new account." Your husband will more likely open up when he feels understood; even if he stays quiet, press on a bit. He'll benefit from hearing you talk openly about emotions he may be feeling.

Warren described his wife as his best friend. "I can talk to her about anything," he told me. "I respect her opinions and know that she always has my best interests in mind, especially when it comes to our son. She often sees things that I don't."

TEMPER YOUR EXPECTATIONS AND CRITICISMS

Men will be men. You've heard that before. But have you embraced the notion? It helps to be patient with your husband and understand his idiosyncrasies. Don't measure his fathering against your mothering. He's a father, not a male mother. Your marriage is a partnership, not a contest. Try to recognize his efforts, compliment him when you can, and don't hesitate to suggest how he can take it up a notch. When a man feels he can please his wife and kids, he feels better about himself.

Lose the baggage. If he hurt you years ago when he played golf on Mother's Day, forgive him. If he forgot about his son's parent-teacher conference, don't hold it against him for weeks. Fathers will make mistakes along the way, and so will mothers. We don't need always to be reminded of them. When your relationship allows for mistakes, you both will be much happier campers.

When we have unrealistic expectations of others, we often criticize them. Excessive criticism has destroyed many marriages. Criticism is not the same as constructive feedback. It's one thing to tell a father how he might do something better. It's another to tell him all that he has done wrong. It puts a wedge between him and you, and often you and your son. Worst of all, attacks often breed counterattacks. The less you criticize, the better off you are.

Cynthia was pretty tough on her husband. Irv worked hard, tried to spend time with his family, and helped around the house when he could, but he'd often retreat to his study to pay bills, read magazines. "God knows what else he does in there," Cynthia told me, irritated by how much time Irv spent in his study. She would often barge in and say, "Are you ever going to come out of this cave?" That wasn't the only thing that bugged her: Irv didn't make enough money. She didn't like the way he dressed. He wasn't always affectionate with their son. Irv told me he had retreated into his study to escape her constant complaints.

In this situation, I was more concerned about Cynthia's issues than Irv's. She was angry and depressed and had unrealistic expectations. After I spent time with Cynthia, I learned that Cynthia's own father was distant and undemonstrative, and she had hoped that her husband would be otherwise. It turned out Irv was more similar to her father than she had thought, and she resented him for it. Her incessant criticism was her way of getting back at her husband for the hurt that she felt over feeling unloved. She eventually expressed those feelings directly to her husband and I helped Irv understand her needs and learn to tune in to them so that he could break away from his defensive posture.

Nagging is less destructive than constant criticism, but it still makes a man feel pushed or controlled. Nina loved her husband, wanted Patrick to be a good father, and did everything she could to promote his relationship with his son. She would ask him to play catch with their son after dinner, and he'd agree. But if he didn't leave the house within ten minutes, she'd remind him again. If Patrick sat down to read the paper, Nina would yell from the kitchen, "When are you going to play catch?" It wasn't much different when it came to Patrick helping with his son's homework, or even household chores. Nina would bug him until he got up.

Nina and Patrick were in therapy together when he exploded at her. "Nina, you spend so much time bugging me about doing things, that it makes me do the opposite." Men like to be asked once and do the task when they're ready. It's a matter of pride. Nina said she wouldn't nag him if he actually got up and did what she asked, which was true, too. So Patrick reassured her that he would be more responsive to her requests. Rather than sitting and reading the paper and waving her off, he'd say, "I'm going to read the paper for ten minutes. Then I'll take him." The reassurance was helpful to her. She needed to know that the family would not collapse if she stopped nagging.

GOOD FATHERING IS A TURN-ON

Sharon came to see me because she found a receipt from a strip club in her husband's wallet. Her husband was often away on business travel, and she had already started to feel distant from him. Now she felt as if she didn't know him. "I know it's a stupid thing guys do," Sharon told me. "He said he was with business associates. Fine. But I can't help but think I was home with his son, feeding him, taking him to the pool, reading him bedtime stories while my husband was out gallivanting.

I said to him, 'What about us?' He just doesn't seem like father material to me anymore." When I asked how her sex life is, she rolled her eyes. "He's interested in me," she says. "But I'm so disgusted. He wasn't thinking of his son or me when he was in that club, and for some reason that keeps me from feeling attracted to him."

Sharon's feelings didn't surprise me. Many women are turned on by fathers who are actively involved with their sons, and they're not so turned on by the ones who aren't. Women can hold back on sex when their husbands don't help them at home and they can make themselves more available when their husbands do. If Francine asked her husband to drive car pool or take his son to the movies, she'd tell her husband that he was earning credit in "the bank." Not only did it get husband and wife flirting, but it gave Francine's husband incentive to improve. Few women tell their husbands that this is a turn-on, but it's helpful when they do.

Sex has a way of inspiring men to be better. Time and time again husbands have confessed that they're more malleable when they feel their wives are sexually responsive to them and abrasive when they're not. Of course, women could make a compelling case for their husbands being too inattentive, and squelching their desires. Some years ago, in my presence, a woman told her husband that the way into her pants was through her heart, not her zipper. Goodwill is contagious in a family. The better your husband feels about you, the more influence you have over him and how he behaves with your son.

Anita was angry at Kenny. He spent too much time at the office, stuck her with too much responsibility, and wasn't very involved with their nine-year-old son. "Sometimes I feel like I'm in this alone," she told me. Kenny said he wished he was around more, and he wished that they had a better relationship.

"Anita doesn't make it easy," he says. "She's critical of me and doesn't give me much of a chance to get back in the door. I guess I've kind of given up."

I asked how often they had sex. Anita scoffed. "I haven't felt in the mood for almost a year now."

Marital stalemates like these are not unusual—and they're difficult to break out of. I suggested that each of them come in for an individual session to speak about these issues further.

Kenny pleaded guilty as charged. He knew that he needed to be more of a husband and a better father. "Believe me, I've been trying. I've been spending more time at home and I make an effort to spend time with my son every weekend—but I can't seem to get past her anger. I feel like she won't forgive me."

My talk with Anita played out differently. She recalled that for several years she wanted to be closer to Kenny, but he just wasn't available. His career came first—family was a distant second. "Can you believe he still tries to have sex with me?" she asked.

"I guess he still wants to be close to you," I said.

"Yeah, because he's horny."

"Well, maybe so, but there are other reasons, too," I said. "I think he wants you and his family back. He's been willing to admit some of his mistakes, and wants to make a go of it. I'm sure that he really cares about your son and wants to do right by him. You must be noticing some effort on his part, right?"

"I guess so," she replied. "But what am I supposed to do at this point?"

"Anita, I think you're both stuck and something has got to give. Kenny's not sure what else he can do. I believe that he needs to be invited back into the relationship. In some respects, you have the power to do so. So I'd like you to consider making a sexual overture to him. It may be difficult, but I think it would be well received. Sometimes, saying yes instead of no can have a powerful impact. It's been helpful for other couples."

Anita grew quiet for a moment and smiled faintly. "I'll have to think about it," she replied.

A week later, Anita and Kenny were back in my office again. Kenny began with a smile. "We broke out of a logjam last week," he reported.

He was a little embarrassed, but we all knew what he was talking about. Anita smiled.

"You mean that you're getting closer again?"

"He's been more attentive," said Anita, "like the old Kenny I used to know."

"You seem pleased."

"I hope it lasts," she said, stealing Kenny a glance.

I encouraged them to keep it up: "This is the happiest I've seen you both since I met you."

As long as it's in a spirit of goodwill, women can use sex as a bargaining tool. Holding back sex as punishment to bad fathering can tear a marriage apart. There's no reason for a father to improve. He'll feel resentful and controlled. He'll wish he was married to someone else and wish that he was having sex with someone else. It's just not healthy.

MY SON, THE HUSBAND

"My husband can't do anything right," Alison exclaimed. She dramatically tossed her purse on my office floor and lay down on the couch. "I'm exhausted. It's come to the point that he can't even manage to take out the trash anymore. I have to get my son to do it. I don't know what I'd do without that kid." Alison had been coming to see me for months. She was frustrated with her husband but determined to stay with him. She couldn't bear to spring a divorce on Eli, their thirteen-year-old. Alison started the session complaining about her husband, but before long we were talking about a recent outburst of Eli's that was bugging her.

Eli could do no wrong. Alison would spend all her free time taking him to museums, out to dinner, to the movies—without her husband. She'd smother him with affection. It wasn't uncommon for Alison to get home from work and kiss her son "hello" and ignore her husband.

But last week, she said, she had been in the kitchen making lasagna when Eli got home from soccer practice. He raided the pantry for cookies and poured himself a glass of milk. He asked where his dad was, and Alison rolled her eyes: "Where do you think?" Eli nodded. Her husband often worked ten-hour days. Eli told his mom that he scored a goal in a practice game. "Dad would have loved it," he said. Alison cut him off.

"If *Dad* ever made it to your games . . . *Dad* needs to start helping me around here or I may lose it," she said. "I wish I'd known that I was marrying someone so lazy."

"It's not like he's not working," Eli said, defensively, as if she were talking about him.

"Yeah, well, I work, too," she said.

Eli threw down his cookie and stormed off. "All you care about is yourself."

Alison couldn't understand why her son got so angry. Eli had never yelled at her before. But I could sense the story behind the words. Alison was using her son to fill a void created by her unhappy marriage, treating her son like her husband. She relied on him for affection, to feel loved and needed. She looked to him to take on some of her husband's responsibilities, like taking out the trash. And she'd badmouth her husband as if her son didn't have a personal stake in the verbal thrashing. It was clear from his outburst that Eli was beginning to resent her.

Mothers can come between fathers and sons, and their relationship often suffers as a result. Alison's example is extreme, but mothers aren't always innocent in their influence. They encourage—and discourage—father and son to spend time together; some mothers like the control this gives them. Some particularly vindictive women have discouraged the father-son relationship when it's convenient for them to do so, say after they've had a fight with their husband. They'll pull their sons closer, hoping to make their husbands feel outnumbered. Alison assumed that her son would see what a jerk his father was, but she was so blind in her frustrations that she didn't consider how she was hurting her son by denigrating his father and male role model.

Women who look to their sons to fill in for absentee husbands are often lonely and unhappy. They obsess over their sons with the hope that they'll create a man who doesn't disappoint them as much—the perfect male prototype. But at the other end of this fawning and attention is a little boy who just wants to be like his dad. Sons are going to feel a tremendous amount of pressure from mothers, causing many to feel smothered. In the early years, a son will go along with his mother's direction. But as he enters adolescence, he'll rebel and grow resentful. He sees how much his mom is trying to control him and how distant he is from his father—and will shut out both. This is often devastating to mothers who spent the last decade or so drawing strength from their relationship with their son.

Mothers sometimes put their sons in the middle of a marriage without even realizing it. Joan often criticized her husband in front of her son. It even happened in my office. She was complaining to me about how her husband stays on the computer until all hours of the night. Her husband denied it. Joan turned to eleven-year-old Darby: "Tell your father I'm right, will you?" she pleaded. Darby's cheeks flushed red. I jumped in and told Joan that involving Darby was not constructive. I asked her if she was happy in her marriage. She said no. Then I asked her husband if he was. Not really, he said. "But you both love your son, right?" They nodded. "Well, it's going to be very hard for him to develop a close relationship with either one of you if you keep at this," I told them. Kids should never feel compelled to take sides, particularly against one parent. But sometimes parents pull their kids between them innocently. Joan never thought Darby cared when she asked him to back her up. "Is that true, Darby?" I asked. He was flicking at a rubber band he had picked up off my desk. "I get scared you're going to get mad at me if I don't agree," he told his mom. "But if I agree then Dad will get mad."

Women sometimes come between father and son in less overt ways. Many wives "run interference" for their husbands. When Dad comes home late from work, they make excuses for him. "Your father is working very hard." If Dad loses his patience and yells at the kids, wives might say, "Don't worry. He's in a bad mood tonight." If Dad forgets about his son's awards dinner, Mom will say, "He's got a lot on his mind." Women do this to smooth over tensions in the father-and-son relationship, and to protect their sons from disappointment. But what they are really doing is enabling their husbands to screw up the same way a loved one enables an alcoholic to keep drinking. Covering Dad's tracks gives him no motivation to change.

Peggy, thirty-seven, is newly married but she and her husband had had a son a few years before. Husband Kirk isn't a natural father and because of that he often shirks his responsibilities. That has never kept Peggy from going to her book club meeting or heading out to the tenis court and leaving their four-year-old behind with him. She felt that her husband needed to learn by trial and error—and she was right. Without her around, her husband was forced to figure things out on his own, and he often did. This may seem like an odd piece of advice but it's something to remember: let your husband screw up. Too many wives follow their husbands around trying to fix their mistakes and making excuses for them. Don't do it. Just let him mess up, ask questions, and figure things out.

Say your husband is taking your son to ice hockey and you notice that he's forgetting to pack his son lunch. I know it's a mother's instinct to rush a brown bag out to the car. Don't. Lunchtime will roll around at the ice rink and dad and son will get hungry and dad will realize he forgot something. It's not like the boy will starve. Dad will have to deal with it on his own. Say your husband is late for his son's school play. When your son asks why, don't make excuses—have your husband explain it when he gets there. Say your husband puts his son's diaper on wrong. Show him the correct way. But if it happens again, don't reattach it yourself. Let disaster strike and let your husband deal with it: "Honey, I think there's something wrong with Jada's diaper . . ." In setting up fathering opportunities, I don't mean that you should overcompensate for your husband by working double-time at home. This is exhausting and unnecessary. Dad won't learn to father unless you allow him to, or even subtly force him to.

This same dynamic—mother as go-between—plays out conversationally. Some well-intentioned mothers advocate for their sons to their husbands rather than urging their sons to speak up for themselves. Sure, there will be times when you need to get involved, such as when Dad is being hardheaded or treating his son unfairly. But it's dangerous because it discourages boys from speaking to their fathers directly, which isn't healthy. It's not a mother's job to explain everything. But if moms continually interpret for fathers and sons during their conversations—or relay messages back and forth between the two—they'll think that it's normal to converse this way and it's not.

Timmy, nine, would often vent to his mother, Angela. "Dad yells at me too much," he'd say. "Dad's not helping me with math." "Dad promised he'd take me to the pool and now he can't." Angela listened when her son complained. She was always understanding and supportive, and she'd often say, "Don't worry. I'll talk to your dad about this." After hearing me speak on this very subject, Angela sent me an e-mail. She explained that she had changed tactics. Today, if her son complains, she says, "I could bring this up with Dad, but it would be better if he hears it from you." Angela said that her son resisted talking to his dad about his feelings, at first—previous chapters have explained why. But he realized that unless he spoke up to his dad, Dad wouldn't know what he was feeling. Their relationship was rocky at first. Dad wasn't used to having to explain himself and felt defensive. Eventually, they learned to communicate directly.

Mothers are typically the primary information gatherers in a family. They watch their sons closely and ask a lot of questions when they're unsure about what's going on, and they don't hesitate to call their friends if they need to. So moms often learn things about their sons before their husbands do. But don't keep Dad out of the loop. Although I encourage you to let your husband screw up, I don't believe in purposely keeping Dad in the dark. Operate under the assumption that your husband is concerned and wants to know everything about your kids, but don't let your role become the only way that your husband gathers information. You're not his press secretary.

Every night after dinner, Celia and Brett would sit down for a few minutes and catch up on the kids. She would tell her husband what their son was up to, how much homework he had, and even whom he played with that afternoon—information Dad might not be privy to. Brett occasionally and unintentionally "tuned out," but Celia would insist he pay attention. He didn't especially enjoy the reminders, but deep down inside Brett knew that he needed them. He learned a lot in those few minutes—and it kept their relationships running smoothly. "My son doesn't seem to mind when I say, 'Mom told me that you . . .' He's just happy that I'm asking." Sound like a symbol of Yin and Yang? It is. Ultimately, mothers and fathers can pick up where the other left off, and create a continuous circle of cooperative parenting.

Make it a point to consult with your husband on big and small decisions for your son. Whether it's the choice of summer camp or whether he should be allowed to go alone to the mall with friends, discuss the events that come up, reach a consensus, and present a united front. Boys are notorious for playing one parent against the other when it suits their needs. Who's not familiar with the teenage boy in the sporting goods store telling his dad, "Mom said it's okay to get a new pair of basketball shoes," but when the savvy dad checks with his wife he hears, "No way, I just got him shoes a month or two ago."

So, moms, keep dads in the loop. In the end, the entire family will grow closer.

TOP TEN TIPS FOR MOMS

1. Promote the father in your life.
2. Don't get resentful about reminding your husband what to do as a parent.
3. Watch the nagging/critical voice.

4. Encourage your son to speak up for himself to his father.
5. Let your husband fail. Don't always compensate for his shortcomings.
6. Be patient with your husband and son.
7. Remember, fathers are not male mothers.
8. Never ask your son to take sides when you argue with his dad.
9. Teach without judgment.
10. Get to the point quickly—then elaborate.

CHAPTER TEN

Top Ten
Fathering Tips

In a hurry to digest the major points of this book? Here is some clear, simple, prescriptive advice about how to improve relationships between fathers and sons. Think of each as a guidepost—a psychological yardstick by which to measure your own progress. If you really want to keep the ball rolling, ask your loved ones how you're doing—then take their feedback to heart. And remember the old saying: "It's nice to be important, but it's more important to be nice."

TOP TEN TIPS FOR DADS

1. Strike a comfortable balance between career and family.
2. Make peace with your own father.
3. Express your feelings openly and encourage your son to do likewise.
4. Be "all there" when you're with your son (no excuses please).
5. Encourage your son to do his best. Remind him that it's good enough.
6. Model the behaviors that you are preaching.
7. Read between the lines. Sons don't always mean what they say ("It's okay, Dad, you don't have to go to my swim meet").
8. Acknowledge your own shortcomings and encourage your son to do the same.

9. Avoid dismissive platitudes: "He knows how much I love him." "I wish I could be there."
10. Never tell your son to "suck it up."

Fathering is your opportunity to reexperience the magic of childhood, the roller coaster of adolescence, and the gradual transition to an adult role. You will hit bumps in the road and times when you feel like the walls of Jericho may be tumbling down. But guess what? They rarely do. When I reflect back on the special moments of my own life, none compares with the joy I felt watching my children laugh, play, and take in the wonders of the world around them. Now I can chuckle at their teenage protestations at my values, lifestyle, and expectations. And maybe they were right, I didn't know as much as I thought I did. But most profoundly, I feel proud watching them grow into fine young adults, launching their ships, and embarking on their own journeys. I know in my heart that I've had a hand in it.

There's so much to being a father. It's an intriguing mixture of simplicity and complexity, toughness and tenderness. You need to be there for your son—love him, listen to him, and guide him. There will be times when the love you give may not be returned in the right way, at the right time, or in the right amount. But as you walk through the autumn of your life, you'll look back on your child-rearing days, and feel the warmth in your heart and the comfort of your soul. Your son will carry the torch for you and fondly remember the greatest gift that you have given him—all of yourself.

I'd like to leave you with some inspiring words from *The Velveteen Rabbit,* a classic children's book I've read many times over the years—to my children, to myself, and to loved ones. It captures the essence of everything I've been trying to convey to fathers and mothers throughout this book. Read it, digest it, and let the words inspire you:

"What is Real," asked the rabbit one day.

"Real isn't how you are made," said the Skin Horse. "It's a thing that happens to you. When a child loves you for a long, long time, not just to play with, but really loves you, then you become Real."

"Does it hurt," asked the rabbit.

"Sometimes," said the Skin Horse, for he was always truthful. "When you are Real you don't mind being hurt."

"Does it happen all at once, like being wound up, or bit by bit?"

"It doesn't happen all at once," said the Skin Horse. "You become. It takes a long time. That's why it doesn't happen often to people who break easily, or who have sharp edges, or have to be carefully kept. Generally, by the time you are Real, most of your hair has been loved off and your eyes drop out and you get loose in the joints and very shabby. But these things don't matter anymore, because once you are Real you can't be ugly, except to people who don't understand."

To dads everywhere: May you all become fully there dads.

Acknowledgments

I am grateful to all the fathers and sons who shared their lives with me over the years. Their sobering and heartwarming stories are the inspiration for this book. For purposes of confidentiality, stories in the text are composites of clients, friends, and men interviewed for this book. Names have been changed and identities obscured. My agent, Gail Ross, was instrumental in developing my ideas and translating them into a viable book proposal. She was there when I needed her and guided me throughout the process.

Special thanks to my co-writer, Brooke Lea Foster, who was an absolute pleasure to work with. She provided invaluable editorial and creative input and is a top-notch writer. Her patience with my ruminations, early choppy writing, and seemingly endless phone calls was greatly appreciated. I'm glad that I found her. And of course, my editor at Free Press, Leslie Meredith, took the pain out of the revision process and provided enormously useful feedback in a timely fashion.

Dr. Susan Gordon, partner, friend, and seasoned therapist, lent her support and professional insight to the creation of this book. And finally, thanks to all my friends and colleagues, especially Marcia Katz, who reviewed the manuscript from a parent's perspective.

Index

abuse, 34, 39, 150
  verbal, 112
academic performance, 73, 78–79,
  85, 86, 87, 88, 89–90, 119,
  120, 183
"ADD dads," 125–26
addiction, Internet, 152–53
adolescence, 23, 71–91, 124, 130,
  219, 222, 226
  academic performance and, 73,
  78–79, 85, 86, 87, 88,
  89–90, 183
  alcohol and drug use in, 72, 73,
  86, 108, 116, 128, 146,
  149
  awakenings and challenges in,
  71–73
  character building in, 88–91
  communicating with sons in,
  10–11, 76–84, 155, 157–58,
  159–62, 174
  expression of feelings in, 11,
  183–84, 187, 188, 189–91,
  197–98
  fathers lacking personal
  knowledge about sons in,
  136–37
  father-son competition in,
  169–70, 173–74
  Internet use in, see Internet
  jockeying and sarcasm in,
  74–75

misbehavior and rebellion in,
  73, 75, 76, 84, 87, 97, 108,
  116–18, 130–32, 219
mood swings in, 75–76
overcontrolling fathers and,
  86–88, 108–9, 130–32
preparing children for, 69–71
setting limits in, 72, 73, 74, 75,
  84–88, 116–18, 131–32, 148
sex and, 72, 147, 159, 161–62
social networking sites and, 141,
  142, 143, 145–49, 155, 156
technology use in, see technology
understanding interests of,
  80–81
Agassi, Andre, 176
alcohol, 37, 38, 49, 106, 128, 160
  adolescents and, 72, 86
All in the Family, 7
American Beauty, 200–201
American Idol, 159
anger, 45, 65–66, 106, 150, 216
  managing of, 195–97
anxiety, 72, 105
  see also fears
apologies, 29, 33, 173, 174
Apple Store, 144

baby talk, 58–59
Barba, Antonella, 159
Best Buy, 144
Best Life, 112

Index

bonding, 54, 56–60, 77
  healthy competition and, 167,
    172
  Internet use as interfering with,
    151–54
  mother's role in promotion of
    father-son, 205–7
  technology and father-son,
    144–51
Braveheart, 166
Breakfast Club, The, 122
bullying, 67–68, 69, 110, 122,
  176–77, 189
  on the Internet, 143
Bunker, Archie, 7, 130

CareerBuilder.com, 18
"Cat's in the Cradle" (Chapin), 103
"cavemen dads," 7–9, 12, 13,
  15–16, 19, 52, 114–16,
  132–34, 204, 206
cell phones, 141, 142, 145, 152
  text messaging on, 141,
    150–51, 152
"CEO dads," 96–97
Chapin, Harry, 103
character building, 88–91
chat rooms, 149, 152, 154–58
chauvinism, 113–16
Chicago Tribune, 146
childhood years, 60–69, 77, 124,
  153–54, 161, 226
  expression of feelings in, 7, 64,
    181–82, 185–86, 187–88,
    196, 199–200
  father-son competition in,
    167–69, 170
  father-son play in, 61–62, 63–64
  father-son talks in, 66–68
  learning to be a "good sport" in,
    176–77
  listening in, 68–69

"male code" and denial of feelings in, 7, 181–82, 186
  managing son's anger in,
    196–97
  misbehavior and setting limits
    in, 61, 63–64
  patience as valuable in, 15, 16,
    17, 64–66, 129–30
  preadolescence and, 69–71
  sex talks in, 66–67, 158–60,
    163
Child Trends Study (2001), 13
Christmas Story, A, 8
Cohen, Richard, 209
communication, 70–71, 175, 221
  with adolescents, 10–11, 76–84,
    155, 157–58, 159–62,
    174
  in e-mail, 149–51, 190
  father-son talks and, 66–68
  making conversation and, 81–84
  in marriage, 207–12
  about sex, 66–67, 158–63
  teaching intimacy and, 155,
    157–58
  withholding information vs.,
    134–36
  see also feelings, expression of
competition, father-son, 165–79
  in adolescence, 169–70,
    173–74
  in childhood, 167–69, 170
  learning to be "good sport" in,
    176–77
  managing of, 171–79
  pushing too hard in, 177–79
  unhealthy forms of, 172–75,
    177
controlling fathers, 96, 108–9
  setting reasonable limits vs.,
    86–88, 108, 130–32
conversation, making, 81–84

Index

couch potatoes, 132–34
critical fathers, 29, 33, 34–35, 38, 39, 78, 118, 121, 122
criticism, in marriage, 213–14, 218, 219, 222
curfews, 84, 85, 88, 130
cursing, 90
"cyberbullies," 143

Dateline NBC, 155
depression, 39, 93, 100, 105, 106, 116
   in adolescence, 72, 73, 137
developmental stages, fathering in, 53–91
   adolescence, 71–91
   childhood years, 60–69
   infancy and toddlers, 53–54, 55–60
   preadolescence, 69–71
   see also specific stages
discipline, 86, 101, 116–18, 131–32
disrespect, 126–28
divorce, 7, 22, 38, 67, 106, 115, 134, 173, 217
   father-son relationship and, 109–10
drugs, 72, 86, 106, 108, 116, 146, 149, 160
drunk driving, 106, 117

e-mail, 149–51, 159, 190
Emerson, Ralph Waldo, 181
empathy, 90–91
E! News, 80
Entertainment Software Association, 144
Estevez, Emilio, 122

Facebook.com, 141, 142, 143, 145–46, 155, 156

"Facebook for Fifty-Somethings!" (Yoffe), 145–46
"father longing," 14, 96, 137
father project, 204–23
   marital communication in, 207–12
   mothers as interfering in father-son relationship and, 217–22
   organizing of husbands in, 206–7
   sex as incentive, 214–15
   tempering expectations and criticisms in, 212–14, 218, 219, 222
   top ten tips in, 222–23
fathers:
   anger and tempers of, 34–35, 38–39, 65–66, 106, 150, 211
   childhood cues for attention and, 60–69
   childraising regrets of, 28–29, 33, 46–48
   as controlling, 86–88, 96, 97, 108–9, 130–32
   defining good parenting for, 22–25
   discipline and punishment by, 86, 101, 116–18, 131–32
   fears and self-doubt of, 23, 24–25, 93–95, 100–118
   generational mistakes of, *see* generational mistakes
   guilt and self-blaming of, 106–10
   "half-there" and periphery parenting of, 12–18, 20–21, 47, 52, 114, 120–21
   as hypercritical of sons, 29, 33, 34–35, 38, 39, 78, 100, 118, 121, 122, 177

Index

fathers (*cont.*)
    as lacking personal knowledge
        about sons, 136–37
    lack of proper role models for, 8,
        12–13, 15–16, 17, 21, 29,
        96, 100, 114, 195
    learning about one's own,
        41–43
    masculine stereotypes imposed
        on sons by, 7, 15–16, 17,
        111–13, 114, 199
    mothers as primary information
        gatherers for, 221–22
    mother's role in promoting
        good, 203–23
    negative thinking of, 100–102,
        104–5
    nurturing and affection by, 54,
        113, 185–86
    as passive or couch potatoes,
        132–34
    provider role focused on by, 6,
        13–14, 17, 96, 97, 98–100,
        124
    rising expectations and "super-
        dad" myths of, 8–9, 19–20,
        24, 52
    sons as hiding feelings from,
        30–33, 119–23, 138, 174
    sons' biggest complaints about,
        123–37
    stereotypical roles and expecta-
        tions of, 7–9, 12, 15–16, 21,
        114–16
    technology as bond for sons and,
        144–51
    top ten tips for, 225–26
    unrealistic expectations held by,
        37, 38, 89–90
    work as more comfortable than
        home for, 14, 95–98
    work vs. family time of, 5–6,
        13–14, 17, 29, 47–48, 50,
        96, 97–98, 120, 123–25, 225
    see also father-son relationship;
        husbands; sons
father-son relationship:
    in adolescent years, see adolescence
    character building and, 88–91,
        176
    in childhood years, see childhood
        years
    communication and expression
        of feelings in, 10–11, 16,
        30–33, 64, 66–68, 70–71,
        76–84, 123–25, 134–36,
        138, 149–51, 155, 157–63,
        175, 181–201, 221
    competition in, 165–79
    divorce and, 109–10
    generational mistakes and, see
        generational mistakes
    "half-there" dads and, 12–18,
        47, 52
    in infancy and toddler years,
        53–54, 55–60
    listening in, 68–69, 75, 125–26,
        138
    misbehavior and setting limits
        in, 61, 63–64, 72
    mothers as interfering in,
        217–22
    mother's role in promoting
        strong, see father project
    mutual respect needed in,
        126–29, 138
    nurturing and affection in, 54,
        113, 185–86
    overworking as strain on, 5–6,
        13–14, 17–18, 29, 47–48,
        50, 97–100, 120–21,
        123–25, 225
    patience as valuable in, 15, 16,
        17, 64–66, 129–30

play and "roughhousing" in,
59–60, 61–62, 63–64
in preadolescent years, 69–71,
122
sex talks in, 66–67, 158–63
"teaching moments" in, 16–17,
64, 68, 155, 157–58, 196
technology as bond for, 144–51
unresolved regrets and impossible reconciliations in, 43–45,
46
withholding information from
son and, 134–36
see also fathers; sons
fears, 93–95, 100–118
admission of, 10–11, 16, 94–95,
198–200
of closet chauvinism, 113–16
managing of, 198–200
self-doubt and negative thinking
as, 100–102
of son's closeness to mothers,
110–13
of son turning out like selves,
103–6
feelings, expression of, 64, 167,
181–201
and admission of fears, 11, 16,
94–95, 198–200
adolescents and, 11, 183–84,
187, 188, 189–91, 197–98
in childhood years, 7, 64,
181–82, 185–86, 187–88,
196, 199–200
on e-mail, 149–51, 190
fathers as reluctant in, 181–84
hugs as, 185–86
identifying feelings and, 192–94
intimacy built by, 182–83, 194
"male code" as opposed to, 7,
121–22, 123, 182, 186, 187,
188–89, 199

managing anger, hurt, and fear
in, 195–200
mothers and, 7, 111–12, 113,
185, 190
in resolving issues with own
father, 30–33
"safe zones" for, 191–92
self-doubt as thwarting of,
189–91, 193
sons as reluctant in, 30–33,
119–23, 138, 174, 181–82,
184, 186, 187, 188–89,
190–91
tips for encouraging of, 187–88
with wives, 193, 194, 212
see also communication
foul language, 90
Friday Night Lights, 126–27

generational mistakes, 27–52, 96,
171, 173, 195, 201
childraising regrets and, 28–29,
33, 46–48
grandfathers as resolving regrets
in, 48–52
identifying patterns of, 35–36,
40–41
learning about one's own father
and, 41–43
and resolving issues with own
father, 30–35, 225
unresolved regrets and impossible reconciliations in, 43–45,
46
Generation Me (Twenge), 72
gifts, 72–73, 80, 110
Gladiator, 166
Gladwell, Malcolm, 145
Godfather, The, 166
Gottlieb, Daniel, 51–52
grandfathers, reclaiming sons by,
48–52

graveside chats, 46
Gray, John, 208
guilt, of fathers, 106–10

half-there dads, 12–18, 21, 47, 52, 115, 120–21
Hebrew, 45
hugs, 185–86
hurt, managing of, 197–98
husbands:
    communication with, 207–12
    expression of feelings by, 193, 194, 212
    "helping out" vs. equal partnership of, 19, 21, 113–16
    nurturing and comfort craved by, 212–13
    sons as stand-ins for, 217–18
    tempering expectations and criticisms of, 212–14, 218, 219, 222
    wives as frustrated and resentful of, 18–22
    wives as "running interference" for, 219–21
    see also fathers; marriage

infancy, 53–54, 55–58
Instant Messenger (IM), 141, 142, 143, 149, 154, 155, 191
Internet, 141, 142, 143, 144
    addiction to, 152–53
    chat rooms and pseudo intimacy on, 154–58
    e-mail and intimacy on, 149–51, 190, 191
    as interfering with family bonding, 151–54
    pornography on, 158–63
    social networking sites on, 141, 142, 143, 145–49, 155, 156

spying vs. monitoring use of, 148–49
iPods, 145, 153–54

Kaiser Family Foundation, 142
Karate Kid, The, 168

Lenhart, Amanda, 146
Letters to Sam (Gottlieb), 51–52
listening, 68–69, 75, 79, 138
    fathers as distracted and failing at, 125–26, 225
    to wives, 208–9

marijuana, 72, 86
marriage, 12
    communication in, 207–12
    compromise in, 205–6
    equal partnership vs. "helping out" in, 19, 21, 113–16
    identifying and expressing feelings in, 193, 194, 212
    tempering expectations and criticisms in, 212–14, 218, 219
    see also husbands; wives
Married with Children, 6
Marriott, Bill, 72
Master and Man (Tolstoy), 11
Men Are from Mars, Women Are from Venus (Gray), 208
misbehavior, 61, 63
    in adolescence, 73, 75, 76, 84, 87, 97, 108, 131–32, 219
mood swings, of adolescents, 75–76
mothers, 12, 59–60, 84
    infants as bonding with, 55–56
    interference in father-son relationship, 217–22
    as primary information gatherers, 221–22

role in promoting good fathers of, *see* father project

as "running interference" for fathers, 219–21

"single parent" trap of, 6, 20, 204, 215

sons as allowed to express feelings by, 7, 111–12, 113, 185

sons as closer to, 110–13, 133

sons as stand-in husbands for, 217–19

stereotypical roles of, 7, 55, 113–16

top ten tips for, 222–23

see also wives

MySpace.com, 143, 145, 146–47, 155, 156

nagging, 214, 222

Nanny 911, 20

National Center for Fathering, 12–13

National Public Radio, 138–39

negative thinking, 100–102, 104–5

New Hampshire, University of, 159

New York, 159, 160

Ofman, Ursula, 160

organizing, of fathers, 206–7

panic attacks, 48

Partnership for a Drug-Free America, 72

passive dads, 132–34

patience, 15, 16, 17, 64–66, 129–30

People, 80

Pew Internet & American Life Project, 143, 146, 151

PlayStation, 144

pornography, 158–63

preadolescence, 69–71, 122

"provider" dads, 6, 13–14, 17, 96, 97, 98–100, 124

Pryor, Richard, 186

puberty, 73–74, 110

punishment, 86, 101, 116–18, 131–32

rebellion, 73, 76, 84, 87, 97, 131–32, 219

reconciliation, as impossible, 43–45

regrets, 28–29, 33, 46–48

grandfathers and resolving of, 48–52

in relationship with own father, 43–45

remarriage, 109

respect, mutual, 126–29, 138

for women, 163

Rolling Stone, 80

"roughhousing," 59–60, 63

schedules, parenting, 206–7

self-blame, 106–10

self-confidence, 39, 65, 89, 175

self-doubt:

expression of feelings as thwarted by, 189–91, 193

of fathers, 100–102

self-esteem, 72, 89

father-son competition and, 169, 175

self-respect, 88–90

self-restraint, teaching of, 69–71

Sesame Street, 59, 186

setting limits, 63–64, 161

in adolescence, 72, 73, 74, 75, 84–88, 116–18, 130–32, 148

setting limits (*cont.*)
  monitoring activities vs. spying
    in, 148–49
  punishment and, 86, 101,
    116–18, 131–32
sex:
  as bargaining tool, 214–15
  talking about, 66–67, 158–63
  teenagers and, 72, 147, 161–62
Slate.com, 145
social networking sites, 141, 142,
  143, 145–49, 155, 156
sons, 119–39
  adolescent, *see* adolescence
  biggest father complaints of,
    123–37
  bullying and, 67–68, 69, 110,
    122, 143, 176–77, 189
  character building for, 88–91,
    176
  as closer to mothers, 110–13,
    133
  developmental stages of, *see*
    developmental stages, father-
    ing in
  discipline and punishment for,
    86, 101, 116–18, 131–32
  effects of uninvolved fathers on,
    14–15, 17, 54, 132–34
  fathers as hypercritical of, 29,
    33, 34–35, 38, 39, 78, 100,
    118, 121, 122, 177
  fathers as lacking personal
    knowledge about, 136–37
  father's fears and self doubt on
    raising of, 23, 24–25, 93–95,
    100–118
  fathers' negative thinking and,
    100–102, 104–5
  hiding of feelings by, 30–33,
    119–23, 138, 174, 181–82,
    184

Internet use of, *see* Internet
listening to, 68–69, 75, 79,
  125–26, 138
masculine stereotypes imposed
  on, 7, 15–16, 17, 111–13,
  114, 182, 199
misbehavior and setting limits
  for, 61, 63–64, 72, 73, 74,
  75, 84–88, 108, 116–18,
  119, 131–32, 219
monitoring activities vs. spying
  on, 148–49
mothers as allowing expression
  of feelings by, 7, 111–12,
  113, 185
mothers as primary information
  gatherers of, 221–22
mothers as "running interference" for fathers and, 219–21
overcontrolling of, 86–88, 96,
  97, 108–9, 130–32
patience as valuable for, 15, 16,
  17, 64–66, 129–30
pornography and, 158–63
in preadolescence, 69–71, 122
self-confidence of, 39, 65, 89,
  175
as stand-in husbands, 217–18
talking about sex with, 66–67,
  158–63
technology use of, *see* technology
understanding interests of,
  80–81
withholding information from,
  134–36
see also fathers; father-son relationship
Sophocles, 103
Spacey, Kevin, 200
SparkNotes.com, 142
suicide, 106
Superman, 8

Index

Tannen, Deborah, 208
technology, 141–63
    as bond for fathers and sons,
        144–51
    see also Internet
teenagers, *see* adolescence
tempers, 34–35, 38–39, 65–66,
    106, 150, 211
    management of, 195–96
Temple, 45
Tennyson, Alfred, 62
text messaging, 141, 150–51,
    152
"Tin Man," 186
Tipping Point, The (Gladwell),
    145
"To Catch a Predator," 155
Today show, 198
toddlers, 54, 57, 59–60
Tolstoy, Leo, 11
Treos, 144
Twain, Mark, 105
tweens, 69–71
Twenge, Jean, 72
20/20, 148

unresolved regrets, 43–45
USA Today, 143

values, 88, 90
Valvano, Jim, 53
Velveteen Rabbit, The (Williams
    and Nicholson), 226–27
verbal abuse, 112
video games, 144, 152
Virginia Tech shootings, 198

Washington Post, 209
Weaver, William, 138–39
Wikipedia.com, 142

wives, 22, 41, 91, 94, 95–96, 100,
    102
    communication with, 207–12
    father-son time set up by, 54,
        204–7
    frustrations of, 18–22
    "helping out" vs. equal partner-
        ship with, 19, 21, 113–16
    husbands as jealous of son's rela-
        tionship with, 56, 110–13
    identifying and expressing feel-
        ings with, 193, 194, 212
    as "running interference" for
        husbands, 219–21
    sex as bargaining tool of,
        214–15
    tempering of expectations and
        criticisms by, 212–14, 218,
        219, 222
    see also marriage; mothers
Wizard of Oz, The, 186–87
women, 8, 12, 28, 56, 111, 113,
    123, 185
    "have it all" expectations on, 9,
        19, 20
    pornography and relationships
        with, 160, 161–62, 163
    teaching respect for, 163
    see also mothers; wives
work:
    family time vs. demands of, 5–6,
        13–14, 17–18, 29, 47–48,
        50, 96, 97–100, 120,
        123–25, 225
    as preferred to home, 14, 95–98

Yoffe, Emily, 145–46
Yom Kippur, 45
You Just Don't Understand (Tannen),
    208

ABOUT THE AUTHOR

NEIL I. BERNSTEIN, PH.D., is a practicing clinical psychologist, author, lecturer, and consultant to the Washington Nationals baseball team. He is based in the Washington, D.C. area, and he is a nationally recognized expert who has spent thirty years guiding children, teens, and families through difficult times. In the past decade he has become increasingly interested in and concerned and involved with the issues that fathers face. He has a grown son and daughter who have survived his parenting nicely and taught him a few things along the way.

Dr. Bernstein's previous books are *How to Keep Your Teenager Out of Trouble and What to Do If You Can't* and *Treating the Unmanageable Adolescent*. He has appeared frequently on the *Today* show, MSNBC News, and other major broadcast media and is a regular interview source for major newspapers and magazines.